Nature, Technology and the Sacred

RELIGION AND SPIRITUALITY IN THE MODERN WORLD

Series Editors: Paul Heelas, Linda Woodhead, *University of Lancaster*

Editorial Adviser: David Martin, *Emeritus Professor of the London School of Economics*

Founding Editors: John Clayton, *University of Boston*, and Ninian Smart, *formerly of University of California – Santa Barbara*

The **Religion and Spirituality in the Modern World** series makes accessible to a wide audience some of the most important work in the study of religion and spirituality today.

The series invites leading scholars to present clear and non-technical contributions to contemporary thinking about religion and spirituality in the modern world. Although the series is geared primarily to the needs of university and college students, the volumes in the **Religion and Spirituality in the Modern World** series will prove invaluable to readers with some background in Religious Studies who wish to keep up with contemporary thinking about religion, theology and spirituality in the modern world, as well as to the general reader who is seeking to learn more about the transformations of religion and spirituality in our time.

Published:

Don Cupitt – *Mysticism After Modernity*
Paul Heelas, with the assistance of David Martin and Paul Morris – *Religion, Modernity and Postmodernity*
Linda Woodhead and Paul Heelas – *Religion in Modern Times*
David Martin – *Pentecostalism: The World Their Parish*
Steve Bruce – *God is Dead*
David Smith – *Hinduism and Modernity*
Peter Berger – *Questions of Faith*
Paul Heelas, Linda Woodhead, Benjamin Seel, Bronislaw Szerszynski and Karin Tusting – *The Spiritual Revolution*
Bronislaw Szerszynski – *Nature, Technology and the Sacred*

Forthcoming:

Simon Coleman – *The Gospel of Health and Wealth*

Nature, Technology and the Sacred

Bronislaw Szerszynski

Blackwell
Publishing

BLACKWELL PUBLISHING
350 Main Street, Malden, MA 02148-5020, USA
108 Cowley Road, Oxford OX4 1JF, UK
550 Swanston Street, Carlton, Victoria 3053, Australia

First published 2005 by Blackwell Publishing Ltd

Library of Congress Cataloging-in-Publication Data

Szerszynski, Bronislaw.
  Nature, technology, and the sacred/Bronislaw Szerszynski.
    p. cm.—(Religion and spirituality in the modern world)
  Includes bibliographical references and index.
  ISBN 0-631-23603-1 (hardcover : alk. paper)—ISBN 0-631-23604-X
  (pbk. : alk. paper)
  1. Nature—Religious aspects. 2. Technology—Religious aspects. I. Title. II. Series.

  BL65.N35S94 2005
  202'.4—dc22

                                                                        2004024181

A catalogue record for this title is available from the British Library.

Set in 10 on 12 pt Galliard
by Kolam Information Services, Pvt. Ltd, Pondicherry, India
Printed and bound in the United Kingdom
by MPG Books, Ltd, Bodmin, Cornwall

The publisher's policy is to use permanent paper from mills that operate a sustainable forestry policy, and which has been manufactured from pulp processed using
acid-free and elementary chlorine-free practices. Furthermore, the publisher ensures
that the text paper and cover board used have met acceptable environmental ac-
creditation standards.

For further information on
Blackwell Publishing, visit our website:
www.blackwellpublishing.com

to my mother,
Sylvia Szerszynski

Contents

viii   Contents

Preface

If this is a book about the present, it is one that is written predominantly in the present perfect tense. By this I mean that although the book is about what is contemporary to us, about our present relations with nature and technology, it insists that these relations can only adequately be described and understood if we are mindful of the way that the meanings of the present have been shaped by those of the past. It is because we have been through the previous stages of our cultural history that we experience nature and technology in the way that is currently the case. Our emplacement in history is always in the form that Gadamer (1975) describes as 'historically effected consciousness'. Our freedom thus should not be thought of as our escaping being shaped by history, as if the latter were a coercive force outside ourselves; far less does freedom consist in transcending finitude itself – imagining we can know the world from a point outside it. Instead, our freedom is constituted by our very historical emplacement – in the way we receive what is passed to us by history, and in the way we pass it on to the future.

In this book I have a particular way of rendering that history – in terms of transformations of 'the sacred'. But I do not simply use the term 'sacred' in the narrow sense of something marked out, extra-mundane, as bearing more than instrumental value; I am using 'sacred' in a more general sense, to understand the ways in which a range of religious framings are involved in our ideas of and dealings with nature and technology. At the theoretical level, 'the sacred' in its different historical orderings plays the primary interpretive and explanatory role in the chapters that follow; it is the ground against which particular historical phenomena or ideas appear as intelligible figures. So, for example, rather than particular orderings of the sacred being a response to a particular experience or understanding of God, I would rather see any particular understanding of God (including the idea that there is no God) as a feature of a particular ordering of the sacred, as only intelligible when that order is grasped as a Gestalt. Any given ordering of the sacred, then, is more than just a particular account of which things, people, places or other beings might have ultimate value; more even than a particular understanding of the divine, whether transcendent or immanent; more even than a cosmology, if by cosmology we understand an account of all that *is* in the world.

Why write such a book? To be sure, this is not a book that is intended to be directly useful in the shaping of public policy in respect of science, technology or the environment – though some of its ideas may well find applications in such domains. It is primarily intended to be useful to those readers who perhaps have a fragmentary sense that contemporary attitudes to nature and technology have religious qualities to them, but do not know quite what to make of this hunch. So on one level what I present in these pages could be seen as a gathering together of examples of the religiose in contemporary ideas and practices concerning nature and technology, that very act of gathering perhaps making more meaningful and significant what separately might have seemed simply cultural curiosities and accidental homologies.

But also the book presents a framework which I think is helpful for making greater sense of our complex attitudes to nature and technology. I hope that by the end of the book the reader will see examples of the explicit sacralization of nature or technology, new forms of spirituality that have sprung up around, say, the Gaia hypothesis or the Internet, as simply more visible and articulated versions of implicitly religious understandings of nature and technology that are widespread in Western societies (on 'implicit religion', see Nesti, 1985; Bailey, 1998). Furthermore, I also hope that at least some readers will come to see even these more diffuse religious understandings as illustrations of an even more general truth: that what Heidegger calls our 'thrownness' in history means that our being-in-the-world is mediated through – no, stronger, is incarnated in – the cultural currents into which we are thrown. And that, whatever character the local eddies might have, the broad swell is always that of the sacred.

In case some readers are starting to worry that they have stumbled into a work of theology, I want to reassure them that the primary disciplinary approach taken by this book is social scientific. The sociology and anthropology of religion will be important reference points, in that I will use the approaches, theories and concepts developed in these areas to explore contemporary relations with nature and technology. But I will also draw widely on theoretical and empirical work from other areas of social and historical research, such as consumption and lifestyle, political and social movements, risk perception, science and technology, and moral behaviour, in order to marshal and illustrate my case.

So, for more directly philosophical or theological treatments of nature, the reader will have to look for other writings by myself and others. However, despite the predominantly social scientific approach, there *are* more metaphysical moves underpinning the analysis. For example, in discussing and problematizing the popular idea of 'the disenchantment of nature', I want to resist the idea of projection – the idea that when humans sacralize nature, when they treat it as more than simply so much stuff, they are simply projecting ideas and values onto it. This way of thinking, that treats all cultural meanings of nature as something added by humans to an essentially meaningless nature, is shared by positivistic, scientific approaches of nature and social constructionism alike (see Ingold, 2000: 208). But as we will see in the chapters to follow, the very idea of nature as the kind of thing that we could project onto, and indeed the idea of the human subject as something that can project, emerge through a long historical process of disentanglement of what we now call the human and the natural. The idea of nature as a blank *tabula rasa* is thus itself part and product of the story of the disenchantment of nature, so cannot be used as a fixed, stable point on which one might build an understanding of that disenchantment.

My relationship with the story of the disenchantment of nature will be a complex one – one neither simply of acceptance nor rejection. Others have claimed that nature is not disenchanted (e.g. Douglas, 1975; Latour, 1993; Bennett, 1997; Milton, 1999). But these writers tend either to identify exceptions to the rule of disenchantment, which nevertheless leave the general claim intact, or to undermine the whole notion of the disenchantment thesis by denying any radical discontinuity or change in the dominant idea of nature. I want to take yet another route, developing an argument for the ongoing sacral ordering of nature which has both a general and a specific level.

At the general level, I will say that nature is always understood in religious terms, even where nature is apparently secularized through technological meanings. The religious meanings that frame the understanding of nature do not disappear over time – they just alter. At a more specific level, I will also try to identify specific domains – consumption, health, lifestyle, politics – in which nature can be seen as bearing sacral meanings in modern culture, and to explore the forms that those meanings take. In this regard I will necessarily have to make reference to explicit attempts to resacralize nature, to new forms of religiosity and spirituality that treat nature as an object of sacral value. But my focus will be more on implicit rather than explicit religion, on the broad, more-or-less mainstream culture of modern Western societies, rather than on the high-water mark of minority religiosities. I do not want just to identify exceptions to a general, assumed disenchantment of nature; instead, I want to propose a shift in the whole way we think of that disenchantment, in terms of an overarching set of transformations in the sacral ordering of the world.

Above all, I hope the book will make a contribution to the much-needed project to discover a more authentic and appropriate response to our present predicament, a predicament at least partially captured by terms such as 'ecological crisis' and 'technological self-endangerment'. Such a project will have to be political, in a way which is only barely recognized by most of what today passes as environmental philosophy and theology. But it will also have to be theological or liturgical: rather than tiresomely repeating the modernist denial of the still-rootedness of modern secular culture in religious history, it must involve a conscious reappropriation of that tradition, in a way that acknowledges the sacral grounding of the social but is also responsive to the demands of the present and the future. The first half of this book is devoted to clarifying and substantiating this argument, while in the second half I start to develop the implications of the argument for the possibility of a critical relationship with contemporary technological society.

In Part I, I set out the approach I take in the book. Chapter 1 introduces the problem which the book addresses – the adequacy of the description of the modern world, and particularly modern 'nature', as disenchanted. Under this description, one reproduced by both defenders and critics of modern society, science is presented as understanding nature in utterly secular terms, as stripping it of sacral meaning or purpose. Modern technology is seen as the product of this rendering of nature – the release of human practical activity which results when the cultural constraints provided by ideas of nature's divinity or sacrality have been removed. While partially endorsing this account, I suggest that it obscures a deeper truth – that this disenchantment of nature is itself a form of enchantment, a very particular sacralization of nature, and one that emerges within a specifically Western religious history.

In Chapter 2, I clarify my own approach to the understanding of religious change, and of the relationship of Western religious history to the emergence of the modern, secular world. After considering a number of different accounts of secularization – the decline of the influence of religion and the rise of secular thought and action – I identify a group of theorists, most notably Max Weber, who are closest to my own approach. These theorists of religion provide useful ways of thinking about religious evolution in terms of the working out of inner contradictions within orderings of the sacred, but also give various accounts of how the secular world is itself produced by that evolutionary process. Among that group is Marcel Gauchet, particularly influential on the argument developed in the book, who differs from the other theorists by seeing Western religious history and the emergence of the secular modern world not as the operation of universal reason bringing about the inevitable, common destiny of humankind, but as a highly contingent branching-off from the mainstream of world religious history. Using Weber, Gauchet and others, I construct my own schematic history of that branching path. Starting from the monistic world of the *primal* sacred characteristic of indigenous cultures, I describe how an *archaic* form of the sacred emerges in parts of the world, concentrating sacral power in certain objects, places and persons, closely linked to new ideas of worldly, political rulership. But with the emergence of historic religions such as Judaism and Christianity comes the emergence of a new transcendent axis in the sacred, as, in what I call the *monotheistic* sacred, supernatural power is gathered together and expelled from a world now understood as empirical. This transcendent axis is radicalized with the emergence of the *Protestant* sacred, in which the stripping away of intermediaries between God and his creation makes that God both more infinite and sublime, and at the same time more intimately involved with both nature and the individual. With the *modern* sacred, the transcendent axis is pulled into the very empirical world that was constituted by its ejection, producing a new immanentist ordering of the sacred in terms of the sacrality of life itself, a sacrality grasped through Enlightenment reason or Romantic sensibility. Finally, in the late twentieth century we start to see the emergence of a *postmodern* sacred, where multiple orderings of the sacred are grounded in the very individual subjectivities that had been made possible by the transcendent axis.

Part II explores how modern ideas of nature and technology can be understood as products of this history of the Western sacred. In Chapter 3, I describe the emergence of the idea of nature. In the primal and archaic sacred, what we would call nature is understood socially. Non-human beings and inanimate objects are not part of a unified realm of cause and effect with which one interacts technologically, but simply part of a larger cosmos ordered through social relations of obligation, compromise and contract. With the monotheistic sacred, nature becomes understood as the creation of a transcendent divinity, and in Christianity this results in a rich semiotics of nature, where nature is approached primarily as a collection of signs from the creator to the faithful, to be interpreted according to scriptural conventions. In the late Middle Ages this 'oral' understanding of nature is made both more 'textual' and more 'material': nature is seen as containing its own ordering, like scripture, but this ordering is also understood as involving causal, magical connections between objects. But with the Reformation and the rise of modern science this ordering of the sacred is displaced by one based on God's absolute transcendence, power and lawfulness, and nature's passivity and dependence on God's will.

In Chapter 4, I trace the emergence of modern ideas of technology. I describe how in the classical world *techne* or craft was seen as associated with an inferior form of knowledge, that of changing particulars, as compared with the timeless, universal truths of contemplative *episteme* or *gnosis*. The crafts were plural, incapable of an overarching rationalization. They required participation with a matter still understood in quasi-animistic terms. And they always threatened to turn their user away from higher reflection on the good, to a dangerous preoccupation with means. But in the Protestant sacred, *techne* was given a new status as the source of the highest form of knowledge, one that required not contemplation but active intervention in the empirical world. And, as 'technology', the practical arts were given a religious, soteriological function, as promising a liberation from finitude and necessity by bringing the certainty of reason itself to humanity's dealings with matter. But in the modern sacred – and particularly in what Foucault describes as the biopolitical ordering of society – the soteriological understanding of technology comes to be rendered in purely technical terms. No longer is technology subservient to either worldly or supernatural ends; technology starts to impose its own immanent ends on its users, as the goal of life is seen as its own reproduction and optimization.

Part III looks in more detail at two key domains of inner and outer nature in which these processes have worked themselves out in Western sacral history, exploring coexistence and competition between competing orderings of the sacred. In Chapter 5, I explore how the body has been a key site of struggle between competing orderings of the sacred. I describe most of the Christian era as involving the coexistence of two models of healing; a 'vertical' one based on dependency on the saints and the sacraments as conduits of transcendent power, and a 'horizontal' model, with its origins in pre-Christian culture, based on the restoration and maintenance of connections with the social and natural environment. Both of these were displaced with the emergence of the Protestant sacred by the development of a more cognitive approach to the self, of a rational disciplining of the body and the creation of coherent inner life-narratives. However, in the nineteenth century, traditional forms of healing were hybridized with Enlightenment ideas of rational nature and revivalist religion to produce individualized soteriological health practices. These were revived and transformed in the 'postmodern' contemporary context in the form of complementary and alternative medicine, which coexists with, and offers an alternative form of embodiment to, the modern biomedicine that dates from the late eighteenth century.

In Chapter 6, I look at the development of a number of ideas of nature that serve as tributaries to the contemporary idea of 'the environment'. I first look at two ideas which emerged most clearly in the context of the immanent sacred of modern, biopolitical society, ideas which see nature as threatened by resource depletion or pollution. Two further ideas of nature as a collection of beings – in terms of sentience and rights, and in terms of rarity or other criteria of value – I argue are rooted in the monotheistic and archaic sacreds respectively. Finally, I explore Romanticist ideas of nature as a moral source, as a realm that offers temporary or permanent escape from technological society.

Against the background established by the previous chapters, Part IV explores contemporary resistance to the technological domination of non-human nature. I argue that, despite the contemporary popularity of immanentist ideas of a sacred nature, ideas with an elective affinity with biopolitical ideas of the immanent reproduction of life itself, technology critique significantly draws on resources from earlier Western religious history, and particularly from the Protestant sacred. In Chapter 7, I explore the emergence of the environmental movement in Western societies in the 1970s, in terms of its inheritance from the Protestant sacred, but also as the product of a postmodernization of the sacred in the 1960s. I also argue that environmental and technological critique is grounded in a 'social distancing' of individuals and groups from the symbolic ordering of societal power over humans and nature, and is thus a continuation and radicalization of the critique of the archaic sacred from the perspective of the monotheistic sacred.

In Chapter 8, I pursue this idea further by exploring how individuals attempt to establish non-technological relationships with nature in their everyday lives through choices about lifestyle and consumption. In particular, I focus on vegetarianism, as a symbolic activity used by individuals to distance themselves from the dominant codings of power in society, and as a practical activity in which they can take up a non-dominative relationship to non-human nature. Against the background of a contrast between a quietist politics of lifestyle and active, public protest, I argue that the vegetarian option has to be understood in terms not of historic shifts from 'emancipatory politics' to 'life politics', or of levels of commitment, but of a particular model of moral excellence, rooted in religious history. I conclude by exploring how in such ethical lifestyles Protestant forms of self-monitoring become hybridized with more collective, Catholic modes of corporate embodiment and ritual, with a constant tension between reflexivity and routine, between social distancing and archaic forms of power.

In Chapter 9, I turn from the private to the public realm, firstly tracing the roots of the public critique of the technological domination of nature in modes of speech and action developed by Protestant Christianity. I then look at the various uses of temporal language in environmental and technological critique, exploring the way they draw on modes of temporality characteristic of particular orderings of the sacred. Finally, I briefly explore the contemporary postmodern sacred in terms of a partial return to the polytheism of the primal and archaic sacred. I suggest that because disagreement and the coexistence of multiple points of view seem to be constitutive of the contemporary technological condition, the only sacralization of nature which could ground an adequate technology critique would be one which could harmonize, yet not homogenize, this diversity.

In Part V, I turn to the future of the sacred. In Chapter 10, I consider the image of the earth as seen from space as a candidate for an icon for the contemporary sacrality of nature. However, by exploring the different receptions and interpretations of such images, I argue that the globe is an unstable sign, an empty signifier, whose immanent sacrality can be recoded in terms which vary from the sacrality of biological life, through that of the biopolitical, technological ordering of society, to that of the sovereign consumer. I close the chapter by locating the emergence of the idea of the global sacred against the history of the sacred, and suggest that in order for it to avoid becoming an archaic and repressive sacralization of life at the scale of the planet itself, we need an ordering of the sacred which preserves difference while avoiding the agonistic violence of pre-modern polytheism.

Finally, Chapter 11 concludes the book by reflecting on where things might go from here. An important implication of my analysis is that the nature of environmental and technological critique needs to be rethought. Most of what passes for such critique, I argue, is still captured by the immanent sacrality of modernity, and does not fully escape technological modes of thought. I suggest that a full embracing of the finitude and historical embeddedness of human existence is not only a prerequisite of an adequate critique of technological existence, but is itself an anti-technological move, a rejection of technology's rejection of human finitude. Such a move involves taking up a new and active relationship with the history of the sacred, but also being sensitive to new forms that the sacred might be taking. While reminding the reader of the contingency of the transformations of the sacred, I nevertheless identify a number of trends in science, technology and society which might be signalling radical transformations in our experience and ontology of nature, technology and the human. I suggest that any emergent ordering of the sacred worth affirming and nurturing must be one which can help us to make sense of such transformations and to re-harness technology to non-technical purposes and values.

Bronislaw Szerszynski
Lancaster, May 2004

Acknowledgements

I have a debt of gratitude to so many people for helping, sometimes unwittingly, with the gestation of this book. Enormous thanks are owed to Peter Scott and two anonymous readers, who all read an earlier draft and provided extremely insightful comments and advice. I must also thank John Hedley Brooke, Rebecca Ellis, Bente Halkier, Dave Horton, Adrian Ivakhiv, Greg Myers, Chris Partridge, Alison Stone and Cain Todd, each of whom read, and provided invaluable comments on, parts of the draft, and Lynn Smith for her careful copy-editing. Ursula Baatz, Emily Brady, Tony Coady, Celia Deane-Drummond, Tristram Engelhardt, Yrjö Haila, Malcolm Hamilton, Michael Hammond, Kevin Hetherington, Mathew Kearnes, Kaie Kotov, Kalevi Kull, Beate Littig, Dave Littlewood, Jim Proctor, Ken Rees, Christoph Rehmann-Sutter, Richard Roberts, Robert Song, Emma Tomalin, Ian Welsh and Brian Wynne also gave me very helpful feedback on my ideas at various stages in the book's gestation. Doubtless there were others to whom I can only apologize for omitting them. Thanks are also owed to John Urry, Linda Woodhead, Paul Heelas, Kevin Hetherington and Vernon Pratt for encouraging me to write this book in the first place, and for helping me identify what it was. I am also grateful to the Economic and Social Research Council (ESRC) for financial support during the writing of my PhD, sections of which form the basis of parts of chapters 6 and 7, and for funding the projects 'Science, Culture and the Environment' and 'Global Citizenship and the Environment', which I have drawn upon in chapters 8 and 10 respectively. I must also express gratitude to the Leverhulme Trust for funding 'The Kendal Project: Patterns of the Sacred in Contemporary Society', findings from which I use in Chapter 5. The Alternative and Complementary Health Research Network (ACHRN), in particular Christine Barry, Linda Gibson, Sara Morris, Alex Ryan, and above all the late Sue Clarke, played an indispensable role by helping me think through some of the ideas for that chapter.

Such is the nature of life at Lancaster University, with its over-abundance of opportunities for interdisciplinary intellectual exploration, that there have been many other conversations with colleagues, especially Robin Grove-White and others at the Centre for the Study of Environmental Change, and with our excellent postgraduate students, which have gone on to inform the ideas in this book. I also must credit my mother, Sylvia Szerszynski, for getting me to rethink the title – thus forcing me to get clearer about the scope and argument of the book. And Donna – she never thought I'd finish it; I'm glad to be able to show her that all the work was, in the end, fruitful!

Part I

Modernity, Nature and the Sacred

Chapter One

The Disenchantment of the World

Dover Beach

The sea is calm to-night.
The tide is full, the moon lies fair
Upon the Straits; – on the French coast, the light
Gleams and is gone; the cliffs of England stand,
Glimmering and vast, out in the tranquil bay.
Come to the window, sweet is the night air!
Only, from the long line of spray
Where the ebb meets the moon-blanch'd sand,
Listen! you hear the grating roar
Of pebbles which the waves draw back, and fling,
At their return, up the high strand,
Begin, and cease, and then again begin,
With tremulous cadence slow, and bring
The eternal note of sadness in.

Sophocles long ago
Heard it on the Aegean, and it brought
Into his mind the turbid ebb and flow
Of human misery; we
Find also in the sound a thought,
Hearing it by this distant northern sea.

The sea of faith
Was once, too, at the full, and round earth's shore
Lay like the folds of a bright girdle furl'd;
But now I only hear
Its melancholy, long, withdrawing roar,
Retreating to the breath

> Of the night-wind down the vast edges drear
> And naked shingles of the world.
>
> Ah, love, let us be true
> To one another! for the world, which seems
> To lie before us like a land of dreams,
> So various, so beautiful, so new,
> Hath really neither joy, nor love, nor light,
> Nor certitude, nor peace, nor help for pain;
> And we are here as on a darkling plain
> Swept with confused alarms of struggle and flight,
> Where ignorant armies clash by night.
>
> Matthew Arnold, 1867

In 'Dover Beach' Arnold gives us a grand and moving metaphor for the decline of religion, for the disenchantment of the world. I quote it here, though, to draw attention to the use of natural imagery within the poem. Like the best metaphors, the key metaphor of the poem illuminates in two directions. Here, the familiar, poignant feel and sound of the retreat of the sea gives flesh to the sense of loss at the fading of faith. But also, the metaphor, like the tide, turns back on itself, helping us to see the retreat of a vital, awesome, natural presence like the sea as a religious event. The sea itself can be seen as a metonym for nature's animacy, withdrawing from the world.

In the poem the sea retreats, leaving behind a world without light or love, a world where nature is denaturalized and inanimate, one whose lingering, faltering animation is only an echo of the disappearing ocean. In the soundscape of the poem the only noise is the retreating roar of the sea, the grating pebbles flung up and tumbling back, borrowing their life temporarily from the tide, then resting in silence. All that's left is the silent, 'naked shingles'. The 'breath of the night-wind' intensifies rather than softens the desolate mood of this 'darkling plain', hostile and meaningless.

This image, I want to suggest, captures well the idea of the desacralization of nature, a narrative that is central to our understanding of the modern world. According to this account, nature has been progressively mechanized and instrumentalized, cleansed of mysterious forces and meanings.[1] Nature is no longer understood as being filled with gods, demons or spirits that might assist, hinder or terrify us. It is no longer shot through with occult connections between one object and another. Neither is it any longer one of the two books of God, filled, like scripture, with signs and lessons for human beings from its creator. As a disenchanted realm, practices towards it that might once have felt appropriate – worship, prayer, magic, interpretation – now seem quaint and futile, to flail around without purchase.

Instead, nature in the modern age seems to present itself to us in very different ways. Nature is mathematical – something to be counted, measured and mapped. Nature is immanent – it operates according to its own internal processes, rather than being shaped or guided by a supernatural hand. It is mechanical, behaving according to cause and effect, not seeking teleological goals. It is a resource, to be owned or held in common, to be used or preserved. It gives up its meanings to careful observation and scientific theory, not to mythology or divination. This is the nature of scientific, industrial modernity, the nature whose being is mastered by science, whose value is measured by economics, and whose potentiality is determined by technology.

Indeed, technology can be seen as a key player in this drama. The rise of modern technology is not just a side effect of nature's desacralization – as if the banishing of nature's spirits merely granted permission for the expansion into nature of technological operations that had been held in check by the threat of supernatural reprisal. Rather, technology *is* the desacralization of nature; it is in technology that nature's disenchantment is most clearly performed. The technological mastery of nature, the turning of nature's potentiality to human purposes, is not just the putting into action of a technological attitude; it in turn validates that attitude, making it seem right and inevitable. And it is only when we approach nature in a technological way – in a way that is concerned above all with prediction and control – that the kinds of knowledge offered by science and economics become intelligible and useful (Habermas, 1971a).

According to this story of the world's disenchantment, then, as technology's powers advance, those of nature withdraw. For some – let us call them the modernists – this is a story to be celebrated. Max Weber, who first gave us the term *die Entzauberung der Welt* (Weber, 1989: 14, 30), used the phrase to describe the way that, in modern societies, sublime, ultimate values withdraw from public life into the private sphere, leaving public life to be organized around notions of instrumental rationality and bureaucratic efficiency (Weber, 1989: 30). The disenchantment of nature is central to Weber's account: in a disenchanted society 'there are in principle no mysterious, incalculable powers at work' – everything is capable of being explained (Weber, 1989: 13). According to the modernists both nature and social relations have been stripped bare, are rendered how they have always been, no longer hidden from view by the confusions of religion and ignorance. Weber, as we shall see later, is interestingly ambivalent about this story. But in the hands of other modernists such as Jürgen Habermas this story becomes more unambiguously a positive narrative of the success of Enlightenment values. Influenced by Hegel's vision of (particularly Western) history as the progressive incarnation of reason or 'Spirit' in human affairs (Hegel, 1977), Habermas narrates the disenchantment of the world as humanity's liberation from superstition and ignorance, from enthrallment to nature and to arbitrary power (Habermas, 1984).[2]

Yet this very same story has also been told by the critics of modernity, this time in a more negative mode, as a kind of fall into darkness. In the nineteenth century we heard this critical version of the disenchantment thesis from the Romantics in Europe and from the Transcendentalists of North America. In the twentieth century the theorists of the Frankfurt School such as Max Horkheimer and Theodor Adorno (1972) offered their own version of this counter-narration, building on Weber's own account of how the growth of modern technical rationality increasingly might leave us not free but caught in an 'iron cage' of bureaucratic reason. And then, in the second half of the twentieth century, various popular social and cultural movements popularized this negative reading of disenchantment; these movements included the hippy counter-culture, the natural health movement, and, perhaps above all, the environmental movement.

For many environmental writers, our alienation from nature lies at the roots of our rootlessness, at the base of our base treatment of nature. Morris Berman, for example, gives a particularly passionate version of this view – that the ecological crisis is one that ultimately is a result of alienation from nature. Once, Berman recounts, humans were participants, at home in a living universe. But the scientific revolution changed everything, destroying the possibility of ultimate meaning and cosmic belonging. For the alienated modern consciousness the human being is largely an observer, not a part of the world. The technological attitude opens up a breach between subject and object, in a process nicely captured by Timothy Reiss in the image of Galileo's telescope as described in his *Sidereus Nuncis* of 1610: the telescope constructed the distance between the human subject and the material world at the same moment that it promised to bridge it (Reiss, 1982: 24–5). For Berman,

> [t]he logical end point of this world view is a feeling of total reification: everything is an object, alien, not-me; and I am ultimately an object too, an alienated 'thing' in a world of other, equally meaningless things. This world is not of my making; the cosmos cares nothing for me, and I do not really feel a sense of belonging to it. What I feel, in fact, is a sickness in the soul. (Berman, 1981: 3)

What is striking here is that both sides – both the champions and the critics of modernity – accept more or less the same story. Both those who see modern rationality and technology as liberating forces, and those who see them as a source of profound alienation, generally accept that nature has become disenchanted, and that the rise of modern technology has been centrally implicated in that disenchantment, as principal beneficiary. But, to paraphrase Mark Twain, what if reports of the death of nature have been greatly exaggerated? What if the narrative of the disenchantment of nature is little more than a creation myth of modern society – a half-truth told in order to secure a sense of modernity's exceptionality, its discontinuity with earlier cultures (Crook, 1991; Latour, 1993)? What if the critics of modernity have sold the pass by even admitting that nature has been stripped of sacrality, and that the modern technological mastery of nature is a wholly secular enterprise?

For on closer examination the narrative of disenchantment reveals a more complex story, one where disenchantment – the rendering of the world as totally profane and without spiritual significance – itself involves and calls forth new forms of enchantment. Consider a few examples. A young protester locks himself to the top of a swaying tree in order to prevent the construction of a new road and the consequent destruction of an area of native woodland. A middle-aged woman sees an acupuncturist in order to unblock the natural 'healing powers' of the human body. A farmer walks out into his fields with a canister of herbicide, determined to eradicate the weeds that are 'invading' his crops. A woman, still smarting after an argument with her partner, stops her car at the roadside on a deserted mountainside to take in the view, and feels able to get things back in proportion. A botanist collates all the data from his experiments, and tries to discover the law that underlies the different patterns of growth he observes in his plants. How does nature appear in these examples – as the 'dead matter' of a mechanized world-view (Merchant, 1980)? Or is it sometimes an object of absolute, intrinsic value, a healing energy, an evil to be subdued, a calming presence, or an obeyer of laws? And, if so, what does this say about ideas of nature's disenchantment (See Milton, 1999, 2002)?

In the rest of this book I will be arguing that contemporary ideas and practices concerning nature and technology remain closely bound up with religious ways of thinking and acting. More specifically, in the next chapter I will argue that these ideas and practices are radically conditioned by the very specific religious history undergone by Western society, by what I want to call the 'long arc' of institutional monotheism. Other, very different, stories could be told about ideas of nature and technology that have developed in cultures outside the West. But because of the central importance of European cultures and their New World offshoots in the emergence of modern society, it is the trajectory of the sacred in these cultures that will be the focus of this book. This trajectory has seen the establishment, rise and fall of a vertical, transcendent axis in thought and cosmology – one that both united and divided the empirical world from a transcendent, other-worldly reality. As this axis emerged, the supernatural powers of ancient divinities were progressively gathered together in the monotheistic God of the Abrahamic faiths of the Near East, and expelled from the empirical world into a supernal reality. This axis, along with its correlate in the philosophical reason of classical Greece, established a new dimension in human experience which had a profound impact on ways of thinking about the world, an impact that was felt across Europe with the adoption of Christianity by Rome. Without such an axis it would just not have become possible, as happened later, to regard nature as *nature* – as a secular realm, ordered according to its own immanent principles, principles that can be discovered through inquiry. Indeed, without this axis it would not have been possible to think of nature as one unified thing at all. It is as if the transcendent axis gave human thought a new vantage point to regard the cosmos, as though from the top of a tower built into the sky.

Contemporary understandings of nature and technology, both secular and sacred, I am suggesting, are impossible to understand without reference to what sociologists call their 'path-dependency' – in this case, to their conditioning by this very specific religious history, and in particular by its central motif, the transcendent axis. Even the very plurality of modern ideas of nature, as illustrated in the vignettes above, is evidence not just that the age of transcendental monotheism has passed, but that we have passed *through* it. For, while this vertical axis no longer casts its shadow across the West, its fragments still litter the cultural landscape. Indeed, the very secularity and immanence of the modern world – the seeming absence of a transcendent dimension, of any reference to an other-worldly reality – came about not through the dismantling of the transcendent axis but through its radicalization. The axis was stretched to infinity, as, after the Reformation, the divine realm came to be understood as even more radically beyond this world, as an absolute and unconditioned divine, to be worshipped for its own sake, without thought of benefit to the worshipper. But then, with the modern age, the corollary of this – the absolute profaneness of the empirical world, its self-sufficiency and immanence – became the central cultural motif. A transcendent God was no longer seen as a necessary being, without which the existence and order of the world was inconceivable. Yet the vertical dimension, which had helped constitute the idea of a secular empirical reality in the first place, was not so much cut loose and discarded as collapsed *into* that reality, as attributes of the divine were reassigned to nature and to the human subject, and intelligibility and value came to be seen not as conferred by creation's relationship with a transcendent God, but as inherent in the confrontation of human consciousness by the empirical world itself.

But, as with all transformations of the sacred in religious history, the emergence of the contemporary sacred did not completely displace earlier understandings of nature and the sacred. Within the contemporary 'absolute profane' – the experience of empirical reality as without a transcendent source or ground of meaning – there also coexists a variety of sacralizations of nature; indeed this plurality is *constitutive* of the contemporary ordering of the sacred. This condition is what I want to call the 'postmodern sacred', one in which plural perceptions of meaning and value coexist. But it is also post-transcendental – not just in the sense of being subsequent to, but also a consequence of, the period of transcendental religion. For it is only at *this* end of the transcendental arc – after the age of transcendental monotheism – that the postmodern sacred can exist.

So it is not the case that the retreat of institutionalized monotheism in Western societies has simply allowed the return of the kind of understandings of nature that dominated in pre-Christian cultures. There is certainly a sense that Arnold's retreating tide of monotheism has deposited us once again on a polytheistic shoreline. Yet, although contemporary societies seem to be enjoying a revival of 'nature religion', forms of religiosity that make nature their central object of concern and sacralization (Pearson et al., 1998), it would be a mistake to see this too literally as a 'return of the repressed', as an eruption of a long-suppressed pagan cosmology and sensibility. Instead, we should understand contemporary ideas of and practices around nature as evidence of a postmodern sacred, a mode of being-in-the-world and a cosmology that is the product of a long and distinctive historical process, and shaped by distinctively contemporary conditions. The long tide of transcendental monotheism has so radically shaped Western culture that its departure leaves us in a very different landscape than the one from which we started.

Chapter Two

Nature, Secularization and the Transformation of the Sacred

What does it mean to ask about the relationship between nature and the sacred? Taken in a Durkheimian sense, to regard something as sacred is to set it apart from the routine and the everyday; to attribute to it some kind of divine or transcendent characteristic, power or significance; to treat it as an end in itself rather than as something that can legitimately be used solely as a means to an end (Durkheim, 1915). However, Kay Milton criticizes this approach to defining sacredness, arguing that such a definition only specifies how sacred things are treated, and says little or nothing about how and in what way they come to be seen as sacred in the first place (Milton, 2002; 157 n. 6).[1] She discusses a number of different approaches to defining how nature can be thought of as sacred. She considers Posey's (1998) argument that indigenous cultures see nature as sacred because they see it as having a close relation to a spirit world, and Gregory Bateson's ideas that sacredness consisted in a wholeness and that it depends on non-communication or non-cognitive processes (Bateson and Bateson, 1987; Bateson, 1991). But Milton finally settles on a definition of the sacred as 'what matters most to people', thereby linking it to her ecologically grounded theory of the emotions (2002: 101–5).

While all these senses of the sacred are helpful in understanding some aspects of the contemporary treatment of nature, I also want to use the term in a broader way in the chapters that follow. Firstly, while Milton's term is very inclusive (recalling as it does Paul Tillich's (1957) definition of religion as involving 'ultimate concern'), it still implies that it is only the *positive* valorization of nature that is of interest here, and that needs to be theorized. The ambitions of this book are such that the alienation from, and fear of, nature must also be amenable to analysis in religious terms. Secondly, I want to look not only at ideas of nature, but also at practices of nature, not just what people think but what they do. Thus, some of what

I would want to term the sacralization of nature involves practices that have religious or quasi-religious aspects to them, practices that do not always comfortably fit Weber's concept of disenchantment in terms of the belief in calculability, in mechanical causation and instrumental rationality. So, by arguing that nature is sacralized in contemporary culture, I will be asking the reader to look at certain features of the modern world in a new way, to see their quasi-religious character. As such, I will be arguing that the sacred has its correlate of what astrophysicists call dark matter – that there is much more of it about than we might think.

But, thirdly – and here I know I may be stretching some readers' already generous hospitality in entertaining my argument so far – I also want to embrace the profane, the secular, in my analysis of the sacred. I will be arguing that the secular treatment of nature has itself to be understood in religious terms. As Hans-Georg Gadamer (1975) argued, the concept of the profane always presupposes the sacred, in however attenuated a sense. They are a pair, and the contrast between them only relative – and one that can be switched around at particular times (van Gennep, 1960). In its original sense in the classical world, the profane or worldly was itself understood religiously;[2] it was only with the Christian banishment of spirits and demons from this world that the profane began to be understood in an absolute, rather than a relative sense, as a space that was *only* profane, that had no relation to the sacred, that did not need a sacral reference point to make it intelligible (Gadamer, 1975: 150; see also Milbank, 1990). Following this line of thought, in Chapter 4 I will explore the way that even the utilitarian exploitation of nature can be seen as having sacral underpinnings.

First, though, I want briefly to survey theories of secularization, particularly as they apply to nature and our relationship with it. Secularization theory, which seeks to chart and explain the diminishing importance of religion in Western society, remains an influential theoretical approach in the sociological study of religion, and one with clear links to the 'desacralization of nature' thesis. If religion – and by extension the sacred – is indeed disappearing from Western society, then one would expect nature to be understood in increasingly secular ways. As we shall see, however, our understanding of the desacralization of nature will be affected not just by whether we think that secularization is unequivocally taking place in Western societies, but also by how we comprehend secularization.

Secularization and Nature

The idea that modern, Western societies are qualitatively different from all other forms of society was a foundation stone of the discipline of sociology as it developed from the nineteenth century onwards. The very legitimacy of the modern age came increasingly to depend on the idea that something special had emerged in Europe in the last few centuries of the second millennium, something that was at the same time both unique and universal: that had made a radical break with earlier societies, but had in doing so freed the universal, liberating force of rationality (Crook, 1991). For the classical sociologists such as Weber, there was an intrinsic relationship between the dynamism of modern society and this 'occidental', secular reason. It was no accident that modern scientific, artistic, political and economic development took off exactly at the point on the globe that was disenchanting the world, abandoning an overarching religious world-view in favour of a secular culture, divided into autonomous realms such as law, science, art and politics, realms which developed according to their own, inner logic (see Weber, 1965, 1985; Habermas, 1987a: 1–2).

Secularization was thus one of the key ideas used to capture the idea of the uniqueness of modern Western society. Bryan Wilson described secularization as:

> the shift from primary preoccupation with the superempirical to the empirical; from transcendent entities to naturalism; from other-worldly goals to this-worldly possibilities; from an orientation to the past as a determining power in life to increasing preoccupation with a planned and determined future; from speculative and 'revealed' knowledge to practical concerns, and from dogmas to falsifiable propositions; from an acceptance of the incidental, spasmodic, random and charismatic manifestations of the divine to the systematic, structured, planned and routinized management of the human. (Wilson, 1985: 14)

It was assumed widely – and argued explicitly by secularization theorists – that this shift was a natural and inevitable outcome of societal development. Echoing the way that Darwinian evolution was widely understood to place human beings at the top of an evolutionary ladder, it was thought that societies, too, could be ranked by how modern they were, with Western societies highest up the societal ladder. And a key criterion for modernity was held to be the loosening of the hold of religion on thought and action, and its replacement by rational, scientific ways of knowing and acting. As all societies moved up this ladder, it was thought, religion would lose its hold and disappear.

However, in recent years this assumption has been questioned both empirically and theoretically. Pointing to the worldwide resurgence of mainline religions such as Islam and evangelical Christianity, and to the widespread and diffuse religiosity and spirituality of modern capitalist societies, critics argued that the prediction of an inevitable end of religion was too simplistic, with secularization theory compromised by its origins in a northern Europe with distinctive patterns of religious decline, and by a dogmatic nineteenth-century faith that religion would disappear and be replaced by the rule of reason (e.g. Kepel, 1994).

Nevertheless, secularization theory remains a very potent framework for thinking about religion and society. Woodhead and Heelas have suggested that secularization theory takes a number of forms today, *disappearance* and *differentiation* being the most frequently promoted, with *de-intensification* and *coexistence* being less common variants (Woodhead and Heelas, 2000: 307–8). Disappearance theorists are closest to nineteenth-century ideas of secularization, suggesting as they do that religious interpretations of the world are rapidly disappearing in the contemporary West. However, according to differentiation approaches to secularization, such as that advocated by Bryan Wilson, religion is not so much disappearing as simply losing its former role in maintaining and steering the social system, being replaced in this by secular, rational, bureaucratic and technical means (Wilson, 1985). According to such interpretations, a decline in religion's significance in the public sphere can coexist with its continuing significance in the private sphere – indeed it might even encourage a spiritual 'inward turn', whereby individuals' inner lives become more elaborate and sacralized (Heelas, 1996). De-intensification theorists see religion as surviving but becoming far less salient and significant in people's lives, becoming for many little more than an item of consumption like any other (Bauman, 1998). For example, Steve Bruce, while being a firm advocate of the idea that religious belief and activity is in overall decline, also argues that much religion or spirituality that does seem to be popular in Western societies, such as New Age spirituality, is in fact of low salience in people's lives (Bruce, 2002). Finally, coexistence theories see the processes of secularization and sacralization occurring simultaneously, in different geographical locations or different areas of life (e.g. Martin, 1993).

What all of these approaches to secularization share is an understanding of the religious that positions it as one phenomenon among others within society. Society – understood fundamentally in secular terms, as a mundane sphere made up of human beings, their ideas and institutions – is seen as the more fundamental, primary phenomenon. Religion – like sport, suicide or marriage – is just one of the many secondary phenomena that happen within society, one of the many things that people do, and one of many social phenomena which grow, shrink or even disappear. Below I want to present a rather different way of thinking of the secular and the sacred, but for now let us explore how the two main versions of secularization theory described above might apply to the natural world.

If the disappearance variant of the secularization thesis held in relation to nature, we would expect nature to be becoming wholly secular, with all traces of sacrality being stripped away. As Marx and Engels put it in the communist manifesto of 1848: 'All that is solid melts into air, all that is holy is profaned, and man is at last compelled to face with sober senses his real conditions of life, and his relations with his kind' (Marx and Engels, 1962: 13). According to this account, in modern societies nature has been increasingly disentangled from religious misunderstandings, and thus has been revealed as it really is. Daniel Bell summarizes the standard view of secularization in this way:

> Religion, in this view, arose out of the fear of nature, both the physical terrors of the environment and the dangers lurking in the inner psyche which were released at night or conjured up by special diviners. The more rational answer – we owe the start, of course, to the Greeks – was philosophy, whose task was to uncover *physis* or the hidden order of nature. (Bell, 1977: 420)

According to the Enlightenment view that Bell is characterizing here, religion is displaced by science and technology, by the rational understanding and manipulation of both inner and outer nature.

However, the differentiation variant of the thesis – which sees religion not as disappearing but as playing an ever smaller role in the steering of society – would allow for nature to remain 'enchanted' in the private sphere. According to Bryan Wilson, traditional societies were 'preoccupied with the supernatural', with super-empirical 'ideas, beings, objects and conditions', whereas in modern societies we see 'the abandonment of mythical, poetic and artistic interpretations of nature and society in favour of matter-of-fact description and, with it, the rigorous separation of evaluative and emotive dispositions from cognitive and positivistic orientations' (Wilson, 1982: 149–51).[3] Wilson sees this separation as resulting in religion losing its influence over social steering, however much it might still empirically survive in private beliefs and practices. If this variant of secularization were true of nature, while in the running of society nature might be increasingly understood as a mere physical resource governed by cause and effect, nevertheless, in people's private lives the non-human world might still be regarded and related to in religious ways. In terms of institutional religion, this may well be the case, in that all of the major traditions have engaged in environmental self-reinterpretation in recent decades, and thus offer sacralized readings of the human relationship with nature (Oelschlaeger, 1994; Gottlieb, 1996). Aside from this, recent decades have seen the emergence of new traditions, such as neopaganism and ecopaganism, which insist on the sacrality of nature (Pearson et al., 1998; Taylor, 2001a, 2001b). And as we will see in later chapters, there are lots of even more informal ways in which nature is sacralized in the private sphere – such as in the aesthetic experience of nature, in contemporary ideas of health and healing, and in green lifestyles.

We can see already that it is not just to what extent secularization is true, but also how secularization is to be understood, that has a bearing on the character of nature in modern societies. But as well as the different variants of secularization theory catalogued by Woodhead and Heelas, there are also some sociologists of religion who do not fit so neatly into these categories. Richard Fenn and James Beckford, for example, argue that secularization does not so much refer to a quantitative change in the amount of religion, but to a qualitative change in its relationship to institutions. In this they are similar to differentiation theorists like Wilson, but unlike them they do not argue that religion has necessarily lost its significance in public life. Fenn suggests that in contemporary societies the sacred is not so much in decline as being fragmented and diffused (Fenn, 1982). Although consensus on the nature and location of the sacred might be in decline, for Fenn this increases rather than decreases the likelihood of individuals and groups basing their claims to social authority on religious grounds (Fenn, 1978: 26). Beckford similarly wants us to see secularization as meaning not the decline of religion but its 'deregulation'. Progressively freed from their institutional moorings, religious symbols, discourse and modes of action do not disappear but instead become a free-floating 'cultural resource', drawn on by individuals and groups in an ever-widening range of contexts (Beckford, 1989: 171–2). This kind of approach to the contemporary sacred – which sees it not as caged but feral, not incarcerated in private, individual subjectivity but roaming abroad across the social and natural landscape – will provide a more fertile approach for thinking about the sacralization of nature in the modern world.

But so too will another literature on secularization, more theoretical in approach, which tries to link the development of a secular society to the broader sweep of religious history. Rather than seeing secularization as something that impinges on the history of religion from outside, as the modernization of society undercuts the 'plausibility structures' of religion, this literature sees secularization as far more intimately related to that his-tory – even to the point of seeing it as a phase *within* that history. In the next section I will draw heavily on that literature – and in particular on the work of Max Weber, Robert Bellah, Jürgen Habermas and Marcel Gauchet, (Bellah, 1970; Habermas, 1984; Weber, 1965, 1985; Gauchet, 1997) – in order to develop the central narrative that will structure the rest of this book.[4] Inevitably, to compress my account into the space available I am going to have to commit gross acts of generalization and conflation, as well as over-simplifying the messy processes whereby one ordering of the sacred is superseded by another. And, while my narrative will be one that might seem to lead inexorably from primal religion, through Judaism, Christianity and the Reformation, to arrive at the modern secular, this is only one branching route taken by the sacred in its transformations. Yet the central narrative I am presenting should be clear – one that leads from the unified sacro-natural cosmos of primal and archaic religions, through the dualistic cosmology characteristic of the monotheistic world religions, within which the idea of nature as a distinct realm first emerges, through the radical dualism of Protestantism and the immanent sacrality of modern society, and arrives finally at the contemporary, postmodern sacred, with its complex of multiple ideas of nature.

The Long Arc of Transcendental Religion

This story starts with what we might call the *primal sacred*. Our under-standing of the kind of religion and cosmology associated with this ordering of the sacred mainly derives from the study of indigenous, small-scale societies that have survived into modern times, such as the aboriginal hunter-gatherer societies of Australia and North America. Yet it seems clear that this kind of ordering of the sacred was widespread before the emer-gence of agricultural and urban societies. Such societies typically inhabit a unified cosmos, one not organized in terms of any distinction between the empirical and the transcendent. Yet the very unity of this kind of cosmos means that its key characteristic is plurality, since there is no way of regarding it as a unified thing, from outside, as it were. In Heideggerian terms, in this kind of cosmos there are (empirical) 'beings' but no concept of (transcendental) 'Being' (Heidegger, 1962). These beings include what we would call both natural and supernatural entities. Yet the mythical beings of the primal sacred, typically ancestral figures, cannot properly be called gods as they do not control the world, and are not approached through worship, but through identification and the acting out of primal myths, or through mundane forms of social interaction. And natural en-tities are not related to naturalistically, in terms of physical causation, but in what we would call a *social* way (Kelsen, 1946). Indeed, the idea of a purely technological operation in the modern sense can hardly be formulated at all in such a cosmos. So, although we would say that such cultures usually (though not always) live with nature in a sustainable way, what secured this was not simply a technical awareness of the effects of particular economic activities, but a cosmology in which human beings find themselves in social relationships with human and non-human, relationships which came with certain obligations and constraints (Rappaport, 1967, 1979).

The aim of primal religion is to secure the sustainable reproduction of life within this world, rather than to escape it or to live according to laws originating from outside (Bellah, 1970: 25–9). Mythical narrative is not seen as referring to a separate, heavenly realm but is woven into the empir-ical details of the physical world, with every natural feature experienced as related to the actions of mythical beings. For example, the hunter-gatherer Mbuti pygmies of the Congo experience their every material need as being met by the forest, which is accordingly addressed as father or mother. They appreciate the extent of their dependence on it ('When we leave the forest, or when the forest dies, we shall die. We are the people of the forest'), but rarely could be said to worship it as such, though they sing to it as they go about their business, and make charms and clothing from its fabric to maintain their intimacy with it. When disasters occur they need just awaken the forest by playing their *molimo* trumpets and singing their sacred songs ('because we want it to awaken happy') (Turnbull, 1974: 224, 84). In their unified sacro-natural cosmos, there is no sharp distinction made between interactions with nature, with humans or with supernatural beings.

Bellah uses the term 'archaic religion' to apply to the religious systems of Africa and Polynesia, but for our purposes the *archaic sacred* is also characteristic of the pagan cultures that preceded the emergence and spread of Judaism, Christianity and Islam in the Middle East and Europe. Like primal religion, archaic religion is similarly monistic in its experience of the world as a unified 'natural-divine cosmos', but here the deities are more definite gods with whom humans must interact in an ordered way. This phase is characterized by a multiplication of cults, engaging in worship and sacrifice, with priests and a fluid membership (Bellah, 1970: 29–32). With the development of priests there is a relative shift from magic to religion proper – from the *ad hoc*, circumstantial meeting of needs and crises to a systematic regulation of relations with supernatural beings (Weber, 1965: 28). But these beings are still understood as inhabiting the empirical world, as caught up directly in the affairs of human beings – and as multiple, rival possible sources of supernatural benefit. Religion is not concerned with otherworldly salvation, but with securing existence in this world. A common characteristic of the archaic sacred that will be increasingly relevant in the chapters that follow is the marking out of certain places, people or objects as having a privileged relationship with the sacred, other things being seen as – relatively – profane. Sacred, natural and worldly hierarchies are seen as continuous – resulting, for example, in African ideas of divine kingship, where an individual is seen as encapsulating sacred order and power.

But a more significant transformation occurs with the emergence of the *monotheistic sacred* of the historic religions, including the world religions of Judaism, Buddhism, Christianity and Islam, but also aspects of Greek philosophical thought. In a radical shift in the understanding of the sacred which occurs across the globe between 800 and 200 BCE, in what Karl Jaspers calls the axial age (Jaspers, 1953), the cosmological monism of earlier religion is progressively reordered around a dualistic distinction between 'this' world and a transcendent reality understood to exist 'above' it. The historic religions are all in some way religions of dualism and world-rejection, involving a turning away from the empirical world, whether through conforming to religious law, through a sacramental system or through mystical exercise (Bellah, 1970: 32–6). With their emergence, religious concern turns from this world to the next one, and for the first time salvation becomes the great preoccupation of religion.

It is in this phase of Western religious history that we see the beginnings of a number of key ideas characteristic of subsequent orderings of the sacred: a single truth, 'nature' and 'society'. Firstly, the breaching of the immanent sacral order and the idea of a transcendent foundation or source for all reality brings for the first time the possibility of philosophical thought about Being – of 'thinking the "One"'' (Gauchet, 1997: 48). But also religious plurality, which had been easily accommodated within the archaic sacred, comes to be seen in a different way – as deviations from truth, in Christian terms as heresy. Secondly, with divinity and agency progressively eradicated from the world of empirical phenomena, nature as a separate principle starts to emerge. With this withdrawal of divinity, nature starts increasingly to be seen as something which humans can and should master – to be shaped in a systematic, technological way, as part of the task of realizing their divine role on earth. Thirdly, it is with the monotheistic sacred, with its starker separation between human beings and the divine and a clearer sense of the empirical human individual, that we begin to see the emergence of the idea of society as a self-organizing association between human beings with their own projects and opinions.

Yet, although the sacred is here being ordered around a new dualism of natural and supernatural, historic religions nevertheless continue to operate through the material and the bodily in ways that echo primal and archaic religion. In medieval Christianity, like the monistic primal sacred, supernatural realities are mapped onto physical features. Relics and places of worship are scattered everywhere – in chapels, springs, fountains, woods, as well as great urban centres – a sacred topography which organized worship and pilgrimage (Muchembled, 1985: 101). But the meanings of these features are apprehended in a different way than they were in primal and archaic religion – as pointing to external, higher realities. According to the symbolist mentality of the Middle Ages, objects, plants and animals were understood as signs, implicated in endless chains of resemblance (Harrison, 1998: 15). Natural objects and not just words were seen as referring, possibly to other objects and events in nature and history, but finally to moral and spiritual truths as laid out in scripture. This semiotic subordination of the natural to the supernatural world – the reading of nature as 'about' spiritual truths – both reinforced and expressed the move away from the monism of the primal and archaic sacred; no longer is life preoccupied with the cyclic, homeostatic maintenance of this world; instead, attention is increasingly turned to the next.

In terms of the body, too, the monotheistic sacred echoes earlier forms of the sacred, but reorders them according to the dualism between nature and supernature.[5] In medieval Christianity the understanding of the body as 'sinful flesh' (Foucault, 1979) coexists with what Mellor and Shilling call an 'open orifice' body, one where individuals continually merge with other people and the material environment. The attempt to discipline this body according to the dualistic ontology of the monotheistic sacred produces a 'flight into physicality no less intense or passionate than its counterpart: the maximum enjoyment of pleasures'. To this end the Church uses a battery of somatic techniques, including fasting, abstinence, flagellation and the use of 'close contact' senses of taste and touch as paths to religious knowledge (Mellor and Shilling, 1997: 37–41).

The reconstitution of the sacred as a transcendent divine, expelled from empirical reality, facilitates the emergence of new forms of sociality, two instances of which will be relevant later. Firstly, the idea of society as a unified whole, a 'society of mankind', emerges only in the era of the monotheistic sacred. The constitution of the transcendent axis gives an external reference point to which all humans have a shared relationship: *all* humans are created; are capable of salvation or enlightenment; and are bound by the same moral law. In the West this abstract, inclusive model of sociality develops decisively with the emergence of the medieval Church, which aims to incorporate all of political and civic life into itself, and is experienced as an imagined community of the faithful, both living and dead – and even, on one level, the whole of humanity (Troeltsch, 1931: 238–9). In this form of the sacred, society as a whole is conceived of as a body – a *corpus mysticum* – or as a family, bound together through relations of sameness and *caritas* (Arendt, 1958: 53–5). Secondly, the expulsion of the divine also makes possible the sect, an ascetic enclave which defines itself in relation to a divine command that puts the sect at odds with the behaviour of empirical society, to the extent that members of the sect perceive themselves as beyond conventional moral law (Troeltsch, 1931: 331; Wilson, 1970: 26–34).

We arrive at the *Protestant sacred* when the Reformation strips away the institutional and supernatural hierarchies that both constituted and spanned the gulf between the transcendent divine and the world, making that gulf at once infinite and infinitesimal, absolute and vanishingly small. With the divine's even more absolute removal from this world, it became apprehended under the figure of the *sublime* – as infinite, unconditioned and unknowable (Mellor and Shilling, 1997: 106–7). But at the same time as the Reformation radicalizes the gulf between the empirical and transcendent worlds, the latter is also brought close to each individual, and to nature. Following Weber (1930), Bellah describes the way that early modern religion flattens out the hierarchies in both the material and supernal worlds, so that the relation between the two worlds is no longer mediated through heavenly or earthly intermediaries. The service of God comes to be thought of not in terms of specialized ascetic and devotional acts but as an inner orientation, the sense of a divine command that has to be acted out in all areas of this profane life. This formulation allows the centred self of the monotheistic sacred to operate *outside* of world-denying practices, amidst the complexities of empirical social reality. Religious action is 'conceived to be identical with the whole of life', and the world is seen as an arena in which to work out the divine command. Over time, religious impulses become disaggregated, and give rise to a number of secular institutions (corporations, social movements, political parties, health and education) that stand outside the state as civil society (Bellah, 1970: 36–9).

This same dynamic – of the simultaneous shifts towards the radical otherness of the divine and towards its intimate entwinement with empirical reality – is also found in the emergent new science of nature. As nature is stripped of symbolic meaning by both Reformation thought and the emerging natural sciences, the divine is at once removed from direct intervention in natural processes, and also given new and intimate roles in relation to the newly discovered mechanical universe. With spiritual agencies no longer present and intervening miraculously in the physical world, the direct action of God himself is seen in the ordinary and routine operations of nature. For Newton, for example, lifeless nature is only animated by God's continuing intimate, active but predictable involvement in the world, as manifest in the operation of forces such as gravity (Deason, 1986). Divine attributes are thus stripped of metaphor and allegory and allotted specific functions in the new scientific understanding of the world – a move which helps lay the grounds for the later erasure of God from Western science (Szerszynski, 2003c). But for the time being there is a sustained attempt to reconcile the truths about nature that were being revealed by new sciences such as geology and natural history with the truths of scripture. Unlike the symbolic approach to nature characteristic of the Middle Ages this 'natural theology' focuses on defending and promoting the truths of Christian religion; truths that had been more or less taken for granted were now being approached as empirical hypotheses (Webb, 1915).

With the *modern sacred*, embracing the Enlightenment and Romanticism, the vertical transcendent axis is increasingly drawn into the empirical world. Instead of Being and order being seen as deriving from a supernatural source external to empirical reality, they are increasingly seen as *properties of that reality itself*. The world thereby comes to be seen as profane in a newly radical sense. In its original sense in the classical world, the profane or worldly was itself understood religiously; indeed, as I have said, 'profane' originally meant the space in front of the temple (*pro-fanum*), and was therefore only relatively less sacred, within an overarching sacral cosmos. In subsequent religious history, some sense of the profane as a sacral category still survived: even the Puritan settlers of North America had seen the apparent wilderness they found there in sacral terms, albeit as 'a kingdom under Satan' (Albanese, 1990: 35). But in the latter stages of the modern sacred the profane begins to be understood in a more radical sense, as a space that is *only* profane, that had no relation to the sacred (Gadamer, 1975: 150; See also Milbank, 1990).

This shift involved a radical departure from the relationships between political power and the sacred that had emerged in the context of the archaic sacred. Gauchet argues that Christianity broke with the 'organic interlocking of the Natural and the Supernatural'; after Christ, Gauchet suggests, no one could claim uniquely to inhabit the fulcrum between the natural and the supernatural. Initially, the monarchs of Christian Europe continued to draw on archaic notions of rule; however, they sought to take on Christ's power through not identification but comparison – a strategy that was vulnerable to it serving to undermine rather than reinforce kingly splendour. In time, secular power found ways of sacralizing itself that reversed the royal function; the role of the monarch was no longer that of 'incarnating sacral dissimilarity' but one of 'realizing the collective body's internal self-congruence' (Gauchet, 1997: 143). The outcome was a new sacralization of the social, of life itself. Rather than the transcendent sacred touching the empirical world at one point, the body of the king, it was folded into the whole empirical world, and the nature of monarchical power changed. Up to the eighteenth century, the absolute monarch had power to decide life and death – whether indirectly by asking subjects to put their lives at risk by defending the state, or directly by putting to death those who transgressed his laws or rose up against him. Power, in this era, was 'a right of seizure: of things, time, bodies and ultimately life itself' (Foucault, 1979: 136). From the eighteenth century onwards, by contrast, power became the right to administer life – not to impede or destroy the forces in society in the name of supernatural splendour, but to bend and optimize them, to make them grow in particular directions. And the objective of this new *biopolitical* ordering of society was the perpetuation of biological existence, of life itself, which became the new location of the sacred.[6] The goal of politics became the efficient functioning of the organism of society. Even the resistance to state power became conceived in the very terms that that power was taking, in terms of life: of the right to life, health and happiness (Foucault, 1979: 154; see also Rose, 2001).

Nevertheless, the transcendent axis, now introjected into the material world as an immanent ordering principle, still operates in a hidden way to maintain the idea of a single truth about the universe. With the Enlightenment an absolute, singular rational nature comes to take on the sublimity of God, as the idea of a rational but absent God is slowly abandoned in favour of the idea of an immanent rationality to nature itself – evidenced not just in an increasingly secular science, but also in wider cultural ideas. In the New World, for example, such a rational, singular nature provides the basis for the emergent civil religion of the American republic, underpinning the Declaration of Independence, with its lofty universalism, belief in natural rights, and contract theory of government. Nature is seen as 'an ideal and metaphysical principle', and conscience as the individualized version of this universal moral law (Albanese, 1990: 50–64). In terms of the experience of nature, Christian natural theology, with its concern with the truths of revealed, biblical religion, is increasingly displaced by an individual appreciation of wild, sublime nature. And in America in particular the sublimity of the monotheistic God – his supra-human grandeur, his indifference to the interests and projects of individual humans – is transferred not only to nature but also to technology, as the human capacity to transform the world starts to be seen not just as the ability to meet empirical needs but as a quasi-salvational collective project (Nye, 1994). But as we shall see in Chapter 4, with the loss of a supernatural reference for either salvation or worldly power, the ends and purposes of this technological project come to be understood in purely technical ways, as requiring the adaptation of the human to technological imperatives.

With Romanticism, by contrast, individuals seek to connect themselves with a singular nature through the recovery of an authentic state of being, one that has been lost due to the artificiality of social existence. Romanticism thus also offers a form of this-worldly salvation: through rediscovering our natural, authentic selves, and thus our interconnectedness with everything else, we can overcome our alienation from others and from the natural world. With both Enlightenment and Romanticist versions of this form of the sacred, it is the idea of the singularity of nature – a nature that had itself been constituted through its contrast and relationship with the transcendent divine – that takes over from the transcendent axis a central organizing role in thought and experience, not just in natural science but also in the ideas of natural rights and of natural authenticity.

Finally, we arrive at what I want to call the *postmodern sacred*, which exhibits a more thoroughgoing collapse of the organizing dualism of the monotheistic and Protestant sacred. But this signals not a return to the monistic, single reality of the primal and archaic sacred, but the emergence of a multiplex reality, one filled with and constituted by different cosmologies and world-views grounded in subjective experience. Rather than religion and cosmology – including ideas of nature – determining who people thought they were and how they experienced the world, instead people feel obliged to fashion or choose religious and cosmological ideas on the basis of their own subjective experience – what 'feels right' to them (see Heelas,

1996; Roof, 1999). The effect of organized religion had been to hold in check the asking of a myriad questions about the meaning and purpose of personal existence; with its withdrawal, such questions do not wither away but rather come to the fore, propelling individuals into personal searches for meaning. With the dropping of the doctrinal certainties and Puritan character ideals of early modern religion, culture and personality are seen as endlessly revisable, and answers to religious questions are sought not just in scripture but in secular art, thought and practices (see Gauchet, 1997: 200–7; Lee and Ackerman, 2002). Religious action thus becomes even more demanding than it was for the Puritans, with a growing imperative for each individual to work out their own religious and spiritual meanings, whether inside or outside the structures of organized religion (Bellah, 1970: 39–44). And under these conditions it is the 'aesthetic community' that is the paradigm form of sociality – a community that 'has no other foundation to rest on but widely shared agreement, explicit or tacit', and that is 'woven entirely from the friable threads of subjective judgements' (Bauman, 2001: 65).

This very plurality of the postmodern sacred also allows it to accommodate echoes of earlier orderings of the sacred. For example, in contemporary society we can see a partial return to the pre-Reformation experience of at least some places as having unique characteristics and powers and thus provoking 'pilgrimages' (see for example Ivakhiv's (2001) study of Glastonbury, England, and Sedona, Arizona). But whereas in medieval Christianity this kind of experience was organized in terms of the vertical relationship between the physical and the supernal world, in contemporary culture the significance of place is more likely to be conceived of in terms of empirical 'characteristics', or at most immanent 'energies' within this world as yet undiscovered by science. And whereas Australian aboriginals and medieval Christians both experienced places in terms of agreed meta-narratives, contemporary 'auratic' places are typically highly contested, with multiple interpretations being promoted by different social groups (Hetherington, 1997).

Sacral Change, Societal Evolution and the Secular

I have used this chapter to set out both the particular approach that I will be taking to secularization and religious change, and the particular narrative of religious and cultural change that I will be using to organize the discussion of nature and technology. But before concluding I want briefly to address the position of the secular in this account. For, as the attentive reader may have observed, I have described modern and postmodern secular society in terms of particular orderings of the sacred – that is, as not really secular at all, in the sense of being independent of any particular religious or sacral beliefs. And certainly the evolutionary approach to religion I have been drawing on above raises important questions about the continuity between religion and the secular. If modern secular society is produced by the later stages of Western religious history just as each of those stages can be seen as emerging from the one prior to it, does that make the secular part of that history or not? Is it just the latest phase in the ongoing transformation of the sacred? Or, once the secular world has emerged out of religion, does the former then become entirely independent of the latter?

Bellah does not tackle this question directly, but nevertheless does in effect describe the secular as a later stage in the transformation of religion. Bellah's schema is not just describing different kinds of religion; later stages of religion are presented as higher and more developed than the earlier ones, in that they are more open to change – indeed can act as motors for social change – and constitute a self that is more autonomous, more clearly separated from its natural and social environment and more reflexively aware of its own possibilities for action and self-reinvention. But Bellah's scheme is also evolutionary in the stronger sense that, in a quasi-Hegelian dialectic, each later stage is in some sense brought forth by the limits and contradictions of the previous one.

Here Bellah is building on the sociology of Weber, who saw rationalization as a process that occurred not just in modern secular society but also in the history of religion – albeit more slowly and haltingly (see Brubaker, 1984). Weber further argues that religious rationalization plays a role in kick-starting secularity; the Protestant Reformation provided a framework for ascetic self-control that was this-worldly rather than other-worldly in orientation, and thus laid the ground for the emergence of capitalism (Weber, 1930). But for Weber, once Protestantism had done its work in accidentally creating the conditions for the secular order and the technological condition, modern reason took off according to its own secular logic:

> For when asceticism was carried out of monastic cells into everyday life, and began to dominate worldly morality, it did its part in building the tremendous cosmos of the modern economic order. This order is now bound to the technical and economic conditions of machine production which today determine the lives of all individuals who are born into this mechanism, not only those directly concerned with economic acquisition, with irresistible force. Perhaps it will so determine them until the last ton of fossilized coal is burnt. (Weber, 1930: 181)

Jürgen Habermas also follows Weber, seeing secular modernity as growing out of the history of religion, but at the same time having become quite autonomous from it. Indeed, for Habermas the history of religion is actually the history of reason. With each phase of religion reason grows stronger, at first working within the bounds of religious tradition and then finally wresting itself free and claiming its post-religious autonomy in the modern world (Habermas, 1984).

Habermas's version of this religious history is highly sophisticated, but his work brings out sharply a controversial aspect of any evolutionary schema of religion – the vulnerability to a charge of ethnocentrism. Because non-Western religions such as Confucianism are represented as belonging to earlier stages of religion, societies organized by such religions are seen as-arrested at a lower level of societal development. The worry here is that what is in fact a very Western story of religious development is being inappropriately used to interpret and judge non-Western societal development. This problem is more acute in Habermas because it is central to his neo-Hegelian philosophical project to identify secular modernity – at least in its ideal, as-yet-unrealized form – with universal reason (Habermas, 1987a). For Habermas, the course of Western religious history has to be more than a contingent, local story, since it has to be – at least in its overall shape if not in every detail – a process of reason creating the conditions for its own flourishing: clearly differentiated societal spheres of science and technology, ethics and law, and art and affective experience; autonomous, self-legislating human selves with heightened levels of communicative competence; and a public sphere which approximates the 'ideal speech situation', one oriented to achieving unforced agreement based on the best argument (Habermas, 1979, 1987b). A defence of secular modernity which is couched in terms of its universal, rather than merely local, legitimacy, but at the same time wants to show it not as arriving fully formed overnight but as emerging gradually in religious history, will inevitably imply a hierarchy of religious maturity which will always be open to contestation.

Marcel Gauchet's account of *The Disenchantment of the World* largely avoids this problem by in effect reversing the evolutionary narrative of Hegel, Weber, Habermas and Bellah. According to Gauchet the history of Western religion is not one of progress and rationalization but one of decline from religion proper, which Gauchet identifies with primitive or 'primeval' religion. Christianity – and particularly the early modern religion of northern European Protestantism – is the religion to end religion, the religion which leads almost inevitably to a world without religion. For Gauchet post-religious society is thus only the present and future of the Protestant world, rather than being some inevitable and universal end-point of societal evolution. For Gauchet, Christianity and the contemporary secular it produced is not an inevitable working out of religious ideas but 'a highly individualized branching off from the shared destiny of the other major religions' (Gauchet, 1997: 104).

In this book I do not intend to engage deeply with questions about how to explain cultural change – whether, for example, economic and material developments produce changes at the level of ideas, or vice versa. I am using the idea of the transformations of the sacred not to *explain* changes in our understandings of nature and technology, but to *understand* them better.[7] Yet, like Gauchet, I do want to resist the idea that this history is the necessary outworking of universal reason. There is something more contingent to the direction of the history of Western religion than Hegel, Weber and Habermas allow. And the small-scale societies that still endure despite the globalization of Western culture should not be seen as anachronistic survivals of some earlier stage of a universal world history, but as coherent forms of life in their own right. But while it might be accurate for Gauchet to describe the modern secular world as post-religious (for example if one confines the term 'religion' to what Bellah calls historical and early modern religion), this does not mean that it is post-sacral. I am arguing that contemporary culture, the background for our exploration of nature and technology, exhibits not the disappearance but a *reorganizing* of the sacred.

The illusion that the sacred has disappeared is arguably a feature of all historical transitions from one form of the sacred to the next in a given society. Each transition can seem like an eclipse of the sacred in the terms in which it was organized in the closing epoch; from a larger historical perspective, however, it can be seen as the emergence of a new sacral ordering. In this respect, the non-sacral appearance of contemporary society is no different from that of earlier epochs when compared with the epochs that preceded them. Yet there are a number of ways in which the secularity of contemporary society *is* different to the apparent irreligiousness that was perceived to have been brought about by earlier transformations in the sacred. Firstly, as mentioned above, the contemporary world is understood as secular or profane in an absolute, not relative sense. It understands itself not as engaging in heresy, idolatry or apostasy, but as *non*religious, to be understood in its own, immanent terms, without reference to religious truth. Rather than the profane being a space within a sacral cosmos, religion (where it survives) is seen to be a social phenomenon within a fundamentally secular world, one thus to be explained by reference to secular realities such as interests or ideology (Milbank, 1990).

But, secondly, this understanding of the secular is itself a product of transformations in the sacred – of the long arc of monotheistic religion. The expulsion of the divine from the world with the emergence of monotheism at the same time constituted the secular, empirical world. Initially, this world was understood only in terms of its ongoing, ontological relation with its divine source, but with the Reformation that understanding changed, laying the ground for the eventual understanding of the secular world as ontologically self-sufficient, as characteristics of the monotheistic divine were incorporated into the understanding of the empirical world. The emergence of this 'absolute profane' thus has to be understood not as the end of the sacred, as the final, closing event of its repeated transformations – the suicide of the sacred, as Gauchet would have us believe. Instead, it is an event *within* the ongoing history of the sacred in the West.

Thirdly, the contemporary sacred has another important feature that marks it out from earlier epochs: its internal plurality. It has always been true that different periods of religious history are not as sharply delimited from one another as schemas such as that of Bellah might imply; each new epoch typically contains traces of the previous one, and can exhibit a partial return of characteristics of earlier epochs. But internal complexity is constitutive of the contemporary, postmodern sacred in a way that was not true of earlier forms of the sacred. As Beckford and Fenn point out, in contemporary society the discourses and practices of the sacred have been set free from their long incarceration in institutionalized monotheism, and have become generally available as a cultural resource (Fenn, 1978, 1982; Beckford, 1989). But what makes this more than a simple return to the primal and archaic sacred (however much contemporary neopagans might wish it were so) is the path-dependency of the postmodern sacred – its conditioning by earlier history. It was the Protestant sacred that constituted the autonomous human subject, by placing the individual in intimate, unmediated relationship to a transcendent ground of Being. In the postmodern sacred, by contrast, in some sense the subject *becomes* that ground of Being, in that religious, moral and even epistemic truth become seen as grounded in, rather than grounding, subjective experience. In such a context the main problem is not that of heresy (what to do with people who depart from the existing consensus about reality and the sacred); instead, the problem is how people might achieve any consensus in the first place.

It is against this background – a contemporary sacred constituted by and in complex relationship with a series of historical transformations of the sacred – that our exploration of nature and technology will proceed. Both nature and technology bear complex sets of positive and negative meanings in contemporary society, meanings which have to be understood in their historical and social context, that of a postmodern sacred, a defining feature of which is the plurality of subjective perspectives. But in order fully to understand those meanings we will also have to trace the trajectory that ideas of nature and technology have followed through other dispositions of the sacred: through the unified sacro-natural cosmos of the primal and archaic sacred, the transcendental dualism of the monotheistic and Protestant sacred, and the immanent sacred of the modern and postmodern sacred. This is the task of Part II of the book.

Part II

Nature and Technology

Chapter Three

Nature, Science and the Death of Pan

> Suddenly from the island of Paxi was heard the voice of someone loudly calling Thamus, so that all were amazed. Thamus was an Egyptian pilot, not known by name even to many on board. Twice he was called and made no reply, but the third time he answered; and the caller, raising his voice, said, 'When you come opposite to Palodes, announce that Great Pan is dead.' ... So, when he came opposite Palodes, and there was neither wind nor wave, Thamus from the stern, looking towards the land, said the words as he had heard them: 'Great Pan is dead.' Even before he had finished there was a great cry of lamentation, not of one person, but of many, mingled with exclamations of amazement. (Plutarch, 1936: 419)

Was the death of Great Pan, as later writers averred, coincident with the crucifixion of Jesus Christ? Was the moment in which Jesus said 'it is finished' (John 19:30) the point at which 'the natural world lost its numinosity, its sacredness', and human beings were set free to exploit nature for their own ends (Hughes, 1986: 21)? Many have written as if the course of history from the birth of Christianity to modern technology and widespread environmental problems proceeds with an inexorable logic.[1] Though the White thesis, as it has come to be known after the seminal 1967 essay by the historian Lynn White jun., has suffered enough criticism in the intervening decades[2] to point out the shortcomings of his 'early spadework' (Ferré, 1986: 2), it is a style of argument that promises to endure.

For in the literature exploring the relationship between religion and the environmental crisis, the displacement of archaic religion by historic religion (particularly Christianity) is usually cited as the moment in religious history that sets European, and later the wider world, on a path leading to the disenchantment and technological domination of nature. For example, White argues that Christianity 'bears a huge burden of guilt' for the contemporary environmental crisis (White, 1968: 90). He describes the victory of Christianity over paganism in Europe as a psychic revolution, one which laid the grounds for the systematic technological despoliation of nature taking place in later centuries. Seeing nature as full of spirits, or as itself divine, suggests White, was the source of various taboos on resource use (White, 1968: 85). And for White, a key problem with Christianity from an ecological point of view is that it makes God transcendent, wholly outside nature. In Western monotheism, the world is brought into being through the spoken word of God, affirming an absolute, ontological distinction between God and nature. Nature neither emanates from God,[3] as it does for neo-Platonism, nor is it 'the appearance of [a] god' (as it is for early Greek religion – see Foster, 1973). Nature thus becomes simply matter, available for technological appropriation, to be used according to human desires and projects.

Friedrich Schiller describes this shift as *die Entgötterung der Nature* – the dedivinization, or more accurately dis-godding, of nature (Berman, 1981: 57).[4] Many commentators (e.g.; Toynbee, 1974: 143–5; Passmore, 1980: 10; Starhawk, 1982: 7) consider that this process made it possible 'to exploit nature in a mood of indifference to the feelings of natural objects' (White, 1968: 86). Stripped of its divinities, tutelary spirits and *genius loci*, nature is made profane, and of only instrumental value.[5] J. Donald Hughes similarly argued that to see nature as divine had an inhibitory effect on environmental exploitation in ancient Europe, and that the replacement of Greek popular religion with Christianity had a correspondingly disastrous effect. The Great Pan, in particular, was identified with nature, or indeed with matter itself. Pictured as a hybrid of goat and man, he captured the tension between the *kosmos* and the *theos* of Greek pantheism, and as the bringer of panic discouraged the misuse of wilderness (Hughes, 1986).

This kind of narrative is still extraordinarily influential in discussions about environment and religion. However, there has been much dispute about various of its elements. Many scholars have raised doubts over whether non-modern societies did in fact protect nature to any significant extent – and, in so far as they did, whether it was their beliefs that ensured this (e.g. Lewis, 1992). But another problem with this dominant view of the relationship between religion and environmental destruction is that the sacral significance of nature is not exhausted by the notion of it as itself divine, or even as the locus of divinity. Christianity may have displaced animistic understandings of nature, but many other minor and major transformations in the sacred were to occur before nature could be seen as so much inert stuff without any sacral significance. So we have to see the death of Pan and the move to a monotheistic sacred simply as a shift within a larger frame, within what might be called the social or personal understanding of nature.

For much anthropological and historical evidence suggests that pre-modern nature is best conceived not as divine but as social (Kelsen, 1946; Descola, 1994; Descola and Pálsson, 1996). The example of Pan above is a case in point. When we look at the more concrete particulars of Hughes's argument, the idea that it was the perception of nature as divine that held environmental depredation in check seems less plausible than that it was an example of what one might call 'social nature'. Hughes himself supports the account of Pan's origin which sees him at first emerging, like Artemis, as a guardian deity of wild animals, whose goodwill needed to be secured for a successful hunt. Such deities developed into helpers of the hunt, and from there into 'quintessential hunters' themselves. This aetiology explains Pan's ambiguity in popular belief. He is a hunter himself, but protects certain species, and the young and weak of all species – punishing, for example, those who robbed the falcon's nest. He is *erémonomos*, the 'lawgiver of the wilderness', to whom are consecrated certain trees, the felling of which incurs serious penalties (Hughes, 1986: 12–15). In popular belief Pan is not understood pantheistically, as identical with the physical universe, but as a powerful and terrifying deity who must be propitiated by those who would make use of the wilderness. The idea of Pan as the universe itself, held for example by the Stoics, is an idea which belongs more to the 'axial' thought of Greek philosophy rather than the archaic sacred characteristic of the popular religion of the time. The Pan of popular belief and practice is neither transcendent nor immanent; he is the guardian of nature rather than nature itself.

The distinctions that Hannah Arendt (1958) makes between 'earth' and 'world', and between 'labour', 'work' and 'action' in her groundbreaking analysis of *The Human Condition* can be useful for clarifying the ways that pre-modern peoples relate to nature – though, as we shall see, we shall have to revise her implicit narrative of human development. Arendt uses 'earth' to refer to the physical and biological environment. The earth is the basis of our animal nature, grounded in the constant, cyclical processes of life, such as birth and death, growth and decay. As *animal laborans*, labouring (and consuming) animals, humans engage with earth, with the realm of biology and necessity, in the constant never-ending process of the meeting of physical needs. However, humans are not *only* labouring animals. Humans also have the capacity to create a 'world', an ensemble of human artefacts that can form an enduring setting for human affairs. The world in this sense is created by human beings, not through labour but through 'work', a goal-directed activity that leaves behind itself lasting artefacts. The world is carved out from the earth by taking materials out of the cycle of growth and decay and converting them into something enduring, useful and meaningful tools and objects. Arendt's 'world' is thus rather like a clearing in a forest, an enduring space for human life that is wrested by violence from nature, and requires a constant process of repair to keep it from returning to the cycles of nature (1958: 139). Finally, the *vita activa* is completed by 'action' – speech and meaningful gesture, self-disclosure, recognition and remembrance. Action is not transitory and repetitive, like labour; but neither does it leave behind a physical product modelled on the blueprint that guided it, like work. Rather, because of the nature of human beings and relations, action sets into train unpredictable and uncontrollable effects, spiralling away from the actor's control.

In *The Human Condition*, then, we have a three-layered, emergent picture of human existence: through labour we engage with and participate in the rhythms of earth, the biophysical substrate; through work we produce the world; and, against the backdrop of that world, we constitute through action the shared, public arena that subsists between individuals. The human world is thus progressively layered over or carved out from brute biophysical nature. However, anthropological accounts of non-modern cultures suggest that this schema is problematic if we treat it as an account of social evolution. To do so would be simply to perpetuate a kind of creation myth for modern urban societies, an example of what Latour calls acts of 'purification' (Latour, 1993). In terms of the human construal of the world, it is not the case that the social is laid over the natural; the anthropological evidence suggests a rather different picture.

Firstly, small-scale societies see their natural environment less in terms of earth than in terms of world. Rather than simply being experienced as a wild realm of blind forces indifferent to humans and their concerns, pre-modern cultures experience the world as an already meaningful dwelling place (Ingold, 2000, part 2). For example, whereas European settlers conceived of the North American landscape as wilderness, Native Americans regarded it as a homely, domestic space (Cronon, 1983). Secondly, pre-modern cultures typically conceive of human interaction with the non-human world not as labour but rather as action. Walter Ong (1982) argues that oral cultures experience the world in terms of verbs rather than nouns, as continuous action and response. He suggests that it was the rise of alphabetic writing and then print which displaced the magical, dramatic world of events and formal causes, and replaced it by the modern world of abstract space and mechanical causation (see Goody, 1977). Viewed in the context of the historic transformation of the sacred, then, Arendt's notion of the purely biological earth, and the narrowly technological labour through which humans interact with it, are in fact modern abstractions from the interplay of action between humans, non-humans and supernatural beings – projections onto pre-modern culture of distinctively modern understandings of nature and technology. Humans are born into a world of action; it is only when we have moved into the 'carpentered' world of the modern mind that we distil ideas of labour and fabrication from the stream of action (see McLuhan, 1962).

Even farming and pastoral cultures do not necessarily have a separate realm of 'necessity', of the technical manipulation of nature. Karl Polanyi suggests that pre-modern societies did not have a separable class of economic or productive activities. Activities which would be so designated in Western culture were embedded in what we would call non-economic institutions and ways of thought – the spiritual, the ethical, and the aesthetic (Polanyi, 1977: 53).[6] However, 'social nature' proper is more characteristic of primal and archaic cultures. For such cultures the environment is a taskscape – 'an array of related activities' – that has ' "collapsed" into an array of features' (Ingold, 2000: 197–8; see also Szerszynski, 2003b: 209–10). For the Pintupi aborigines of the Gibson Desert in Western Australia, the landscape is not a given substrate but 'the congelation of past activity' of humans and ancestral beings (Ingold, 2000: 53–4). Similarly for Amazonian peoples like the Piaroa of the Orinoco basin, the landscape is sedimented action, signs of actions performed by the gods in primordial time (see Eliade, 1954; Overing Kaplan, 1975). For such peoples, Arendt's foundational narrative is reversed. They do not fabricate an artificial world, and then dwell in it; world-making emerges out of daily quotidian activity – food collecting, cooking, childminding. Even the buildings of such culture are not architecture in the sense of being conceived of, then fabricated, and only then dwelt in. Instead, they emerge out of social activity itself (Ingold, 2000: 172–88).

In order better to understand how nature and technological intervention might have been conceived of in the world of the primal and archaic sacred, we can explore the world of the Micmac, a tribe of eastern Canadian hunter-gatherers, as described by Calvin Martin. For the Micmac the environment is seen not as a mechanism but as a society, in which animals, plants, and even inanimate objects are, in the words of Murray Wax, ' "fellows" with whom the individual or band may have a more or less advantageous relationship' (Martin, 1978: 33–4). However, these beings are not perceived naturalistically, but as examples of the 'super-human forces and beings' which make up the Indian world. These anthropomorphic spirits, which even reside in human artefacts, are called *manitous* in Algonquian, a term also used to refer to the spiritual potency of a thing. Various taboos exist regarding the treatment of animal remains, which are elaborated in the case of bears into 'bear ceremonialism', including conciliatory speeches. These taboos and ceremonies are described as being marks of respect for the dead animal, but the main motivation for their observance is the fear of supernatural reprisal by the spirit of the slain animal, or more likely the appropriate 'keeper of the game', if the taboos are not observed. These 'keepers' or 'masters', later simply known as 'bosses', are minor manitous, sometimes heard among the noises of a forest but rarely seen, which lead and protect each species of animal. Like Great Pan and Artemis in popular Greek religion, the manitous are tutelary deities of the hunt, to be ritually propitiated if the hunt is to succeed.

For the Ojibwa, another hunter-gatherer society discussed by Martin, nature is a 'congeries of societies', each species or 'society' of plant or animal being led by 'keepers of the game' (Martin, 1978: 71). Human beings are seen as possessing no natural pre-eminence, since many other animals outstrip their abilities in many ways. Since they understand their way of life to depend on the co-operation of the animals they hunt, they exhibit no arrogant assumption that the world is a great banquet laid on just for them.[7] But American Indian belief also picks out human uniqueness, through its equivalent of the biblical injunction to have dominion over nature. For the American Indian, human society is just one of many societies which inhabit the world, but uniquely 'has the awesome right to harvest Nature'. The other species 'were to yield themselves up to man for his needs', willing sacrifices to his arrows. This belief may, of course, be explained as functioning to deflect guilt for the killing away from the hunter, and the existence of similar beliefs in ancient Rome, imperial China (Clark, 1984: 121) and seventeenth-century England (Thomas, 1984: 29) may serve to support this suggestion. But, whatever its function or aetiology, this expectation of willing surrender is qualified by corresponding expectations that the American Indians respect certain restrictions placed on their behaviour towards animals, forbidding practices such as overhunting, torturing and insulting them. American Indians are guaranteed *pima-daziwin*, the good life, but only if they pay 'scrupulous attention to innumerable details of comportment' (Martin, 1978: 73).

For the eastern Canadian Indian hunting is no mere technological activity, but a 'holy occupation'. Success in the hunt depends on the co-operation of supernatural forces, and the hunter's role as the harvester of nature is not mechanically assured. Like the *imago* of Genesis 1:26–7, it is not integral to his essence but somehow superadded, and so revocable. Only magical operations can secure the co-operation of the animal and its 'keeper', so that the former willingly surrenders itself to the hunter (Martin, 1978: 114–16). The 'dreaming, divination, singing, drumming, sweating, and other forms of hunting magic' overcome the resistance of the game spiritually, after which process its physical dispatching is inevitable. The process is in effect 'contractual', more social than natural, since the acquiescence of the prey is conditional on both the hunter and the prey fulfilling their obligations both before and after the killing. For the hunter's part, failure to observe the taboos about disposal of the animal's remains would make the hunt illicit, and the hunter would be subjected to supernatural reprisals (1978: 120–1).

We can see here that interactions with nature in pre-modern societies take the form not of 'labour' but of 'action'. Hunter-gatherers see hunting not as a 'technical manipulation of the natural world but as a kind of interpersonal dialogue' (Ingold, 2000: 48). The hunt is seen as a social interaction, whose outcome is inherently unpredictable yet can be secured by each side fulfilling propriety through appropriate forms of speaking such as promising and apologizing. Arendt herself suggests that the only way that the irreversibility and unpredictability of human action can be tamed is through binding speech acts such as forgiving (in which the past is reversed) and promising (in which the future is secured) (1958: 236–47). The very presence of these speech acts in pre-modern interactions with nature underscores the social and action-like character of such inter-actions.

Yet just because pre-modern societies interact with nature in a social way, this does not mean that they regard nature ethically, as consisting of sentient beings who should be treated as ends in themselves. To argue this way is anachronistically to project modern ideas of ethics onto cultures for whom they would make little sense. This can be illustrated by two examples. The Baiga, a tribe of primitive hillfarmers in Deccan, India, believe it to be sinful to 'use a plough and thereby lacerate the breasts of Mother Earth'. Yet the tribe imposes no penalty on those who do, regarding it not as a moral offence but a ritual one, which may cause disease and death (Fürer-Haimendorf, 1967: 50). The second example concerns the Lele of Zaire and the Nuer of the Nile. The hunting Lele conceive the wild forest as a realm of spiritual forces and symbols, the Nuer regard it in a dispassionate way. Yet it is the pastoral Nuer who could more exactly be said to respect wild animals, and find hunting distasteful (Willis, 1974: 21–2). The 'social nature' of pre-modern cultures may encourage ritual limitations on the treatment of the non-human, but does not seem to encourage ethical or sentimental relations in the modern sense. As we shall see, for nature to be regarded ethically it was necessary for a transformation in the sacred to occur, one which replaced the social understanding of nature characteristic of primal and archaic religion with a new ordering of the sacred according to a vertical, transcendent dimension. So if transformations in the sacred laid the conditions for the instrumental exploitation of nature, the same transformations also made possible the ethical counter-reactions to that exploitation which would later emerge.

Monotheism and Nature

If the birth of the Christian era marked the death of Pan, it could be said that he took a long time to die. Theologically speaking, the crucifixion of Christ may have been the end of the archaic sacred, the close of the age of magic and miracles. But it is really only with the Reformation and

Counter-Reformation of the sixteenth century that the sacral presence and power of nature starts significantly to wane. Nevertheless, in its locating of divinity outside nature, Christianity stands firmly in the religious lineage descending from Hebrew monotheism, with its equation between the tribal God who makes a covenant with Israel, and the supreme God of Creation, who brings the universe into being out of nothing. Before this, ancient religions, when they recognized the notion of an ultimate creator god, tended, as African religions do, to think of him, as 'remote and unapproachable, a creator who, having created, stands back and watches rather than participates' (Turnbull, 1978: 135). By contrast, the Old Testament experience of nature, exemplified in Psalms, is one dramatically shaped by the belief that the personal God of the covenant with Israel is also the creator of the world. The result is an idea of a moral order underlying the whole of creation, one distorted by human perversity, but ultimately to be restored.[8]

For the Abrahamic, monotheistic faiths of Judaism, Christianity and Islam, the Creator God was thus brought to the foreground of the religious life. Vriezen argues that this meant that 'the secondary religious world was thrust into the background' (Vriezen, 1960: 224). It is true that, although belief in the spirits of nature and of the household continue throughout the biblical period and beyond, there is hardly any place in official Yahwism or Christianity for contact with them. However, it would be more accurate to say that what monotheism now regarded as the 'secondary religious world' of invisible supernatural presences was reoriented around the new transcendent axis. Classical and medieval Catholicism thus found a place for earthly spiritual power in the form of the saints; yet, as we shall see in Chapter 5, their powers were progressively disconnected from natural places, gathered into the basilicas, churches and other places of Christian worship, and seen as vehicles for divine, unearthly power (Brown, 1981, 1987).

The people of the first few centuries of the Christian era in Europe understood their lives in terms of intimate relationships with invisible companions such as gods, spirits and angels, a notion which was shaped by the late Roman experience of friendship and patronage between living individuals as well as by the idea of a chain of intermediary beings linking the individual with God. In a Christian context, this gave rise to the cult of the saints, whereby personal identity and moral experience were vitalized by felt bonds with 'the very special dead' – individual human beings who had become so intimate with God that friendship with them could enable individuals to bypass the huge chain of mediating entities above them in the cosmic hierarchy, and thus link themselves directly with the divine (Brown, 1981: 61). Just like priests, kings and popes on earth, such beings could be sought out 'as alternative objects of loyalty and affection or as intermediate sources of power and fortune', far more accessible than the dizzy heights of the heavenly throne (Walzer, 1968: 152). As well as serving as moral examples, and as companions, the saints could thus bring aid to the individual, in respect of both worldly problems and spiritual ones. Such was the saints' overflowing personal store of merit that they were able to intercede on behalf of the sinner, and assist their quest for eternal life (Hawley, 1987). Even official monotheism thus retained the archaic sacred's positing of specific points of connection between supernatural and worldly power; but the expulsion of the divine from this world meant that the sacred was understood in terms of relations with a transcendent realm.

As Michael Northcott (1996) and Alister McGrath (2002) have argued, this 'dis-godding' of nature does not by itself result in a disenchanted nature, understood in the material and mechanical terms characteristic of secular modernity. Nevertheless, with the gradual displacement of paganism from Europe by Christianity, the animacy of nature was progressively understood in a rather different way. Firstly, whereas the pagan understanding of nature had been oriented to the meeting of physical needs, for official Christianity at least the focus was on the edification of the soul. The shift from the archaic to the monotheistic sacred involved a reorientation of religious action away from the reproduction of existence in this world and towards the securing of eternal life in the next. In the Christian world, nature came to be approached primarily as a realm in which supernatural truths can be discerned. According to this symbolist mentality, objects, plants and animals were understood as *signs*. The key for interpreting nature was allegory, originally developed by Greek philosophers as a method to sanitize myth, but adopted by Christians as a method for interpreting scripture and nature. Systems of hermeneutic interpretation were developed: for example, as developed by Alexandrian Platonists, and later codified by Origen and Augustine, the medieval *Quadriga* gave rules for the interpretation of both scripture and nature, in terms of literal, allegorical, moral and supernatural levels of meaning. In an interpretation of scripture according to the *Quadriga, historia* referred to the literal deed being reported, *allegoria* to relations to past or future events, *analogia* to moral truths, and *anagogia* to spiritual truths in the transcendent realm (Harrison, 1998: 15–30).

Augustine added a new theoretical foundation for Origen's hermeneutics: rather than words bearing multiple meanings, they are unequivocal in their reference to their object; it is rather the things to which words refer that are open to different interpretations. After Augustine, then, allegorical interpretation is seen as finding multiple meanings not in words, but in the things to which they refer; allegory thus becomes a theory not of language but of *objects*. Objects are not wholly unstable in their meanings, which are determined by relations of likeness or similitude; but it is only scripture that can correctly stabilize meaning and reveal the true meaning of objects.[9] Idolatry, for Augustine, consists not so much in attaching transcendent meanings to things but in failing to attach them, being enslaved by the literal meaning of objects. 'He is a slave to a sign who uses or worships a significant thing without knowing what it signifies.'

Through this method of interpretation natural objects and not just words were seen as referring to moral and spiritual truths as laid out in scripture. The focus of elite thought about nature throughout the patristic and medieval period is structured not in terms of *action* – as social intercourse between natural or supernatural beings – but *signification*. However, nature was not yet interpreted as a text; if nature was approached as language, it was as *parole*, not *langue* – an assemblage of individual signs, messages from the creator to his creatures, rather than an interconnected system with its own syntax. Augustine's theoretical hermeneutics ensured that nature was interpreted according to vertical relations between empirical things and the transcendent realm, rather than through horizontal relations between things and other things. Nature was seen as having no inherent grammar; the intelligibility of nature was only possible through the scriptural exegesis of nature.

But in the twelfth and thirteenth centuries, in the context of a valorization of the physical in Christian culture, there was a growing sense of nature having its own inherent intelligibility – and one that could be manipulated for earthly benefit. Firstly, there was a renewed interest in horizontal relations of similitude between things and other things. Secondly, there was an emergent sense of nature not just as a collection of signs but as an entity in itself – as a text. The idea of scripture as a unified whole, animated by principles of hermeneutic interpretation that related part to part and part to whole, was also applied to nature. Nature became a whole, and the human being was seen as belonging to it in a new way, part of its grammar. Thirdly, the connections between things were understood as not just semantic but causal, with objects in the world acting on each other through relations of similitude (Foucault, 1970; Harrison, 1998: 32–50).

The human body thus came to be seen as part of a natural world that was organized in a grammar such that any element could act on another – such that 'a gesture can loose a tempest'. A range of taboos, protective rites, premonitions and practical spells could be deployed in order to manipulate and control this visible and invisible world (Muchembled, 1985: 71–9). At the level of popular religion, medieval practice had retained many of the characteristics of the archaic sacred, with its moral ambiguity and specific points of fusion of natural and supernatural power; the Church had been only partly successful in reordering the sacred in the terms of a transcendent, benevolent God. For medieval society, 'an immense dispersion of the sacred invested the entire universe with forces...that were neither benevolent or malevolent a priori, but that were all apt to be dangerous' (Muchembled, 1985: 28–9). Relics and places of worship were scattered across the countryside as well as in the great urban centres – in chapels, springs, fountains, at niches with effigies at crossroads, in springs and woods protected by saints. This sacred topography was common knowledge, mobilized during times of pilgrimage as well as out of every-day, local concern for soul and body (Muchembled, 1985: 101). Rituals were specific to particular places – and could even be used to manipulate space, such as in the processions used to bind together sixteenth-century Lyons (Davis, 1981). Late medieval popular culture also placed an em-phasis on the lower body as joyful, and as a locus of connection with nature through functions such as reproduction and the fertilization of the soil (Muchembled, 1985: 93). The ecclesiastical authorities themselves oper-ated in tandem with such understandings, attempting to reorder medieval individuals' understanding of the sacred by using the 'close contact' senses of taste and touch as paths to religious knowledge (Mellor and Shilling, 1997: 38–9).

For the medieval faithful the Church was seen as a bearer of miraculous potentialities. At the level of official doctrine, the Church was seen as possessing a treasury of grace and merit, from which it derived the power to remit the sins of its members; the sacraments were seen as a vehicle through which this grace, as if it was a miraculous substance, could be distributed to the faithful (Troeltsch, 1931: 338, 468; Bossy, 1985: 54–5). But religious, salvational action blurred into magical intervention in the natural world; relics and images were routinely credited with magical effi-cacy – even holy water and consecrated hosts regularly being used to pro-tect the health of people, crops and livestock (Thomas, 1973: 32). Robert Scribner (1987) identifies three kinds of operative magic used in sixteenth-century Germany: *sacraments*, such as baptism, the Eucharist and marriage; *sacramentals*, the use of palms, candles and herbs; and *conjur-ations*, prayers, ritual formulae, and the use of objects, especially natural objects, to bring about magical effects. Sacred power was understood in a material way, and material intervention was understood in terms of the operations of sacred power.

The Reformation and Nature

Let me recapitulate the chapter so far. I have suggested that the transform-ation of ideas of nature from pre-modern to modern societies is best understood not as dedivinization, disenchantment or secularization but de-socializing or depersonalization. Relations with nature in pre-modern soci-eties were not seen as a clearly separate category of technological relations distinct from the social and the cultural; they were understood using categories and concepts that today we would largely reserve for social relationships, such as reciprocity, intention, action and meaning. In pre-Christian societies, the social, spiritual and natural worlds were not distinguished; nature was full of agencies which needed to be bargained with. What for the modern mind would be conceived as technological or economic activities such as hunting and gathering were seen as a social encounter, a bargain with non-humans or with the supernatural beings charged with their protection. Much of this way of thinking survived well into the medieval period, only slightly modified by the positing of a transcendent divinity as the source of all sacred power, and by a new emphasis on eternal salvation as the goal of religion.

With the gradual Christianization of Europe, however, this rendering of nature was gradually displaced by a neo-Platonic understanding of nature as *sign* – intercourse with nature was a contemplative encounter with a collection of signs. In the late medieval period this was materialized. Nature was revalorized, and increasingly seen as a singular whole (Williams, 1980). The relations of part–whole seen as organizing scriptural meaning were also seen as obtaining in nature, and understood as causal as well as semantic. Sympathetic magical relations were understood to exist between different parts of nature. Such ideas were to play a part in the emergence of science (the search for the inner grammar of nature) and technology (the capacity to manipulate nature). But certainly we are still a long way from the supposedly disenchanted nature of secular modernity. It seems that even to the extent that the monotheistic sacred with its transcendent axis did displace the tutelary spirits of the archaic sacred in the Christian era, the result was not a dead and meaningless nature, but one that was alive with sacral meaning.

So if it was not the nailing of Christ to the cross that disenchanted nature, maybe it was another act of nailing that sealed nature's coffin – the legendary nailing of the 95 theses to the door of the castle church in Wittenberg on 31 October 1517 by Martin Luther, an act which precipitated the Reformation. Michael Northcott argues that it is not the arrival of Christianity but its virtual departure in the modern era that constitutes the source of the contemporary environmental crisis, suggesting that in fact '[t]he traditional religious world-view of the Middle Ages tended to preserve the natural world from excessive human interference' (Northcott, 1996: 84). For Northcott the stage for secularization and the resulting ecological crisis was set by the Protestant Reformation, which insisted that the concern of God is for the individual human soul alone, not for the fallen creation. Northcott argues that 'the rise of instrumental views of nature has gone hand in hand with the demise of the traditional Christian view of creation as the sphere of God's providential ordering, and with the gradual secularization of European civilization which began at the close of the Middle Ages and reaches its nadir in secularized modernity' (North-cott, 1996: 83–4).

While disputing Northcott's analysis of the nature of secular modernity, he is right to trace a continuity between Protestantism and secular modern-ity; in terms of orderings of the sacred, they share far more than divides them. But for my purposes I want to focus on the links between the Reformation reordering of the sacred and the rise of the scientific view of nature. And to do that we have to go back to another proclamation – the condemnation issued by the Vatican in 1277 of a number of propositions in circulation at the time among scholastic philosophers. Under the influ-ence of Aristotelian and neo-Platonic ideas, many scholastics had been sug-gesting that God could not but have created the world in the way that he had. For neo-Platonists, for example, to argue that there was anything arbitrary about the universe was to introduce the contingent into the sub-lime unconditionedness of the One. This not only meant that the world was necessary – was a *plenum* – and that its nature could thus be ascer-tained through scholastic reasoning; it also implied that God's power was constrained. Against such ideas, the Vatican asserted the voluntarist doc-trine that God could have created any world that he wanted. This gave support to the nominalist understanding of language – that only particulars exist, not universals. Natural objects were seen not as entities existing in their own right, with their own innate essences and the powers of develop-ment to realize them. Instead, they had no independent being, but were held in existence by God's continuing activity.

So even at this stage in the transformation of the sacred in the West we have not left behind a personalist view of the universe. Indeed, in voluntar-ism we can see a radicalization of this view, one in which all events in nature are seen as the direct activity of God's mind. But at the same time this is the very same branching of the sacred which leads to modern science and its understanding of nature. From the beginning, this growing current of theological voluntarism and nominalism encouraged different ways of thinking about nature. For a start, the idea that God was free to create any world he liked encouraged hypothetical thought, eroding Aristotelian and neo-Platonic certainties. Thought experiments became not just permitted but pious: the universe could have been created without an absolute centre; the universe could have been made infinite; there could be other universes; there might be a void outside the cosmos – or even in it. Initially, such speculation was presented as just that, hypothetical speculation, and at-tracted no criticism so long as it was not asserted categorically (Grant, 1986: 56–7, 68–9). In the seventeenth century, of course, it was Giordano Bruno with his affirmation of plural worlds, and later Galileo with the heliocentric universe, who most publicly contested this model of hypothesis when they presented their ideas not as speculation but as fact.

But voluntarism also meant that the investigation of nature should involve empirical observation. Unlike the neo-Platonic God who necessarily emanated the universe from his very being, the voluntarist God could have chosen to stop creating at any point. Only empirical observation could determine how he had in fact created the universe. Initially, however, the result of the growing power of nominalist ideas was a weakening of confidence in certain truth. The rejection of the idea of creation as necessary had meant that reason was unable to determine the true ordering of nature; but on the other hand experience could not provide certain knowledge either, as God could always choose to change the way he was acting at any time. So the world of fourteenth-century voluntarism was a radically contingent one. To observing nature was not to discover the essences and *telos* of natural things, but to directly observe the continuing creative activity of God, which could alter at any moment.

In such a cosmos, there could only be probable knowledge; the contingent cosmos of the voluntarists thus seems no more hospitable to scientific modes of thought than the necessary cosmos of the neo-Platonists (Grant, 1986: 58–9). But what made science seem worth pursuing was the voluntarist interpretation of the idea of God as a lawgiver, which implied that there was an order to be discovered (Oakley, 1969). Biblical language about God offered many images of his creative power where, rather than creating *ex nihilo*, he is presented as imposing laws onto matter: 'God made a law for the rain' (Job 28:26); 'The Lord says to the sea, hitherto thou may come and no further' (Job 38:11); 'The law has bounded sea with sand by perpetual decree' (Jeremiah 5:22). Voluntarism meant that, rather than natural objects being investigated in terms of God's communication with man through allegory and symbol, they were examined to find the direct operations of God's mind (White, 1968: 88–9). The scientist was not just seeking to know the world from within, as an empirical being among others; he was seeking to know the world as God, its creator, knew it. And, although God had absolute power to act as he wished in creating and upholding the world, there was a difference between his absolute power and his ordained power. In fact, God was rational, and chose to behave lawfully. This language of 'laws' would later be used by scientists from Descartes to Newton, as they sought to discover the laws that God had impressed on passive matter (Deason, 1986).

For more than three centuries voluntarism remained a minor tradition of thought in European culture. But by the sixteenth century a profound transformation was under way in Europe, one which laid the grounds for its revival. The views of Chastellain, the fifteenth-century historian of the Burgundian nobility, summed up the theistic sociology that was being swept away by events. Each estate or stratum of society, he felt, had been created by God expressly for the function which they fulfilled in society:

the common people to cultivate the soil and to trade, the clergy to perform religious duties, and the nobility to maintain justice and to provide a virtuous model towards which the rest of society could aspire (Huizinga, 1924: 48–9). Such views are typical of the period, not least in their failure to acknowledge that real power by this time was moving elsewhere, to the merchants and absolutist monarchs. European society was changing rapidly, moving away from social organicism and towards markets, despotism and democracy. The centralization of power by absolutist monarchs undermined local social and judicial autonomy. This, coupled with extravagance, loss of income and inflation, drastically weakened the aristocracy. Finally, the growing ease of credit, and capitalist innovations like joint-stock companies, facilitated an explosion in the late sixteenth and early seventeenth centuries of mercantile and industrial activity, so that social relations such as those between landlord and tenant became increasingly economic and less and less customary in nature (Kamen, 1984: 105–10, 69–79).

It was in this context that the Protestant reformers reject medieval organicism in favour of the absolute omnipotence of God, and revive voluntarist thought in a new and potent form. Gone is the idea of the great chain of being (Lovejoy, 1936); gone, indeed, is the idea of any intermediary at all between the individual and God, except for the Bible and Christ himself. As Michael Walzer puts it, 'the Calvinist God . . . establishes his own omnipotence by leveling the cosmos, by destroying the intermediate power of the angels, of the Blessed Virgin and the saints, of the pope, the bishops, and finally even the king'. Divine rule over creation, like the political rule of an absolute monarch over his subjects, is no longer seen in the donative terms in which it was conceived in medieval thought; no longer is rulership the partial giving away of power in the very moment of its exercise (Milbank, 2004). Like the absolute monarch who simply sits at the centre and commands, thereby diminishing rather than increasing the being of his subjects (Arendt, 1958: 188–90), the voluntarist God reigns as a despot over 'a single, unified domain', and all beings and institutions only have powers inasmuch as he continuously bestowed them (Walzer, 1968: 152).

The Reformation in turn drives profound shifts of emphasis in northern European culture, shifts from image to word (Duffy, 1992: 591) and from allegorical to literal meaning, enabling the emergence of a radically new way of conceiving of nature, that of modern science. The search by Protestant reformers for a stable, unambiguous religious authority in the Bible leads to an insistence that it should be interpreted literally, cutting away three of the *Quadriga*'s levels of meaning, dismantling the method for interpreting the material world, and thus withdrawing intelligibility and meaning away from objects themselves and reserving such properties for words alone:

The sacred rite which had lain at the heart of medieval culture was replaced by a text, symbolic objects gave way to words, ritual practices were eclipsed by propositional beliefs and dogmas. In the course of this process, that unified interpretive endeavour which had given meanings to both natural world and sacred text began to disintegrate. Meaning and intelligibility were ascribed to words and texts, but denied to living things and inanimate objects. The natural world, once the indispensable medium between words and eternal truths, lost its meanings, and became opaque to those hermeneutical procedures which had once elucidated it. (Harrison, 1998: 120)

However, the collapse of the *Quadriga* not only broke the chains of meaning which embedded the medieval individual in their environment; it also laid nature open to radically new modes of ordering, ones based not on similitude and analogy, but on the precise comparison of sameness and difference through mathematics and taxonomy. This new ordering of nature brought language and the world together in a new way, in relations not of symbol and allegory but of reference, as truth was conceived as consisting solely in accurate correspondence between language and reality (Reiss, 1982). Thus, made possible by the contingent history of the sacred in the West, modern science was born.

Nature in the Scientific Revolution

Contrary to many accounts, the scientific revolution of the sixteenth and seventeenth centuries is only inadequately described in terms of the separation of science and religion. As the historian Amos Funkenstein has convincingly argued, the work of Galileo and Descartes, Newton and Leibniz, Hobbes and Vico can in fact be seen as a high point of convergence between science, philosophy and theology. Funkenstein describes the activity of these and other natural philosophers of the time as a 'secular theology', in two senses. Firstly, theirs was a theology practised by the laity rather than by clergymen, and by those without advanced degrees in divinity. Secularization of theology in this sense, its appropriation by laymen, had of course been encouraged by the Reformation. But secondly, this was a theology oriented to the 'world' in a way that had not been the case before, a world increasingly seen not as a transient stage for the development of human souls, but as having its own religious value, both as a dwelling place and as a creation whose study can reveal the mind of its creator. As Funkenstein puts it, '[t]he world turned into God's temple, and the layman into its priests'. From the fourteenth century onwards, barriers between disciplines had been progressively eroded, not least with the rise of the peripatetic programme as a competing model of transmission to that of the medieval university. The idea of a unified system of thought and knowledge, conceived as 'a set of interdependent propositions', and based on a unified method of enquiry, gained currency from the seventeenth century. As part of this system, theology was expected to import ideas and forms of reasoning from other disciplines, such as mathematics, and in turn 'God ceased to be the monopoly of theologians' (Funkenstein, 1986: 6).

Funkenstein describes modern science as the convergence of four ideals – homogeneity, univocity, mathematization and mechanization (Funkenstein, 1986: 28–42). Each of these ideals have an often long history prior to the seventeenth century, but in modern science they came together in a distinctive and powerful way. The ideal of homogeneity assumes simplicity in *things*, that the universe is the same everywhere – the same matter, the same kinds of motion, ultimately the same laws. Univocity requires simplicity in *language* – that terms unambiguously denote their referent in terms of relations of identity and non-identity, rather than through similitude, analogy and metaphor. Mathematization involves not as it had for Plato and Pythagoras that *things* were mathematical, in the sense that nature takes simple, geometric forms, but that scientific *language* should be mathematical in order to refer correctly to nature. Finally, mechanization required the expulsion of teleology, final causes and intentions from nature; matter was conceived as passive, its behaviour determined by causal relations and natural laws.

There are a number of ironies here. Firstly, the 'disenchantment of nature' is also the *emergence* of nature in the modern sense (see Scott, 2003: 8–16). One could almost say that there was no nature to disenchant before it was disenchanted. The modern idea of nature as a coherent, uniform entity, as matter following its own mathematical and causal laws of behaviour – this emerges at the same time that it is investigated. But, secondly, modern science approaches the world in a way that was deeply conditioned by the religious history of the West. The ejection of the divine from the empirical world had at the same time constituted that empirical world as something that could be thought of as a whole. With the Reformation the radicalization of that transcendent dualism made it possible to think of matter as simply matter – as following the laws impressed on it by the divine, as being connected causes rather than meanings. Nature as understood by science thus has its own hidden theology. And the 'disenchantment' of nature is thus itself a form of enchantment.

The scientific revolution did not in itself dispose of God; however, its proponents changed the meaning of theological language about God, changes which allowed him to be eventually incorporated into the empirical world (see Latour, 1993: 32–4). Their desire for univocity involved the refiguring of theological discourse in the same way that they had refigured natural history, stripping it of the analogical and symbolic relations between signs, ideas and things that had been central to the main currents of theological reasoning for centuries. Whereas for Thomas Aquinas all talk of

God's attributes – even concerning his very existence – could only be analogical, Descartes, Newton, More and Leibniz aspired for a clarity and distinctness in their ideas about God which paralleled that which they sought in relation to nature. Language about God's attributes, about his very being, had to be stripped of its analogical character and rendered univocal; similarly, talk of the relation between God and his creation has to be clarified and purged of mystery. 'God's relation to the world had to be given a concrete physical meaning' (Funkenstein, 1986: 116).

For example, it was necessary for the secular theologians to reject medieval ideas of God co-operating with vital principles immanent within nature. One of the preconditions of their project of the mechanical description of the world according to mathematical laws was that matter had to be seen as wholly passive, containing no vital force or *nisus*. Mechanical philosophers such as Boyle and Newton thus stressed the absolute sovereignty of God and the dependency of matter on him for its continued existence and movement.[10] But it is not merely the case that the theology of Boyle and Newton was being shaped by their science; with echoes of scholastic arguments deducing the nature of God's creation from the nature of God, they also built their scientific principles on theological foundations. In the late sixteenth century Giordano Bruno had argued that, because God is infinite, he must have created an infinite universe;[11] similarly, Descartes deduced his principle of linear inertia – of sustained movement in a straight line – from the immutability and lack of arbitrariness of God.

Thus, far from the birth of modern science consisting of a radical break with religion, it constituted an intensification of theological reflection in relation to the natural world. Up to the seventeenth century natural religion had been seen as a lesser form of religion, for the ignorant and the illiterate, one incapable of revealing the higher theological truths. But from the eighteenth century nature came to be seen as a *superior* religious authority, and one readable by everyone (Harrison, 1998: 200–1). Now we are all in principle capable of reading nature in a scientific way; however, the theology that shapes our reading of nature is a very particular one, produced by one branching of a complex and contingent historical process, and put in place by the secular theologians of the scientific revolution.

It has always been easy to point to exceptions to the modern disenchantment of nature (Bennett, 1997). However, what has been neglected is the way that this very disenchantment involves its *own* ordering of the sacred. The Newtonian world-view depended upon a particular ordering of the sacred; the very constitution of the world as inert matter behaving according to mathematical laws in absolute space required a specific transformation of religious meanings, one that involved a newly literal approach not just to matter, but also to God. The melancholy of the modern world, the 'vast gulf between the sublime and the painful, lonely and finite world of humans' (Mellor and Shilling, 1997: 107), is thus the result not of the abandonment of the sacred, but of the adoption of a particular ordering of it, one made possible by the axial religions' ordering of the sacred in terms of a vertical, transcendent axis, and by the subsequent radicalization of this axis by the sixteenth-century reformers and seventeenth-century natural philosophers in terms of an absolutely powerful divine on the one hand and utterly passive material creation on the other. This complex, branching path taken by the Western sacred – from the social nature that is still inhabited by surviving primal and archaic cultures, through the allegorical nature of symbols and magical interconnections characteristic of the Middle Ages, through the nominalist nature of God's direct activity posited by voluntarist theologians and taken up and later made atheistic by natural science – is not one in which the sacred is withdrawn like a protective mantle from the world, leaving a pre-existing nature bare and exposed to exploitation. It is rather one in which nature and the sacred emerge as separate principles for the first time, and then are fused back together in a quite new ordering of the sacred. Modernity is thus constituted by a 'religion of nature' that changes both religion and nature.

But this of course is not the end of the transformation of the sacred in the West; there are further changes which will be of particular importance in subsequent chapters, changes which involve in part the emergence and fate of the modern conception of the individual as a unique locus of consciousness. The emergence of the axial religions had already laid the ground for this by positing a transcendent non-empirical 'One' to which each existing being could be related, for example as creature to creator. The Reformation had taken this a step further, with its emphasis on the interior life of each Christian as an unfolding personal biography. But as the sense of spiritual power and semiotic meaning in the natural world grows yet feebler in the eighteenth century, we see the emergence of the recognizably modern individual, understood as controlled by impulses coming from within. Tracing changes in the English language over the next two centuries, Owen Barfield describes this as a process of 'internalization', 'the shifting of the centre of gravity of consciousness from the cosmos around him into the personal human being himself'. 'All this time', Barfield writes, 'the European "ego" appears to be engaged, unawares, in disentangling itself from its environment – becoming less and less of the actor, more and more of both the author and the spectator' (Barfield, 1954: 166–7).

As Louis Dupré argues, the constitution of nature as object and the self as subject that we see Descartes (1968) wrestling with in his *Meditations* are one and the same move. The self is no longer being thought of as a microcosm of the whole cosmos; instead, the relation between self and world is one of observer and observed, subject and object. No longer is God the necessary being – that being whose existence it is logically impossible to deny – as he had been for Anselm and other medieval theologians. In the *Cogito* it is the human thinking subject which is necessary, as 'a mere function of the objectifying process' (Dupré, 1993: 93). Thus, as one enchantment of nature passes from history, as the natural world loses its allegorical significance and magical powers, another enchantment takes its place, as nature is reinterpreted according to a theology of absolute divine transcendence and power, one whose God commands rather than co-operates with his creation. So too is the human being subject to another enchantment; no longer able to 'loose a tempest' as he or she could in the medieval cosmos, he or she displays instead the even more awesome power of the God of Descartes, Newton and Boyle: the power to know the world in a univocal sense, in terms not of allegory and metaphor but measurement and lawful regularity.

Yet as we shall see in the chapters to come, in many ways this mutual stability of the world as object and the human as observing subject was not to be a permanent state of affairs. First of all, the objects of science underwent a radical reconceptualization in the early nineteenth century. As Foucault recounts, many sciences underwent a transformation at this time, departing from the methods of reductionistic analysis that had characterized their operations in the seventeenth and eighteenth centuries. Rather than areas of knowledge being organized in terms of relations of observable similarities and differences, many of them started to be reorganized according to the idea of hidden unities lying underneath a surface of differences (Foucault, 1970: 251). In Cuvier's biology, for example, beneath the surface of the differences between species, and between organisms and their environment, lie the great unities of function – respiration, digestion, sensation and so on – not reducible to constituent material elements or visible to the senses, but nevertheless in many ways more ontologically fundamental. At the same time metaphors of mechanism started giving way to more historical, processual understandings of nature, which were to culminate in Darwin's theory of evolution by natural selection (Collingwood, 1945).

These new ideas of nature as 'life' brought the sciences more in line with the changing nature of society. With the growth of industrial capitalism and liberal democracy, political rule was increasingly conceived in terms that had less to with maintaining contact with transcendent supernatural norms and power, and more with maintaining and shaping the immanent self-reproduction of society. In such a context the clarity and distinctness of objects before the knowing mind of God, or the philosopher or scientist, was far less important than their function in the reproduction of the social order. Reorganized in terms of ideas of process and function, in the nineteenth and twentieth centuries science would find itself taking an increasing role in the technological administration of the life process, but – as we shall see in the next chapter – in a way that compromised both nature as stable object and the human as sovereign subject.

Chapter Four

Modern Technology and the Sacred

In the last chapter I argued that scientific ideas of nature are a product of the contingent, branching trajectory of the Western sacred, rather than a timeless set of truths which were simply waiting in the wings of history for cultural conditions conducive to their discovery. Nevertheless, it might be supposed that, once science has contingently emerged, the technological exploitation of nature is an almost necessary outcome – that if not science, then technology was waiting off-stage, an always existing potential of human beings to transform nature, only held in check by religious beliefs and practices which were inimical to the instrumental use of nature. Morris Berman implies such a view when, like Barfield (1954), he suggests that the disenchantment of the world leaves human beings in a passive relationship with nature. The pre-modern cosmos was 'a place of *belonging*', and a member of this cosmos was 'a direct participant in its drama'. By contrast, the modern world is a world of 'meaningless things', and humans just alienated observers (Berman, 1981: 2–3). For Berman the frenzied activity of the modern age is simply a reaction to the meaninglessness and hollowness of this disenchanted modern world.

However, in this chapter I want to argue that the activity of the modern world, and in particular the technological transformation of nature, is more integral to the story of the ongoing sacralization of nature than Berman's account implies. Far from being a reaction to nature's loss of sacral meaning, technology is a 'calling', a vocation with its own theological underpinnings, and one that is integral to the modern sacralization of nature. The modern observer does not just stand back and observe. The passive contemplation of nature characteristic of the modern scientist is but one moment in a more general cultural whole, whose overall character is profoundly active. As Heidegger argues, although chronologically modern science (seventeenth century) precedes modern technology (nineteenth and twentieth centuries), in a more fundamental sense technology is prior. For Heidegger, science is the 'herald' of technology; it arrives first, but it serves technology by ordering nature to 'report' in a technological way, to stand before humanity as a 'calculable coherence of forces' made ready for technological intervention (Heidegger, 2003: 258). To say this is not to say that technology was always the destiny of the West. On the contrary, I will argue that the technological transformation of nature, no less than science, is a contingent product of the West's specific sacral history. Furthermore, I will suggest that placing modern technology against the background of the ongoing transformation of the sacred in the West can help us understand the various meanings attached to modern technology in Western societies.

Reflection about technology can be traced at least back to classical Greece, when Socrates, Plato and Aristotle all deliberated about the relationship between *technai*, the arts and crafts, and *episteme*, knowledge. For both Plato and Aristotle *technai* were activities involving the making of things in a way which was guided by *logos*, by reason, and could thus be talked or reasoned about, and hence taught. Their linking of art with reason shows the 'axial' characteristics of the classical Greek world, in contrast to the 'social' understanding of nature and technology characteristic of the primal and archaic sacred; yet, as Carl Mitcham points out, Greek *techne* is still a long way from modern ideas of technology. Firstly, *techne* is 'fundamentally oriented to particulars instead of toward the efficient production of many things'. Secondly, for classical thinkers *techne* provided an inferior kind of knowledge compared to that promised by contemplation, because of its concern with particulars rather than universals, and with changing rather than unchanging things. Thirdly, at that time the *technai* were regarded as separate crafts with no overarching set of general principles, and as intrinsically uncertain and unpredictable in their outcomes. This was partly to do with an almost animistic conception of matter as having its own desires, its own *telos*. Matter, unlike form, is *agnosis*, cannot be perfectly known. *Logos*, or reason, can only guide the understanding of the form and function of the artefact, not of the matter out of which it will be made. Form can only imperfectly be combined with matter in the finished product; the art of this combination of form and matter cannot be codified in speech and reason but only learnt through experience (Mitcham, 1994: 118–23).

Classical Greece inherited a widespread suspicion of the arts from archaic cultures, with their myths of the punishment of technological hubris, such as those of Babel, Prometheus and Icarus. The over-reaching of technological ambition is seen as disastrously disconnecting those who wielded it from the wider sacral order. But in the axial culture of classical Greece this hostility is reformulated in terms of the vertical axis – in terms of the relationship between *techne* and philosophical knowledge, and in particular the inferiority of fabrication when compared with contemplation (Arendt, 1958). For the Athenian philosophers, technology can only tell us how to do something; technical knowledge must always be subordinated to philosophical and political discussion about the good. An unhealthy focus on *techne* diverts a person from reflection about the good life, makes people morally lazy by producing affluence, and focuses on knowledge of the lower and the ignoble. Furthermore, technological objects are inferior to nature, imperfectly combining matter and form, lacking an innate *telos*, incapable of orienting their activity to an inherent goal, and requiring goals to be imposed on them from outside (Mitcham, 1990).

Whereas Eastern Orthodox Christianity broadly continues this contemplative suspicion of technological activity, in the West Christianity places greater emphasis on the will, thus focusing not on contemplation but action. For the Greeks, sin is to be understood as ignorance, and salvation lies in illumination, contemplation and thought. For the Latins, by contrast, sin is moral evil, a problem of the will, and salvation is to be found through right conduct (White, 1968: 87–8). For White, this theological difference predisposed western Europe to feel that salvation required action, thus laying the ground for the later technological transformation of nature. However, the Christian's allegiance to supernatural over natural ends meant that for at least a millennium this relationship was at most a theoretical possibility. As Ellul (1964: 34) writes of the coincidence of the rise of Christianity and the decline of Rome, '[t]he Emperor Julian was certainly justified in accusing the Christians of ruining the industry of the empire'.

Nevertheless, the activist tendency of occidental Christianity did play a role in the later emergence of techno-scientific understandings of nature. Monasticism in particular provided a context for the development of ideas which would become important in the later revaluation of manual labour and the transformation of nature (Ovitt, 1987). But it was the Reformation which provided the turning-point, by changing the meaning of asceticism. Rather than being conceived as an other-worldly high-water mark of religious achievement which assumed a contrast with average, worldly morality, asceticism became recast as a straightforward refusal of worldly pleasures in favour of purposive conduct within the world (Troeltsch, 1931: 332; Weber, 1985: 118–19).[1] The same need to confirm holiness through worldly activity that encouraged the rise of mercantile and industrial capitalism (Weber, 1930) may also have helped encourage the scientific exploration of nature (Merton, 1970).[2] For, certainly, the scientific revolution, despite seeing the study of nature as a religious activity, did not interpret it as a form of passive contemplation. Indeed, it could be argued that scientific knowledge is only intelligible in the context of an active orientation to the world, one with an interest in prediction and control; such an orientation is assumed by that knowledge, whether or not that activity is indeed carried out (Habermas, 1971a). Seventeenth-century natural history involved finding order in nature not through the passive reading of meanings, but by an active investigation, itself seen as a religious duty – thus reversing the classical privileging of contemplation over action, and of *episteme* over *techne*. It was also believed that the study of nature could restore the human race to its pre-lapsarian state (Harrison, 1998: 269–70). Modern science and technology thus reinterpreted the salvation history of the Bible in terms of a literal history, and one that could be brought about by human action.

Underpinning much of the post-Reformation, activist orientation to nature is what might be called a negative sacralization of nature. Protestant natural theology divided into two fairly distinct variants, with Anglicans generally emphasizing the goodness of creation, and evangelicals its fallenness (Hilton, 1988). As we have seen, in earlier European tradition, nature was seen as full of lesser spiritual beings – both benign and malign. By contrast, for many after the Reformation nature was sacralized under a negative sign. Nature had lost the capacity it had had under the archaic sacred to be bargained with. It had also lost the power it had had in the medieval period to represent complex theological truths. If anything, natural theology experienced a revival after the Reformation. But for the Protestants, nature could only teach a limited number of divine attributes – that there is a God, or that God is great, for example – thus throwing them back on scripture for salvation (Harrison, 1998: 201–3). And for some – even as late as the Victorian era – it was the very disfigurement of nature that spoke most powerfully of God's judgement on those who would stray from righteousness (Brooke, 2004). Armed with this kind of natural theology, the Puritan settlers of America had regarded the nature they found as a hideous wilderness (Nash, 1973). However, they were able to link their own destiny with biblical ideas of the desert as a place for testing and spiritual purification, giving a positive reading to this negative sacralization of nature as 'a kingdom under Satan' (Albanese, 1990: 35–40).

Yet even here we are still not quite arrived at modern technology as it presents itself today. The Reformation may have elevated the *vita activa* and thus given a new dignity to worldly action, and the secular theology of Newton and Boyle might have rendered matter passive and knowable in a way it could not have been for the Greeks. But technology during the Reformation is still largely seen as simply a means to an end, as incapable of guiding action. Similarly, for Protestants, economic activity is able to serve as a sign of spiritual election, and technology is used to pursue religious aims. But the technological has not yet become a whole way of thinking; the arts may be being regarded in a newly positive way, but in the

Reformation period they are still conceived in terms similar to those of the classical period. In this traditional view, tools were subordinated to human goals. As Robert W. Daly put it, using Aristotle's fourfold model of causation, the tool user was the 'efficient cause' of the final product, the resource substance used the 'material cause', the specific goal of the technological intervention the 'formal cause', and lifeworld context within which that goal was intelligible the 'final cause'. In sum, 'an identifiable man [*sic.*] uses a tool as a means to achieve a goal in a comprehensible ends-context' – that is, a context construed in terms of non-technical understandings of human interests, desires or purpose (Daly, 1970: 419).

But by the eighteenth century *techne* was giving way to 'technology', through shifts in the ordering of the sacred that parallel the ones involved in the emergence of modern science, as discussed in the previous chapter. I described there the way that the birth of scientific 'nature' involved a complex modification of religious meanings whereby God became at once more transcendent and more closely involved with the material world – an absolute sovereign commanding passive matter to obey the laws of his creation. At the same time, the languages of natural philosophy and theology were brought together, stripped of their metaphorical layers of meaning, and given new characteristics of univocality and precision. That the technical arts underwent similar shifts should not be surprising, given the close connection between scientific epistemology and the activity of fabrication (Pérez-Ramos, 1988). But at least from Francis Bacon's *Advancement of Learning* ([1605] 1960) onwards, technology also had its own theological framing as a soteriological project, one which sought to bestow upon the practical arts the certainty that was characteristic of reason itself, and thus to liberate humankind from finitude and necessity, allowing it to share in the unconditionedness of an increasingly sublime deity (Noble, 1999; Song, 2003). In the process, the traditional hierarchy of *techne* and *episteme* was reversed – the highest, most certain knowledge derives not from contemplation but from active intervention.

The slow emergence of the term 'technology' itself helps us to trace these changes. Aristotle had only conjoined the words *techne* and *logos* once, and this in the *Rhetoric*, seeming to use the term to refer to the way that words, divorced from their, in our terms, vertical relation to universal reason, could be used solely as a means to quotidian, horizontal ends. The Greek word *technologousi* was used in this sense up to the twelfth century – not as craft subordinated to reason, but as reasoning subordinated to craft and artfulness. But with the Reformation, and particularly with Puritanism, came a new emphasis on reducing the arts to universal, univocal methodological principles – on finding the *logos* of *techne* itself, the science that defines all the arts, and thus overcoming the recalcitrance of matter and making it subservient to *logos*. *Technologia*, and its synonym *technometria*, emerged as Latin terms in the work of the sixteenth-century French Protestant rhetorician Peter Ramus, who used them in the more modern sense of 'the *logos* of the relations among all *technai*'. But it was in the eighteenth century, for example in the work of Johann Beckamann, that the concept of technology as 'a functional description of the process of production' emerges in its recognizably modern sense (Mitcham, 1994: 128–31).

These changes constitute the extension of *logos*, of speech and reason, deeper into the fabrication process, expunging the residual animism that was involved in conceiving the craftworker as having to co-operate with matter. In the Protestant sacred, matter has been reconceived as the passive recipient of laws impressed on it by a sovereign creator, by one who knows his creatures by making them. The scientist too can claim this 'maker's knowledge' through adopting the experimental attitude to nature, and thus coming to know the laws by which it was made. And almost in the same gesture, as the technical intervention into nature allows the scientist to know it in this new sense, as the sovereign voluntarist God knows it, so too does the scientific knowledge of nature allow the technologist to intervene in it in a sovereign manner – commanding nature through a following of it which is now conceived as following God's laws and thus God himself. Thus it is now not only, or even principally, the ends and form of artefacts that are amenable to *logos*, but the very process of manufacture itself. The constitution of a technology in this way requires what Andrew Feenberg calls a 'primary instrumentalization' which involves the transformation both of the materials out of which the technology is constructed, and of the wielder of the technology. On the one hand, the raw materials have to be decontextualized out of their naturalistic context (as, for example, rocks in the ground) and reduced to primary qualities (such as brittleness and homogeneity). On the other, the user of the technology has to be 'autonomized', insulated from the effects of technical action on an object, and positioned in a way that they can control objects through knowledge of the latter's laws (Feenberg, 1999: 203–5). In this new ordering of nature and technology *homo faber*, the human as fabricator, is no longer one who co-operates with matter as another creature with its own desires and goals; instead, he acts on it from outside, yet as one who knows it more intimately than it does itself, as if its creator.

But Martin Heidegger gives us further insight into the technological condition of modern human existence. In *Being and Time* (1962) he describes two ways of relating to entities. For Heidegger, the more fundamental of the two is *Zuhandenheit*, usually translated as readiness-to-hand. This is the quotidian, everyday 'equipmental' relating to objects through use, in which the instrument we are using 'withdraws' and we are just aware of the world through it rather than aware of the instrument itself – for example, as a visually impaired person is aware not of the stick they are holding but of the surfaces and objects that they feel through it. By contrast, Heidegger argues, scientific ways of knowing involve a secondary way of knowing objects, *Vorhandenheit* (presence-at-hand). In this orientation to the world we know not through using but through looking at, and the object appears to us not as a set of possibilities and uses but as an object to which we attach predicates – extension, mass, density, and so on. Heidegger's conception of the relation between these two orientations to the world means that the presencing at hand of objects offered by modern science is itself only made possible by the more primary praxical, equipmental relation to the world of readiness-to-hand. Indeed, for Heidegger, equipment, tools and objects can only become present-at-hand when they malfunction, becoming just brute obstinate objects, and the human subject withdraws from practical engagement in the world and instead knows its objects in a different way, from outside the lifeworld (Ihde, 2003: 289). *Vorhandenheit* thus echoes the image of the transcendent, sovereign God of post-Reformation voluntarist theology, engaging with his creation not socially, as giver of being and receiver of praise, but through his sheer will, which is at once the mode and instrument of his knowledge of the creation.

But it is Heidegger's 1954 essay 'The Question Concerning Technology' that is most concerned with modern technology itself, and that excavates more exactly the consequences of the further transformations of the sacred that occurred after the emergence of modern science. He presents modern technology as a fusion of *Zuhandenheit* and *Vorhandenheit*, of practical engagement in the world and abstract forms of scientific knowledge. He contrasts a hydroelectric plant on the Rhine with the old wooden bridge 'that joined bank with bank for hundreds of years', to try to convey how modern technology as an 'ontic' possibility in the world itself depends on a very specific 'ontological' ordering of the world, a historically specific form of *alethia* (truth, or 'unconcealedness'). Heidegger uses the German word *Gestell* (enframing) to describe this deeper ordering of the world that makes the technological attitude possible. *Gestell* is 'a challenging of nature' to be unlocked, transformed, stored, distributed, and used. Unlike the tree felled by a carpenter to be made into a table, the flow of the Rhine is transformed into power, to be distributed, to serve something else. In this enframing, objects once again withdraw, as they do in the primal everyday orientation of *Zuhandenheit*. But instead of them being absorbed into the everyday practical relationship with the world, they are turned into 'standing-reserve' (*Bestand*), ready to be incorporated into a technological system. And the reason that human beings challenge nature in this way is because they too are 'claimed', challenged by enframing. As part of an economic system, the forester 'is made subordinate to the orderability of cellulose, which for its part is challenged forth by the need for paper, which is then delivered to newspapers and illustrated magazines'. Human beings thus take part in the challenging of nature as standing-reserve, but they cannot control it (Heidegger, 2003).

What Heidegger is describing here is in effect how technology as a phenomenon is further transformed in the modern period, as the transcendent axis, radicalized by the Reformation and modern science, is itself introjected into the empirical world. During this period sovereignty comes to be conceived in terms not of transcendence and difference, but of the maintenance of society's own immanent coherence. 'Life itself' (Franklin et al., 2000: 188 ff.) becomes sacred, as what Foucault describes as the 'biopolitical' ordering of modern society emerges from the end of the eighteenth century. Foucault developed this analysis in *Discipline and Punish* (1977) and *The History of Sexuality* vol. 1 (1979), connecting new forms of state disciplinary power that developed during the eighteenth century with the emergence of a more 'biological' understanding of the human.[3] Foucault argues that it is at this time that life is first thought of as an object to be administered, and that this new power over life took two forms. The first, anatomo-politics, focused on the administration of the individual human body, regarded as a machine to be measured, disciplined and optimized. The second, biopolitics, emerged later, and focused on populations, the management of life, of what Karl Marx called the 'species body'.[4] Both of these, Foucault notes, were vital for the emergence and growth of capitalism, so that bodies and populations could be effectively inserted into productive and economic processes. Law, too, became less focused on displays of 'murderous splendour' for those who transgress sovereign power, and simply part of an array of technical apparatuses regulating and measuring life, trying to bring it to the norm. For Foucault, this was 'the entry of life into history'; rather than the biological exerting pressure on society from outside in the form of epidemics and famines, it was increasingly an object of control *within* society. Life was at once placed *outside* history, by being conceived in biological, natural terms, and *inside* it, in that it was subjected to politics (Foucault, 1979: 139–43).

In terms of the sacred, this represents a shift away from the understanding of this world as pointing towards the next one – as both symbolizing transcendent truths, and preparing the faithful for eternal life. Instead, there is a focus on the endless reproduction of life-processes within *this* world. Here, the natural and biological takes on a new immanence and self-sufficiency. The natural had itself been constituted with the construction of the vertical transcendent axis – as the empirical counterpart to the transcendent divine. In so far as they were *creatures*, created beings, things had a nature. But the creature was never solely biological, merely natural. Within earlier orderings of the sacred, to be solely biological was to be stripped of sacral or social status, to be in a state of deprivation of legal status or religious communion with the divine, characteristic of the slave, apostate or person convicted of a heinous crime (Arendt, 1958: 84; Agamben, 1998: 71–4). In the modern period, by contrast, the biological becomes seen as a self-sufficient mode of existence; what modern power administers is no longer 'legal subjects' but 'living beings' (Foucault, 1979: 142–3). And in such societies technology alters radically from the forms it took in pre-modern times. Technology becomes systematized, with an explosion in the scope and purchase of technique, and its harnessing to the goal of shaping and optimizing life itself.

In *The Technological Society* Jacques Ellul seeks to capture features of this new technological condition – both the way that technology in modern society seems to promise a this-worldly salvation by removing uncertainty from human affairs, and its distinctive, self-reproducing dynamic. He distinguishes between traditional 'technical operations' and the 'technical phenomenon', in terms of the way that the latter takes what was tentative and *agnosis* and 'brings it to the realm of clear, voluntary and reasoned concepts' (1964: 20). The technical phenomenon (*la technique*) is a uniquely modern form of making and using artefacts – '*the totality of methods rationally arrived at and having absolute efficiency*...in *every* field of human activity' (1964: xxv, emphasis in original). He explores the way that technique resists incorporation into non-technical contexts, and becomes the measure for itself. Traditional *technai* were located in the context of a non-technical matrix of human ends, with accounts of human flourishing, incorporating ideas of beauty, justice and contemplation. But with modern technique, the ends-context of any specific technological application is itself construed in technical terms, so that there is no non-technical context to which technology is understood as subordinate. Technique thus becomes 'self-directing', a closed, self-determining phenomenon. Further, technique expands, linking together different techniques in relations of mutual dependency, and absorbs non-technical activities into its orbit. Fundamentally, technique becomes an end in itself, in which elements are functional – adapted not to specific ends but to the needs of the system as a whole (1964: 79–147).[5] Thus no individual steers the technological process; rather than individuals being the wielders and directors of technology, they are 'responsible only for seeing that the technical act is done correctly' (Daly, 1970: 419, 420). To use Heidegger's terms, in challenging nature to act as standing reserve, they are themselves challenged.

Technology and the Sublime

Another way to capture this change is to say that technology became sublime. The concept of the sublime originated with the first-century writer Longinus, who used the term to describe a characteristic of certain performances of rhetorical expression (Longinus, 1964). For Longinus the sublime was not something to be contrasted with beauty, but an *extreme* of beauty. After a long period of dormancy, interest in the sublime as an aesthetic figure was revived by the publication of a translation of Longinus's essay on the sublime by Nicolas Boileau in 1674. Longinus's vocabulary of ideas seemed to resonate with post-Reformation and Enlightenment culture. For example, the concept of the sublime seemed to provide a language for expressing God's distant, inaccessible grandeur after his removal from involvement with this world by the Protestant reformers (Mellor and Shilling, 1997: 106–7). And the sublimity of the divine seemed to correlate with a growing sense of the finitude and alienness of this world, and with melancholy as a defining mood of modern culture (Turner, 1987).

The concept took a decisive turn with the publication in 1756 of *A Philosophical Enquiry into the Origin of our Ideas of the Sublime and Beautiful* by Edmund Burke (Burke, 1987). Burke was not the first to make the sublime a separate aesthetic principle to that of beauty, or to locate it outside human language and expression and in nature; John Dennis had done this in his *Miscellanies* (1693). But Burke grounds his account empirically – in the characteristics of natural objects and scenes, and in human biology. He tries to identify external features that produce the distinctive pleasures of the sublime: obscurity, darkness; power; privations (e.g. silence); vastness, especially depth; infinity, or apparent infinity; seeming expenditure of effort; magnificence (e.g. stars, profusion, chaos) (Monk, 1935: 85–93). And Burke makes terror central to the sublime; whereas beauty is social, linked to love, sublime is linked to self-preservation and pain, but this is pain and terror 'modified . . . not carried to violence . . . delightful horror'. 'Its highest degree', writes Burke, 'I call astonishment; the subordinate degrees are awe, reverence, and respect' (Burke 1987, part 4, section 7). In 1790 Kant's *Critique of Judgement* takes Burke's distinctions between beauty and the sublime, stripping them of their affinity with empirical psychology, and incorporates them into his transcendental philosophical project. In particular, with Kant, although the sublime starts with a sense of shocked wonder and awe, the result is an affirmation of human rational autonomy and moral worth (Kant, 1978).

The shifting place of terror in the concept of the sublime helps us better to locate it within the ongoing transformation of the sacred. In the primal and archaic sacred, fear and dread are evoked by the mysterious supernatural presence that according to Rudolf Otto 'loiters in the secret dread of hollows or caves . . . calling forth the sense of awe, the *numen* of the deserts and of regions of terror, of the mountain and the ravine, of haunted places and of overpowering natural phenomena' (quoted by Proudfoot, 1985: 64). But in the axial religions of Judaism, Islam and Christianity, the divine is ejected from this world along a vertical pole, as the cosmological monism of earlier religion is replaced by a dualistic distinction between 'this' world and a transcendent realm, and religious concern turned from the maintenance of life in this world to salvation in the next. The *numen* is progressively transformed, de-mythicized, stripped of particularity, and becomes the transcendent, numinous God, experience of whom evokes feelings of both dread and blessedness (Otto, 1950). Then, in the Protestant sacred, the numinous is displaced by the absolute sublime, as the divine is increasingly understood as infinite, unrepresentable and unfathomable, and to be worshipped for its own sake only, without reference to self-interest (Milbank, 1998). Finally, this reformulated sublimity is merged into the very 'empirical' world that had been constituted by the ejection of the divine from the cosmos in the first place – into nature, which overawes us and absorbs us into its mystery, and into the abstract human reason of modern subjectivity. Awe has been wrested from its animic object, directed along the transcendent axis, purified and transformed, then pulled back to find its new object in the sublimity of autonomous human reason and its categorical imperative.

But it is not only human contemplation but also the practical arts that find themselves a new object of 'delightful horror', particularly in the New World context. As the sublime crossed the Atlantic, and was adapted from its European roots to fit it for American conditions, it took on a newly public and spectacular form, and found a new object in technology. David Nye lists a number of crucial changes the sublime underwent as it crossed the Atlantic: it became less a philosophical idea and more a feature of practice; it spread progressively from elite, educated society to popular culture; it turned from a solitary experience to one available to crowds; it shifted its framing and language from transcendental philosophy to revivalist religion; it became an occasion for feelings not of individual moral worth but national greatness; and crucially it became associated not just with nature but also with technology (Nye, 1994: 43). The sublime thus became a key figure for the self-understanding of America, able not only to underscore the 'lofty universalism' of the Jeffersonian vision of government (Albanese, 1990: 63–4), but also to combine a sense of the unique grandeur of the vast natural landscape of the new country with a celebration of the human capacity to transform the same landscape. A very specific 'technological sublime', exalting the power to dominate nature, provided a new, non-denominational civil religion to unite a pluralistic nation through awestruck moments of Durkheimian collective effervescence in front of public technological projects such as bridges and skyscrapers, and later atom bombs and rocket launches.

Nye narrates shifts in the values evoked by the evolving technological sublime in America. Whereas the moment of astonishment in sublime experience is universal, the moment of re-establishing equilibrium, when the subject grasps the sublime object through new meanings, changes through history. The nineteenth- and early-twentieth-century technological sublime had celebrated rationality, production and the unique power of America to create a destined world. It has also been republican, manifesting powerful echoes of classical culture with its valuation of democracy and public life. Later, however, the growth of corporate capitalism stripped the technological sublime of its classicism and sense of collective democratic endeavour. Nye describes the exhibits at the 1939 world's fair in New York to illustrate this shift. These 'corporate rituals', exhibits that were not designed to sell particular products but 'to synthesize technological, electrical and geometrical sublimes into one form that modelled the future', displayed possible new futures with few vestiges of classical values (Nye, 1994: 223). Later events marked by the technological sublime, such as the launch of Apollo 11 in 1969 or the rededication of the Statue of Liberty in 1986, were 'nearly empty of the contents of political life required by republicanism', with little reference to virtue or moral elevation (Nye, 1994: 279).

Nye's narrative illustrates a few important features of the technological sublime. Firstly, as an aesthetic and theological figure it can serve to make the kind of specific linkages between worldly and spiritual power which were characteristic of the archaic sacred. The collective awestruck moments experienced by Americans in the face of 'their' nature and technology seemed to mark out the American nation as having a privileged connection to the universal destiny of humankind. Secondly, in the nineteenth and early twentieth centuries, the American technological sublime was also made to carry humanist democratic values. The English architectural sublime had been feudal in character, emphasizing social hierarchy; massive factories and warehouses had been built, 'striking terror into the observer'. In America, by contrast, not architects but engineers built sublime structures, and these were generally public works, celebrating the democratic dynamism of the new nation (Nye, 1994: xviii-ix, xix). But by the late twentieth century this had changed. The technological sublime shifted to the empty liminality of the consumer experience, or to the seeming technological determinism of a technological future determined by private corporations or the military. In both of these renderings of the technological sublime, the place of the individual is that of a passive enjoyer or sufferer of technological change. It is not the American people but technology itself which has 'manifest destiny'; the technological 'stake of the century'[6] has granted technique a self-determination, an autonomy, that trumps and overawes the rational autonomy prized by Kant.

At this point Nye's analysis has to be developed to include not just spectacular technologies, but also the invisible and distributed characteristics of modern technological systems. The very inferiority of technological artefacts in the classical view meant that the danger they posed was always constrained. As they had no inherent purpose, they could not impose this purpose on their users; the worst that might happen was that the user, like Icarus, would be dazzled by the very means and thus forget to reflect about the wisdom of applying it. But technologies like the television or the aeroplane are not just a kind of machine; they are complex technological systems consisting of a range of different specific technologies, sciences, institutions, legal and financial structures, and so on. The complexity and invisibility of such systems constitute a different, invisible sublimity. Such systems can seem to offer populations a form of secular salvation if they allow their lives to be ordered through and by them. Technological systems' grounding in seemingly autonomous technology makes them appear in imperative mode, projecting a technological promise into the future in a way which demands action in the present and thus becomes self-determining (van Lente, 2000).

Technologies granted this form of sublimity advance without any awareness of questions of purpose which lie outside their own way of framing the world; questions like 'why?' hang in the air, with no expectation of an answer (Szerszynski, 2003a). The psychiatrist Robert W. Daly has written about what he calls 'spectres of technology', where technological systems are imbued with quasi-supernatural agency and power (Daly, 1970). For Daly, belief in such spectres arises from 'a *sense of domination by mysterious agencies or forces* which are, or were, *linked to technological enterprises* but which are now *apprehended as being beyond the control of any particular man or collection of men*' (Daly, 1970: 421, emphasis in original). Daly illustrates the different form such spectres can take using case studies from psychopathology, but argues that belief in technological spectres is widespread among psychologically normal individuals, and is even passed down through conventional processes of cultural transmission. The sublimity of technology can thus take the form of its autonomous development, its indifference to human projects and happiness. Here, with echoes of the shifts in the understanding of God in early modern religion (Milbank, 1998: 265), the sublimity of technology becomes sundered from its potential beauty – technology is loved for itself, apart from its fitness for human life and purpose.

The transformations of the Western sacred, then, have led the West a long way from the primal and archaic sacred, within which the crafts were understood in the social terms of contract or gift exchange between humans and non-human nature. The classical world first started understanding craft in terms of its relationship with reason, but its continuity with primal and archaic ideas of nature's animacy meant that the arts' potential for rationalization was seen as strictly limited. It was the emergence of the

Protestant sacred, with its transcendent, sovereign deity and passive matter, which enabled the development of technology in the modern sense. Technology came to be seen not just as a way of easing the human condition, but of radically transforming it, of returning to the pre-lapsarian condition of ease and harmony between humans and nature – ultimately, as a fusion of art and reason, of *techne* and *logos*, which promised to bring the certainty of reason to humanity's technical dealings with matter. Technological activity became displaced from its lowly social location in the artisan sector of society, and increasingly taken up by the emerging scientific elite. But initially at least technology was still understood as subservient to human or divine ends. Even when technological projects took over liturgical functions in society in the form of the technological sublime, they were not just regarded in terms of their sheer technical efficacy but also 'unconcealed' the deeper ontology of the Baconian soteriological project, the promise of granting certainty to the arts.

It was only with the collapse of the sacred into the empirical world, the shift from an ordering of society according to the transcendent axis to a biopolitical, immanent ordering of the social, that technology took on the self-steering character that Ellul identifies, and began to constitute things in the world as Heidegger's 'standing-reserve'. The ultimate purpose of society was no longer the praise of the creator but the reproduction of itself; numerous sciences and technologies emerged to provide the knowledges necessary to ensure the continuation and optimization of the life process. The last vestiges of classical and Christian meanings in the technological sublime were all but swept away. Technology became measured against neither quotidian nor supernal human needs and interests, but against its own, technical criteria. Technology became the measure of man – became autonomous, became sublime.

In Part I of the book I described the task taken up by this book as the exploration of contemporary ideas of nature and technology in terms of their continuing relationship with the sacred; I explained my understanding of the sacred, and set out the historical narrative of the transformation of the sacred that would inform the rest of the book. In Part II, I have been exploring how the emergence of both scientific ideas of nature and modern technological practices can be understood against the background of this narrative. And now that the main arguments of the book have been established, they can be applied to help understand the character of our contemporary relations with nature and technology. Thus, Part III will explore how the dynamics described in Part II have worked themselves out in relation to the two domains of inner and outer nature – the human body, and the outer world conceived as 'environment'. These more detailed explorations will enable us to be more sensitive to the complexity and contestedness of sacral history.

Part III

The Body and its Environment

Chapter Five

The Body, Healing and the Sacred

In his study of *The Cult of the Saints* Peter Brown paints a vivid picture of exorcism in sixth-century Catholic Europe. Christian shrines, especially those where saints were entombed, were typically places where, as Jerome wrote, one could expect to see 'men howling like wolves, barking like dogs, roaring like lions, hissing like snakes'. Such events proved to the faithful the power of the saints and their God. The demons within people, often understood as pagan gods, recognized the power of the saints and submitted to their interrogation. In this way the possessed were brought under the power of exorcists like Saint Martin of Tours, made to perform useful roles in society while the possession persisted, but eventually delivered from demonic control and readmitted into the social fold to the accompaniment of the resonant Christian symbolism of prayers of exorcism, pronouncing that 'he who fixed the bounds of light and dark is he who drives black chaos from the martyrs' tombs' (Brown, 1981: 106–13).

Yet in late antiquity, as today, the individual suffering from dis-ease had a choice of approaches to healing. For some presenting ailments, people would throw themselves at the mercy of inquisitorial exorcists like Saint Martin. For others, however, people would be more likely to turn to very different forms of therapy, such as those offered by the physician Marcellus of Bourdeaux. Marcellus's book *De medicamentis* catalogued a range of folk remedies, listing spells, incantations and medical plants in a kind of self-help health manual (Brown, 1981: 113–16). The coexistence of Saint Martin and Marcellus was a case not just of Christian and pagan ideas and practices existing side by side in late antiquity, but also of a historic situation which seems to prefigure the medical pluralism obtaining in Western societies today.

Yet the difference between the ministrations of Saint Martin and Marcellus was not simply that the first was robustly Christian, the second defiantly pagan. Brown also brings out the way that these two therapeutic systems involved very different models of healing and dependency. The Christian model required the sufferer to place himself or herself in a relation of dependency to specific individuals; the pagan model, by contrast, was predicated on an autarky in which the individual had to work out his or her own therapeutic course on the basis of the materials made available to him or her. The first involved a vertical model of dependence, in which the process of exorcism and healing placed the sufferer in a relation of personal obligation to the saint, and through him or her to the Church and divine power; the second held fast to a horizontal model of healing which tied the patient 'by a web of Lilliputian threads to the diffuse and seemingly bottomless traditions of his own environment' (Brown, 1981: 118).

There are historical complexities in this account that cannot concern us here: the existence of vertical healing cults in Roman society; the way that Roman Christianity modelled the relationship with the saints on late Roman practices of patronage and judicial inquiry; and the fact that, in the later development of Christianity, the principle of individual conscience and interpretation of faith was to work itself out more fully than Brown finds in sixth-century Europe. But what will be very instructive will be to trace the transformations in the tension between these two models of healing, between the vertical and the horizontal, from the time of Saint Martin and Marcellus to the present day. For their time was one where the transcendental dualism of the monotheistic sacred was still actively asserting itself over the more material forms of sacrality characteristic of the primal and archaic sacred. Marcellus's world was a horizontal one of minor powers in the environment that could be drawn on in modest ways to correct the infelicities of life – 'a prayer on seeing the first swallow, accompanied by bathing the eyes in spring water' in order to ward off eye diseases, for example (Brown, 1981: 118). Saint Martin's world, by contrast, shares the archaic sacred's places of intensity in the co-mingling of sacral and earthly powers, but reorders them according to the powerful new vertical dimension imposed by the expulsion of divinity from the empirical world. To be healed by Marcellus is to restore one's links with one's natural and cultural environment; to be healed by Saint Martin is to break those links, to commit oneself to relations with the invisible presences of Christ and the saints which are to be found at the sacred sites, and to learn a whole new ceremonial comportment in life which involves a continual alignment with the realities of the Christian supernatural world. Compared with the quotidian craft techniques of Marcellus, Saint Martin's is a grand 'technology of the self' (Foucault, 1988) which attempts to bring about a dramatic reordering of the self and its world in relation to the transcendent axis.

What historical parallels and threads can we trace between Brown's study and the contemporary situation? It is certainly the case that today conventional medicine coexists with a range of complementary and alternative therapies with quite different models of healing. In 1997 total out-of-pocket expenditure by individuals on complementary therapy in the USA was estimated at between $27 billion and $34 billion – comparable in size to the out-of-pocket expenditure on all conventional medical services (Eisenberg, 2001: 380). Yet I want to suggest that this contemporary medical pluralism, while sharing many features of the situation Brown describes, is nevertheless organized by a rather different competition between orderings of the sacred. While modern scientific medicine shares with the late Roman cult of the saints the vertical relationships of dependency which Brown describes, the modern patient is dependent not on the personal *potentia* of the saint but on the impersonal truths of medical science. The vertical transcendent pole that symbolically organized the exorcisms of Saint Martin has in modern medical science been stretched to infinity, rendered sublime and impersonal; the modern patient, when accepting a diagnosis and treatment, submits himself or herself not to relationships of personal obligation, but to impersonal technical operations. The foreign agencies responsible for ill health have to be made to submit to the power of the healing agent, but this is not through judicial inquisition, by forcing demons to declare spiritual truths, but by technological and natural processes that have been rendered absolutely profane by the radicalization of divine transcendence that leads from the Protestant to the modern sacred.

And, similarly, the complementary and alternative medicine of today is both like and unlike the folk medicine of Marcellus. Whereas conventional medicine disciplines individual bodies in ways that typically erase individuals' uniqueness and fail to recognize that they are embedded in relationships, the holistic therapies of today, like the folk medicine of the classical and medieval eras, offer techniques for reinforcing the horizontal embeddedness of the individual in his or her social and natural milieu.[1] Both thus reject a technological model of health, one predicated on an artificial intervention which realigns the body using energies and principles external to the body itself. Yet at the same time complementary and alternative medicine often involve a salvational model of health which owes more to Christian than pagan models of healing – a model of individual spiritual conversion and balancing of cosmic energies which, like Saint Martin's exorcisms, promise not just the amelioration of ailments but a profound spiritual transformation. And complementary therapies also often involve a far greater personalization of the healing power within the person of the healer, a *potentia* similar to that of the saints. The *quaestio* of the late classical exorcist – the juridical interrogation of the possessing demon – is replaced by the post-Freudian therapeutic collaborative investigation of the deeper meanings of an affliction. But in both cases the inquisitor is often seen as possessing special powers, placing the afflicted in a relationship of supplication and dependency.

Such a blending of healing paradigms, as we shall see, is partly due to the hybridization of folk healing with popular, evangelical Christianity and Enlightenment ideas about nature that occurred in the nineteenth century. But contemporary ideas and practices of healing also owe much of their character to the contemporary postmodern sacred. Indeed, despite their important legacies from earlier orderings of the sacred, we can see contemporary alternative therapies as important techniques for reordering people's sense of the sacred in a postmodern direction: away from the idea of a singular, external reality which had been an important by-product of the monotheistic sacred, towards a sacralization of the self as the origin and guarantor of reality; towards this-worldly forms of salvation; and towards forms of 'aesthetic' sociality based on the sheer similitude of individual perspectives. As we shall see, during times when orderings of the sacred are in competition with each other, one of the central means for the establishment of the new disposition of the sacred is through altering the dominant forms of embodiment. The body is a site in which ideas of nature and technology are repeatedly worked through and struggled over, in the process constituting contrasting ideas about human sociality and responsibility.

Medieval, Protestant and Modern Healing

Regimes of care for the self had existed in the pre-Christian world (Foucault, 1986); but in the context of the monotheistic sacred these practices were reorganized according to the vertical, transcendent axis, in terms of the need to transform the flesh, now seen as fallen and sinful. Yet, as Mellor and Shilling (1997: 36–41) recount, this produced not a flight *from* carnality but one further *into* it. Medieval society was organized through a sacramental experience of body and community; the presence of the transcendental realm was perceived in the material and sensuous. The ecclesiastical authorities sought to control the volatility of medieval bodies immersed in this sacralized material world by the deployment of 'physical religion' – the ordering of the sacred according to the transcendent dimension through the ordering of corporeal reality. Ascetic bodily regimes were used by the spiritual elite of society (monks and ascetics). For the laity, other forms of carnal religiosity were employed to regulate their immersion in the sacred: the eating and drinking in the Eucharist, baptism's preparation and immersion of the body, fasting, sexual abstinence, vigils, prayers and exorcisms.

One feature that distinguishes this from the forms of physical religion that emerged in the nineteenth century and inform contemporary ideas of healing and the body is the lack of emphasis on the individual. The carnal spiritualities of nineteenth-century Christian physiology and medical sectarianism deployed Enlightenment, republican ideas of rational nature to offer new forms of individual salvation, correcting the individual body's deviation from natural harmony and realigning it with the immanent unity of natural law (Albanese, 1990: 118–20). Since the late twentieth century, complementary and alternative therapies have offered similarly corporeal techniques for reordering the sacred – one that is now grounded in the interiority of individual subjectivity rather than the exteriority of rational nature. Yet both nineteenth-century and contemporary forms of alternative healing, like the cognitive bodily disciplines of Protestantism, worked through constructing forms of individuality; medieval physical religion, by contrast, worked through the creation of forms of community. There was no encouragement for people to take individual responsibility for their bodies; instead, through excesses of indulgence and purging such as the festivities of carnival and the fasting of Lent, they were made to feel part of a collective body being brought into relation with divine power (Bossy, 1985).

Yet the coexistence that Brown described of Christian and pre-Christian regimes of healing in the sixth century continued throughout the Middle Ages. Alongside the 'canonical' carnal rituals of the liturgical calendar was a range of more 'indexical' rites which people used in response to specific problems (Rappaport, 1993). Christina Larner's study of sixteenth- and seventeenth-century Scotland and England describes two forms of healing as existing alongside the official, scientific forms of healing that were sanctioned by and taught in the universities of the day. Firstly, there was practical and common-sense folk medicine, employing herbs and minerals. There was some concentration of expertise in local individuals, but most people had some knowledge; however, there was little interest in how any particular form of healing worked. Secondly, there was ritual healing, using spells and charms, which relied on the power of the cunning man or woman (Larner, 1992: 26). Keith Thomas describes three basic assumptions behind this popular healing: disease was thought of as a foreign presence that needs to be conjured out; religious language was understood as a mystical power available to anyone who can recite the correct words; and some charms and potions were thought to owe their power to the healer, the spell just being the medium to transmit the healer's power (Thomas, 1973: 215).

But the Reformation's shift to the Protestant sacred required the displacement of both liturgical and popular forms of physical religion. The corporate, carnal sacrality of the Catholic sacraments was inconsistent with the move towards an idea of God as sublime. Protestant nominalism severed the relationship between words and objects, and between objects and spiritual truths. The logic underlying sacramental religion was thus broken; the relationship with God became not physical, external and corporate but mental, internal and individual. At the same time, the move to this new form of the sacred also required the individual to close off their bodily connectedness with other people and with nature, to orient themselves to a radicalized transcendent axis through reflection and prayer, not carnal practices. Protestantism thus attempted to finally eradicate the horizontal forms of healing that involved the restoration of the individual's embeddedness in his or her social and natural environment. At the same time it sought to replace one vertical model of healing with another – to displace the corporeal and collective bodily techniques of Saint Martin's exorcisms and medieval sacramentalism with new, individual techniques of self-monitoring and control.

Protestant religion had inherited the medieval idea of nature and the body as unstable and dangerous (Mellor and Shilling, 1997: 39). But medieval Christianity had seen this instability as a necessary part of the human condition – indeed, welcoming the howling of Saint Martin's possessed, or the bodily emissions from the cadavers of the saints, as signs of saintly power (Brown, 1981: 109–10; Camporesi, 1988: 5). For Protestantism, by contrast, this instability has to be expunged. And as the Protestant sacred develops further, this construal of nature as a fallen realm to be mastered reinforces the Baconian project of the practical and theoretical domination of nature. The idea of rational medicine thus emerges in the seventeenth century, with the establishment of the royal colleges of physicians; nevertheless, through that and the next century a broad medical pluralism still persists in society (Saks, 1996: 29–30).

However, at the close of the eighteenth century there is a dramatic shift in medicine. Even in official medicine, up to this time there had been little or no place for detailed knowledge of the interior of bodies; diseases were identified and treatments chosen through the interpretation of sets of symptoms of individual patients. But in the nineteenth century the transmission of medical knowledge shifts from the lecture hall to the hospital, and finally to the laboratory. The experience of intervening in the interior of living and dead bodies becomes central to the conceptualization of disease and health, placing an emphasis not on interpretations but on visible signs (Foucault, 1976; Saks, 1996; 32), and the sick person is converted to a 'case' (Freund and McGuire, 1995: 234–41). Borrowing Foucault's language, Ursula Sharma suggests that in orthodox medicine at this time the body becomes at once an opaque mass and a penetrable space, with the nature and origins of disease not available as symptoms to the senses but inscribed on the organs, and thus only visible to the professional gaze (Sharma, 1995: 45). Forms of healing which did not fit this emergent 'medical gaze' were simply not incorporated into the medical establishment (McGuire, 1988: 7).

This reorganization of medical perception was closely related to the professionalization of medicine. The early nineteenth century saw the foundation of Britain's Provincial Medical and Surgical Association, which lobbied for a register of medical practitioners and launched attacks on the medically unorthodox such as homeopaths and hydropaths. This culminated in the 1858 Medical Registration Act, which triggered a state-legitimated assault on unorthodox medicine (Saks, 1996: 30–1). The resulting centralization of medical practice placed the individual in new relations of vertical dependency – not, as had been the case in early and medieval Christianity, on the dead, but on the living. And these living persons on whom the sick were now dependent had the power to heal not because of the personal charisma characteristic of the archaic sacred, but due to their capacity to mediate the sublime, universal knowledge of nature's laws.

In the post-Reformation period, healing was still organized in terms of the transcendent axis; Protestant cognitive body regimes may have had the effect of creating individuals suitable for the productivist demands of capitalist society, but their primary aim was to align individuals with the moral demands placed on them by God (Weber, 1930). But as the divine was expelled even further from the empirical world, was construed as sublime, unconditioned and unknowable, it was at the same time pulled ever closer, to the point that the empirical world, understood now as the endless performance of life, became itself sacred. Health was no longer conceived in the horizontal, pagan terms of piecemeal adjustments to one's embeddedness in the social and natural world, nor in the vertical, Christian terms of the transcendent axis, but was understood in terms of the demand of normalization, to be maximally suited for insertion in the productivist social body. Medicine lost its final links with transcendent religion (Douglas, 1994: 25), becoming instead a primary instrument of anatomo-politics in the service of the immanent sacrality of the ongoing social order (Foucault, 1979; 139).

The Rise of the Natural Body

But the existence in contemporary society of alternative regimes of health and healing is not simply a case of their survival against orthodoxy's attempts to eradicate them. Alternative understandings of the body also underwent their own development in the modern period, incorporating new developments in the ongoing transformation of the sacred. Contemporary forms of alternative medicine, with their belief in nature as a healing force, derive their ideas from a complex set of religious and secular tributaries. These include eighteenth-century Enlightenment notions of reason and nature, and of progressive control over the human condition, and also

74 The Body and its Environment

Romantic notions of a nature from which modern society is becomingly increasingly alienated. These came together in a view of nature as itself providential, a view that was increasingly common in the popular religion of America and Europe in the nineteenth century, and which, combined in turn with revivalist notions of sin and grace, formed a new 'physical religion' for the modern age (Albanese, 1990).

In nineteenth-century America alternative healing became something it had not been before – a 'utopian technology' (Weinberger, 1985). This was partly due to its absorption of Enlightenment ideas of reason. In Europe, as the seventeenth century gave way to the eighteenth, and the radically transcendent Protestant sacred started its transition into the immanentist modern sacred, there was a broad shift away from the idea of nature as the fallen counterpart to the purity of the supernatural divine, and towards a re-evaluation of the natural as the source not just of happiness but also of virtue (Pilkington, 1986). In the form of an Enlightenment equation of nature with reason, such ideas played a key role in the development of American civil religion, from the Declaration of Independence onwards. But in the nineteenth century these currents in American culture took a distinctive turn. Enlightenment ideas of nature were combined not just with new and refashioned forms of alternative healing but also with the religion of evangelical revivalism. The resulting therapies represented health as a natural property of the body and illness as a disturbance caused by living unnaturally, and invoked a 'state of nature' account of a pre-civilized state where illness was unknown. The resulting physical religion relocated theological concepts in nature and the body: grace came from nature; sin was behaving against it and brought about bodily dysfunction (Albanese, 1990: 120). These theological elements combined with Enlightenment ideas of nature and reason to produce a concept of health which offered not just cures but the promise of physical perfectibility.

These new kinds of popular healing took various forms. The 'Christian physiology' of figures like Sylvester Graham and William Alcott was a kind of privatized millennialism: a golden age of health was at hand, but one that was to be attained by individuals through their own efforts. Rejecting the 'invasion' model of medieval popular healing, disease was seen as an immanent derangement of vital functions brought about through failure to live in the right way. Disease was thus not a punishment or a test from God, but the result of the individual's own decisions. Also drawing, if less explicitly, on evangelical Christianity was a further range of medical sectarians – herbalists, homeopaths, hydropaths, osteopaths and chiropractors – who offered a range of techniques for a this-worldly salvation, an existence without disease which people could enjoy if only they would align themselves with the operations of nature (Albanese, 1990: 123–49). In a remarkable fusion of the worlds of Saint Martin and Marcellus, then, a new nature religion was born.

Contemporary Alternative Healing and the Sacred

These cultural currents, lying fairly dormant for much of the twentieth century, have undergone an extraordinary revival in Western societies since the 1970s. In terms of the overall use of complementary and alternative medicine (CAM), including people seeing practitioners as well as those simply buying remedies over the counter, Astin (1998) reported that 40 per cent of US respondents had used some form of alternative medicine during the past year, while Eisenberg et al. (1998) estimated 42.1 per cent of respondents had used at least one of sixteen listed therapies in 1997. Of these, 46.3 per cent saw a practitioner on at least one occasion, which would mean that 19.5 per cent of the US population saw an alternative therapist in 1997. As regards the UK, a British Broadcasting Corporation (BBC) survey of complementary medicine use in the UK estimated that 20 per cent had used CAM, whether purchased over the counter or through practitioners, in the previous twelve months (Ernst and White, 2000). And Thomas et al. (2001) found that 28.3 per cent of the population of England used at least one of eight well-established therapies, or practised self-care using remedies purchased over the counter, in 1998. They estimate that 13.6 per cent of the adult population of England visited at least one therapist providing one of eight named therapies in the past twelve months.[2]

Contemporary alternative therapies are extraordinarily diverse in character and origin. Some have been imported more or less wholesale from non-Western cultures; others have been home grown. Anyinam (1990: 70) suggests a classification into comprehensive systems (such as anthroposophy and ayurveda), dietary therapies (herbalism, macrobiotics), diagnostic therapies (iridology, dowsing), meridian therapies and energy work (acupuncture, shiatsu, psychic healing), manipulation and muscle retraining (yoga, tai chi, osteopathy, Alexander technique), and psychotherapy and counselling (Gestalt, transcendental meditation).

One thing that is striking is the commonalities in the ideas of healing involved, even between therapies that emerged quite independently. Proponents of CAM would explain this by reference to a single set of timeless underlying principles of holistic health on which all therapies in some way depend if they are going to work. Sociologically, these similarities might be explained in terms of an underlying *episteme*, a way of thinking about and intervening in the world, that might be specific to a particular historical period (see Foucault, 1970).[3] Either way, Stephen Fulder (1996: 5–7) sums up the ideas of healing involved in CAM under eight themes:[4]

1 'Working with, not against, symptoms' – symptoms are to be managed not suppressed; they can be a guide to the origin of an upset, and serve as milestones on the journey to a cure.

2   'Individuality' – each person, condition, constitution and treatment is different; no statistical norms are to be used.
3   'The integrated human being' – there are no barriers between mind, body and spirit, or between society and individual; all are relevant in both diagnosis and therapy.
4   There is 'no defined or determined state of illness where treatment must begin or wellness where treatment must end' – CAM operates with a broad definition of health in terms of physical, mental and spiritual well-being.
5   'Safety is sacred' – therapies are 'minimally interventionist' and harmless, by working with rather than against the normal functioning of the body.
6   'Areas of competence' – CAM is better at 'chronic, psychosomatic, early-stage, musculoskeletal, immunological, non-specific/multi-origin, environmental conditions as opposed to acute, traumatic, infectious, genetic, tropical conditions'. CAM is thus complementary rather than an alternative to conventional medicine.
7   'Patient is partner' – 'the status differential is less than in conventional medicine, and the tone of the consultation is more of a dialogue, less of a pronouncement by the dominant professional'.
8   'Alternative world views' – therapies posit patterns of relationship between creatures and their environment, which can be subtle and energetic.

Summarizing, Fulder suggests that alternative therapies work by stimulating the body's self-healing powers, work with rather than against symptoms, and regard human beings as 'part of the flow of nature and not necessarily at its control centre' (Fulder, 1995: 51–2, 55). Others who have written about CAM emphasize the processual understanding of illness and health in complementary medicine.[5] Illness itself is a process of transformation (Duff, 1994). Diagnosis is an art, involving reading the particular sequential patterns of events and symptoms (see Sharma, 1995; Fulder, 1996: 7–9). Cure involves the creation of order out of personal narratives more than it does the physical alleviation of symptoms (Lebeer, 1993). Others again stress the relationship between healer and client – for example, that the social dimensions of healing cannot be separated from the directly therapeutic intervention (Wynne, 1989: 1294). Whereas some therapists 'emulated the medical profession in its professional distance and charges for services rendered' (McGuire, 1988: 172), others recognize the danger to the 'charisma' of the healer posed by adopting an expert model (Cant, 1996). Most therapists adopt a model of themselves as a 'wounded healer', an idea influenced by Christian ideas of the person (Power, 1991: 157).

In terms of the different historical relations between the body and the sacred catalogued by Mellor and Shilling (1997), these characteristics of complementary and alternative medicine suggest it can be seen as a 'baroque modern' form of embodiment, in that it combines features of the sensuous forms of embodiment characteristic of the medieval period with the more cognitive orientation to the body which was developed by Protestantism and passed on to secular modernity. In its more somatic and symbolic aspects, and its engagement with the material, natural world, alternative medicine seems to exhibit a partial return to the 'open-orifice' body of medieval culture, in constant material and spiritual communion with its surroundings. Yet at the same time the body in complementary and alternative medicine retains features of the Protestant body. For example, despite holistic health's insistence on the relational aspects of human well-being, it exhibits an overwhelming emphasis on the individual. Not only do the therapies operate almost exclusively on the individual, but there is an emphasis on the patient constructing a coherent self-narrative as part of the therapy (Johannessen, 1996). This recalls the emphasis on introspection and diary keeping among Puritans. Unlike Catholics, whose sanctity was guaranteed by their participation in the sacraments of the Church, Protestants were made to fall back on forms of spiritual self-accreditation, with spiritual autobiographies playing a crucial role in determining believers' Christian credentials by revealing the operation of providence in their lives (Mellor and Shilling, 1997: 126).

But the understandings of the body and healing implicit in complementary and alternative medicine are not simply a blend of medieval and Protestant ideas of the body; they are also essentially contemporary in their rejection of the transcendental dualism that underlay both sets of ideas. In both contemporary and historical forms of Christian healing, healing can be demonic as well as divine (McGuire, 1988, ch. 3). Nature is no saving power; it is fallen, and in need of saving from outside by the powers of the transcendent deity (see Allen and Wallis, 1992). By contrast, in CAM the transcendent axis has been flattened into immanent nature; there is only one possible source of healing – nature and nature's powers. Even when divine power is invoked, as in psychic healing, this is less a personal deity to be aligned with than a power in the universe that can be drawn upon by anyone (McGuire, 1988: 150). CAM thus displays not just the history but also the present of the Western sacred.

It is true, however, that many of the therapies and therapeutic systems in operation today clearly have their origins outside the Western world. Yet when they are transplanted in the West they have typically been adapted to Western cultural conditions. James Spickard (1995) offers an example of this process in his study of a Japanese-American healing church, the Church of World Messianity (Sekai Kyusei-kyo), on Hawaii and the West Coast of the USA. Central to the activities of the church was the ritual practice *johrei*, in which invisible light was said to be emitted out of the palms of the hands. Spickard identifies three different groups, all attracted by *johrei* but imposing on it very different theologies. The first group were second generation Japanese-Americans, who had a very pragmatic orientation to the ritual. For these church members *johrei* was treated as a supernatural medical tool, as God reaching into bodies and bringing about physical well-being. The second group were older Caucasians, who had previously been religious seekers involved in what Campbell calls the cultic milieu (Campbell, 1972). For this group, *johrei* was prayer in action, resulting in spiritual rather than physical results, and to be given rather than received. The third group of younger Caucasians, 1960s counter-culturalists and hippies, regarded *johrei* as a way of spiritually cleansing the world and bringing in the Age of Aquarius. They would practice *johrei* both openly and covertly at home, at work, and in places polluted by industrial activity. Whereas the Japanese-Americans were practising *johrei* in a way that was similar to the quasi-pagan folk religiosity of the Middle Ages, the Westerners reinterpreted it in (different) ways which drew on the later transformations of the Western sacred.

Explaining Complementary Medicine

Although I have said that the primary aim of this book is not to explain contemporary ideas of nature and technology but simply to understand them better, there are points at which this distinction becomes artificial. This is one such point: in order to understand what is happening in complementary and alternative medicine we need to speculate about why it has become so widespread in Western societies, and why it has taken the forms that it has. And one way to start to construct such an explanation is to see the rise of complementary and alternative medicine as part of a more general 'turn to life' in what in Chapter 2 I called the postmodern sacred (Woodhead and Heelas, 2000). In a recent research project, I and other colleagues tested that idea by exploring the various forms of religion and spirituality in a typical English market town (Heelas et al., 2004).[6] As well as studying organized (largely Christian) religion in Kendal, Cumbria, we tried to understand the complex and diffuse patterns of alternative spirituality taking place there, including those involving alternative healing. We found that in general the religions and spiritualities that are growing are those which help to resource the individual. They are concerned more with the here and now than with the afterlife; they nurture the unique, individual, lived life rather than simply promote life in a particular prescribed social role; and they may pay more attention to 'natural' life – to the environment and the body. The suggestion is not just that organized religions are shrinking at the expense of a growing alternative sector (although that is the case), but rather that one can detect a turn to life occurring *across the board* – within church and chapel, in forms of alternative spirituality, and also in the more diffuse spiritualities and sensibilities of wider culture.

The growth in complementary and alternative therapies, vigorously alive and well in Kendal as elsewhere, illustrate and benefit from this turn to life in two ways. Firstly, CAM benefits from the turn to life that is taking place within religion. Consistent with the emergence of the postmodern sacred, organized religion in Kendal as elsewhere has shifted towards the offering of experiences and resources that help individuals to lead their own lives, whether in the sense of enabling them to cope and feel happier, or by offering challenging experiences and ideas which may help them to grow and develop as people (Woodhead, 2001). As Zygmunt Bauman puts it, in the postmodern condition men and women feel not an other-worldly un-certainty about eternity but a this-worldly uncertainty about their own lives. They do not seek reflection on death, but resources to equip them for this world's uncertainities – not religious experts but identity experts (Bauman, 1998: 67–8). According to this view, people are attracted to complementary therapies because they are well placed – perhaps better than the churches – to meet the spiritual needs of people today, needs which have shifted away from preparation for the next life and toward the desire to find meaning, purpose and well-being in this one.[7] People are also seeking ways of being spiritually resourced without being preached at; unlike church services, healing rituals such as those provided by CAM provide new 'self-validating experiences, without narrowly specifying norms' (McGuire, 1988: 254).

Secondly, CAM also benefits, as it were, from a turn to life within medi-cine. The relationship between orthodox medicine and CAM bears a striking similarity to that between 'harder' forms of religion, emphasizing transcend-ence, hierarchy, external authority and doing one's duty, and the newer experiential spiritualities of 'life'. Critics of orthodox medicine complain that in orthodox medicine there is a strong emphasis on the hierarchical authority of the doctor; the patient is not treated as a unique individual; their case is made to fit into an abstract class of cases, as an example of this disease or that condition; there is little empowerment of the individual to take control of his or her own life; treatment of sickness is understood as a process of normal-ization, of returning to a static, standardized model of healthy functioning, rather than health being seen as a dynamic process of personal development and discovery. And these are much the same as the criticisms that are made of 'hard', transcendental forms of religion by those in Kendal who have left them in favour of the 'softer' spiritualities of life.

Talcott Parsons developed the idea of the 'sick role' to capture the bundle of expectations and permissions that are given to the individual at the point when they become a patient in orthodox Western medicine. This sick role represents a departure from Protestant forms of embodiment in a number of ways: modern medicine's absolution of the patient from any blame for his or her illness contrasts with Protestantism's emphasis on individual responsibility for sin; and the assumption that the patient is in need of outside help from an authorized source contravenes the cognitive and hermeneutic autonomy of the individual that is at the heart of the Reformation. But Parson's sick role nevertheless manifests many continuities with the vertical, Christian model of healing that we have traced from Saint Martin onwards.

The drift away from orthodox medicine and towards CAM can be seen as a turn to life within the domain of health and illness: a 'softening' of medicine that parallels the contemporary 'softening' of religion. According to research carried out by Kajsa Ahlstrand, Christian belief and practice in Sweden exhibits a profound softening, as evidenced by a number of shifts: from a picture of God as a distant Lord and King to one of God as life and love within; from seeing humans as sinners in need of forgiveness to seeing them as wounded and in need of healing; from an ethic of obedience to one of creativity; from understanding salvation as for the few to seeing it as universal; and from a hierarchical understanding of authority to one based on personal experience (Ahlstrand, 2001). The increasing dissatisfaction with the experience of orthodox medicine, and what people say about what they value in CAM, parallels these findings very closely. CAM offers a pronounced reduction in the hierarchical status differential between therapist and client (Power, 1991; Lowenberg and Davis, 1994); clients generally feel themselves to be empowered rather than disempowered (Braathen, 1996); complementary therapies focus on the unique individual lived life, rather than trying to fit the individual into a pre-set sick role (Johannessen, 1996); health is understood as a diachronic and open-ended performance, rather than a normalized state of functioning.

But is it enough to say that complementary and alternative therapies have grown in popularity because of the wider turn to life in contemporary culture? If CAM *is* meeting many of the needs of contemporary individuals better than transcendental religion or orthodox medicine, why is this the case? Are those needs different today than they were in the past – and, if so, why? Unless we want to give autonomous agency to the ongoing transformation of the sacred, it is not enough to suggest that it is because the sacred has changed that spiritual practice has changed. We need to identify more historically contingent events and changes that might be driving this transformation in the sacred. Ideas can certainly shape practice: alterations at the level of ideas will make certain practices seem more appropriate than others. But also changes at the level of material and social organization will affect the credibility of different ideas.

Albanese attempts to explain the rise of the physical religion of nineteenth-century America in terms of the internalization of philosophies

of social harmony as the new society was unsettled by rapid industrialization and development. Rejecting the feudal hierarchies of Europe, republican America was a society that had been built on the Enlightenment
assumptions that autonomous individuals would naturally work in harmony
with each other, 'that democracy would be the smooth and oiled running
of the great political machine that conformed to nature'. But as American
society grew and became more complex, these ideas lost their plausibility at
the communal level and became privatized and somatized; 'the individual
body, for many, became the ground for complaint or celebration. Here
was a place that, conceivably, could be mastered and made perfect' (Albanese, 1990: 120). Robert Crawford constructs a similar argument about the
later resurgence of alternative healing in the 1970s, suggesting that the
failure of 1960s political and cultural radicalism to transform society
prompted a defeatist turn towards the cultivation of the self (Crawford,
1980: 377).

However fruitful such arguments may prove, perhaps alternative medicine is not simply a vehicle for abandonment of the social body. Recall that
Peter Brown analysed early Christian exorcism as a technology not just for
detaching individuals from their pagan embedding in the social and natural
world, but also for imparting a new Christian comportment towards this
world and the next, and thus implicating them in a new Christian social
order. Could not CAM be performing a similar role in the contemporary
transformation of the sacred, reshaping bodies for a different mode of
insertion in the world?

Some commentators have speculated whether alternative medicine can be
seen as a new form of the anatomo-political disciplining of the population,
part of the wider 'medicalization' project of modernity. Contemporary alternative medicine could certainly be seen as an extension of the Protestant
project of rationally controlling the body (McGuire, 1988: 257). The very
modes of incorporation developed in the Reformation and the later modern
period involved becoming part of a 'speaking association' in contrast to the
more sensuous forms of collective embodiment characteristic of the medieval
Catholic Church (Mellor and Shilling, 1997: 128 n. 3). Most alternative
therapies similarly rely heavily not only on language but also on bringing the
operations of the body under more conscious control, and could thus be
seen, ironically, as a normalizing technological project.

However, Robert Crawford distinguishes two broad meanings of 'medicalization': 'an expansion of professional power over wider spheres of life',
and 'the extension of the range of social phenomena mediated by the
concepts of health and illness' (Crawford, 1980: 369). McGuire (1988:
247) suggests that alternative therapies exhibit medicalization in Crawford's second sense, which she also terms 'spiritualization', in that,
although medical metaphors are being applied to more areas of life, the

therapists are nevertheless advocating largely non-medical responses to people's problems. At first glance, medicalization in Crawford's first sense does not seem to apply to CAM, given its as-yet unprofessionalized character. Indeed, Lowenberg and Davis argue that the relationship between therapist and patient is more one of *demedicalization* – as evidenced, for example, in the decrease in status differential between therapist and patient. However, CAM could be seen as a 'soft' disciplinary project, in which the very egalitarian relationship between healer and client might be said to be constructing the client in new ways.

One of the most significant factors in the growth of CAM and the turn to life more broadly may be the dramatic changes in the economic structuring of Western societies in the late twentieth century, changes which are captured under the general heading of post-Fordism (Lash and Urry, 1987; Harvey, 1989). These changes have involved a seemingly relentless shift away from large-scale industrial operations offering jobs for life to whole communities; individuals are increasingly thrown back on their own resources to construct their own coherent life-narratives. More and more areas of people's lives – occupational choice, geographical residence, marital partnership and so on – have been set free from their perception of being natural and inevitable and have become understood as subject to choice and calculation (Beck, 1992). The forms of sacrality that are appropriate to this context seem to be ones that equip the individual with what might be called transferable spiritual skills – internal capacities for creating meaning and coherence across an increasingly unpredictable life course. The shift towards a consumer-led capitalism encourages and requires the development of inner imaginative capacities in tension with the disciplined, responsible normalized individual of productivist capitalism (Bell, 1979; Campbell, 1987) – even to the extent of encouraging a sacralization of the self as the creator *ex nihilo* of reality (Heelas, 1992, 1996). Similarly, the contraction of manufacturing and the steady expansion of jobs in the service sector has produced a socio-economic context which values co-operation, communication and creativity – just the kind of capacities which are nurtured in the milieu of alternative health practices (see Martin, 1981: 185 ff.; McGuire, 1988: 253). As such, although the practices of complementary and alternative medicine may constitute a form of resistance to certain disciplinary modes of insertion in the social order, they may be playing a subtle role in helping make possible one that is even more conducive to the maintenance of contemporary technological society.

But to complete Part III we must turn from the body to its milieu, exploring the complex of technological and anti-technological sacralizations of nature as 'environment'. In Chapter 6, I look at the way that specific ideas of nature – as a system to be protected, as a collection of beings, and as a moral source – emerged in particular social and cultural contexts in the modern period, and were later gathered together in the contemporary discourse of the environment. As we saw with the body, we shall see how alternative sacralizations of external nature can coexist and compete with each other. In Part IV this complexity and competition of the sacred will take on a renewed significance when we see how nature was politicized in the late twentieth century, and turned into a key site of struggle over orderings of the sacred.

Chapter Six

The Birth of 'the Environment'

Over recent decades, but most markedly since the late 1980s, there has been a profound change in public life in many Western countries, as 'the environment' has come to take a prominent, and seemingly permanent, place in political discourse. The strength of public concern about issues as diverse as rainforest logging, whaling, ozone depletion and global climate change has brought about profound effects on the behaviour not just of the public themselves, but also of industry, commerce and government. Environmental non-governmental organizations (NGOs) have experienced massive growth in public support, and have come to wield substantial influence on policy makers. The notion of sustainable development, defined as 'development that meets the needs of the present without compromising the ability of future generations to meet their own needs' (World Commission on Environment and Development, 1987: 43), has been kept on the global stage by the earth summits at Stockholm in 1972, at Rio de Janeiro in 1992, and at Johannesburg in 2002, and has significant influence on policies at international, national and sub-national levels.

But it would be a mistake to think that it is the condition of the natural world itself that has brought about these deep cultural, social and political changes – that they have simply been driven by growing evidence about the damaging effects of our present industrial practices on natural systems. The emergence of environmentalism as a potent social force in the late twentieth century cannot simply be explained by reference to the extent of environmental damage, or even to the strength of our scientific understanding of such damage. There have always been what we would now call environmental problems, but they were not always seen as such at the time. They might have been seen as discrete problems, rightly addressed within the context of strictly bounded social and economic practices. They might not have been seen as problems at all, simply as the effects of human activity on nature, the inevitable and unpredictable side-effects of *techne*. Doubtless they were often not even understood as being due to human activity at all. Before they could be understood as aspects of an 'environmental crisis' the environment had to be *constructed*, as a coherent discourse.

For example, as Charles T. Rubin has pointed out, the sight of a factory chimney pouring out smoke was once more likely to be viewed as a sign, not of pollution and danger, but of progress, employment and societal well-being. Furthermore, '[c]hanging the public perception of pollution has required the adoption of a perspective from which brown air and smelly streams can be viewed as a coherent set of problems that have certain kinds of solutions – without such a change, there would have been "stream conservation," "beach renewal," "air purification," etc., rather than "environmentalism"' (Rubin, 1989: 30). Rubin is describing two related cultural shifts here – firstly the redescription of a range of phenomena as being environmental problems rather than simply environmental change, and secondly the gathering up of all of these as parts of one overarching problem, the environmental crisis. Both of these shifts are clearly necessary for the emergence of 'the environment' as a coherent political discourse, and both have taken place over the course of the twentieth century.

Central to the dynamics of these discursive changes has been the emergence and persistence of a vociferous environmental movement in the countries of the industrialized West. This movement, which brought to the attention of an inattentive world a crisis in the making, was an open-ended and creative social phenomenon which both intentionally and unintentionally generated new understandings and new languages (Melucci, 1996; Jamison, 2001). Through its discursive labour a new and powerfully resonant discourse of 'the environment' was brought into being. Yet this did not emerge *de novo*. As Eyerman and Jamison rightly insist, the cognitive praxis of the environmental movement owes a lot to the space opened up by the 1960s new left before them (Eyerman and Jamison, 1991: 91). But the movement also took up many representations of nature from earlier periods and overlaid them with new levels of meaning. This chapter will explore this prehistory of environmentalism, seeking to understand the way that these proto-environmentalist ideas of nature arose in the context of the ongoing transformation of the sacred.

In the broadest terms, environmental ideas and debates seem to draw on two main groups of ideas from Western religious thought. The first group is based on Hebrew ideas of creation, particularly as described in the first three chapters of Genesis. Creation is here described as *ex nihilo*, from nothing, placing the very nature, existence and activity of the physical world in radical and direct dependency on God. The ends and functions of created things thus depend solely on the purposes that God has designated for them. As we saw in Chapter 3, this way of thinking about nature, particularly in the variant that sees God as impressing laws upon his creation, played a key role in the emergence of experimental science in the seventeenth century. But the doctrine of creation also sees humanity, created in God's image, as his specially appointed representatives on earth, as having been entrusted with special rights and responsibilities over the rest of creation (Glacken, 1967: 163–8). While the interpretation of the passages in Genesis as giving the non-human world over to humanity for its own use has been subjected to much critical discussion (e.g. Barr, 1974; Westermann, 1974), nevertheless it is that interpretation of the doctrine of creation that has dominated, at least in recent centuries.

The second group of ideas contain important elements from Greek thought, particularly neo-Platonism. The third-century writer Plotinus took the Platonic concept of the realm of ideas beyond the empirical world and crafted out of it a cosmology in which all beings participate in some way in transcendent Being (Lovejoy, 1936: 63–6; Glacken, 1967: 76–9). Plotinus distinguishes three main principles in the world. Out of the infinite, formless One emanates Nous, from which in turn flows the world Soul which gives form and order to the material world. Plotinus's One is a divinity that cannot but create the Many, the beings of the empirical world; its very perfection requires it to generate other beings – and not to stop until it has generated all possible such beings. Plotinus's universe is an organic whole, permeated by a dynamic, divine life principle that ceaselessly creates variety – ideas that seem to presage many interpretations of ecological science, not least James Lovelock's Gaia hypothesis, which conceives of the whole earth as a massive, self-regulating organism (Lovelock, 1987).

In the nineteenth century neo-Platonic ideas underwent a dramatic revival with the emergence of Transcendentalism and Romanticism. For the American Transcendentalists Ralph Waldo Emerson and Henry David Thoreau, nature was itself absolute, filled with divine significance. But at the same time both saw nature as pointing beyond itself to an unconditioned infinite. Emerson, for example, saw a perfect correspondence between nature's processes and human ends, making nature both mother and teacher to humanity. But Emerson was also drawn to an idealism that saw the most significant moments as those which involve 'the reverential withdrawing of nature before its God', as the human individual recognized both the illusory character of nature and their own god-like transcendence of it. Echoing the medieval *Quadriga*, Emerson saw nature as having three levels of use, practical, aesthetic and symbolic; the highest 'use of the world' comprising all three and leading the soul to God (Stoll, 1997: 104–5). Similarly, despite Thoreau's more consistent attention to the particularities of nature, and the adoption of Hindu and pagan ideas, central to his thought was the idea of 'Higher Laws' to which one must ascetically subject oneself (Albanese, 1990, ch. 3). Such tensions within

Transcendentalist thought reveal the Judeo-Christian foundations on which they were built. Preserving many of the features of traditional Christian cosmology, such as humanity's place as the peak and point of creation, and the moral and religious truths to be found in nature, Transcendentalists nevertheless collapsed the dualistic cosmos of Christianity into a monistic ontology where there was only nature. But no genuinely secular idea of the cosmos could have satisfied their quest for a sacramental approach to nature; instead they folded characteristics of the transcendent One of neo-Platonism, and of God the transcendent law-giver of Hebrew thought, into nature itself. In Transcendentalist thought nature thus replaces Christ as the revealed image of God that offers salvation to those that follow it (Stoll, 1997: 106–7).

In a comparable vein, English Romantics like Wordsworth thought that 'where wilderness asserts itself there the spirit of humanity survives', thus valorizing the solitary, contemplative individual communing with the sub-limity of wild nature (Bate, 1991: 34). The experience of nature described by Wordsworth in 1798 in his 'Lines composed a few miles above Tintern Abbey' evokes neo-Platonic ideas of the world soul:

> And I have felt
> A presence that disturbs me with the joy
> Of elevated thoughts; a sense sublime
> Of something far more deeply interfused,
> Whose dwelling is the light of setting suns,
> And the round ocean and the living air,
> And the blue sky, and in the mind of man:
> A motion and a spirit, that impels
> All thinking things, all objects of all thought,
> And rolls through all things.
>   Wordsworth (1965)

These two strands, the Hebrew and the Greek, were woven together in medieval Christian theology. However, in modern Protestant theology they have tended to unravel, with liberal Christianity turning more and more to neo-Platonic ideas of immanence, and evangelical Christianity becoming more resolutely Hebrew, returning to the commanding, sovereign God who can be discerned in the Bible. Stoll describes environmental politics in America as evidencing this divorce: those advocating environmental protec-tion are more likely to draw on neo-Platonic ideas of nature, or similar understandings from non-Western cultures, while those seeking to justify the exploitation of nature tend to draw more on the Hebrew, biblical strand of Christianity (Stoll, 1997: 189). One might be forgiven for con-cluding that the frequent alliance between evangelical Protestantism and business interests in America seems to confirm Lynn White's (1967) claim about the elective affinity between the biblical tradition and the industrial exploitation of nature. However, as we shall see in Part IV, contemporary cultural and social movements that place themselves in opposition to the technological domination of nature also draw heavily on the Protestant religious tradition.

These two strands in Christian thought about nature, the Hebrew and the Greek, do not simply pass unchanged down the centuries; as society changes, and the sacred itself undergoes a series of transformations, they come to take on new meanings. Two developments in the constitution of the sacred are central to these changes, and work their way through to the ideas of nature discussed in this chapter. The first concerns the emergence and transformation of concepts of political rule. According to Gauchet, rulership is initially constituted in the context of the archaic sacred, by the making of explicit connections between specific empirical people, objects and places with divine power, the paradigm case of this being African ideas of divine kingship. By contrast, Gauchet argues that Christianity brings to fruition one of the central implications of the political logic of the monotheistic sacred, that of the separation of earthly and heavenly power. Unlike the warrior messiahs predicted by many Jewish cults, Jesus is an 'inverted Messiah', in whom divine power was identified not with the highest, the sovereign, but the lowest, the weak and excluded. In contrast to the divine kingship of the archaic sacred, this shows not a continuity but a radical gulf between heaven and earth (Gauchet, 1997: 118–24). As Christianity develops, the very positing by the Church of a form of spiritual power independent of temporal power later constitutes a space for a competing form of sacrality. Gradually, European monarchy moves to occupy this space; rather than being marked out as different, as filled with divine radiance, the monarch has to take responsibility for collective life, connecting this whole together through practices of administration and representation (Gauchet, 1997: 140–3). The eventual outcome of this is what Arendt calls 'no-man rule' (Arendt, 1958: 40). With the modern liberal state the monarch thus becomes a crossed-out ~~monarch~~ corresponding to the crossed-out ~~God~~ of the modern sacred (Latour, 1993: 32–4); in modern democracies society is ruled not in the interests of each and every empirical being but in those of an imagined abstract person, by an anonymous system of administration grounded in sublime reason.

In terms of the broad shifts in practical and normative relationships with nature discussed so far in the book, the general pattern is a change from nature being seen as the visible activity of supernatural beings (primal sacred), to specific parts of nature being guarded by tutelary spirits (archaic sacred), to nature as a creation of a transcendent deity and as revealing supernatural truths (monotheistic sacred), to a self-sufficient nature which is to be protected for the good of the social body or for the abstract contemplation of the non-ruler of democratic society (modern sacred). Revealingly anomalous in this story, however, is the popularity in early modern Europe of the protection of areas of nature for the royal hunt, linked to the archaic sacred logic of medieval monarchy. But as the European monarchy shifted to claiming not a Christological but a political sacrality, laying the ground for representative democracy, the logic was that nature should be protected not for the divine king but for an abstract, sublime 'no-man' for and by whom society was governed. Modern science supplied the grammar for such a portioning of nature, by providing an Archimedean viewpoint on nature, one that enabled the description of nature from a point outside the lifeworld of everyday human meanings (Arendt, 1958: 257–68). It is the imaginative construction of that sublime viewpoint by the scientific revolution that enables us to think today of protecting nature for 'its own sake' – in fact, for an abstract, objective contemplator of nature. The modern protection of abstract nature is thus a correlate to the abstract ruler of society.

The second key transformation involves the emergence of the individual, which Gauchet argues has roots in the Christian reordering of the sacred. Whereas a traditional messiah would have preached war, and thus re-affirmed the primacy of the collective, Christ preached love and peace, constituting an interiority to human experience which distanced individuals from the social bond. Similarly the infinite distance of the Christian God and the refusal of the demonstrations of magical power characteristic of the archaic sacred demands of the individual acts of faith and conversion based on a denial and surpassing of the senses.[1] But this radical separation from communal sociality was counterbalanced by the apocalyptic expectation that worldly and divine power would be merged in the second coming, an expectation that was eventually converted into an endlessly deferred, eschatological fusion of the two kingdoms of the human and the divine (Gauchet, 1997: 120–2).

Gauchet describes how this new ordering of the sacred brought forth correspondingly new forms of collective being, where distanced indi-viduals were gathered together into a salvation community distinct from political power – the Church. Because, as discussed above, the Incarnation had taken a form which broke with the sacral continuities of the archaic sacred, a yawning gap was opened up between divine and earthly truth. The Church at once symbolized and promised to fill that gap by organizing dogma and policing souls; 'what legitimated the Church's existence – the human understanding's uncertainty about revealed truth – simultaneously justifies challenging its authority'. At the same time, the separation of sacred and earthly authority did not just put the Christian in tension between what Augustine (1960–72) called the two cities of man and God; the very existence of the Church and its continual tension with worldly administration showed how the absolute otherness of God meant that there could not be one legitimate worldly order (Gauchet, 1997: 120–2, 130–44).

The conflicting imperatives of outward belonging and inward distancing from worldly power and the emphasis on the impossibility of certain knowledge of spiritual truth and the demands of salvation, thus started to shape what would become the modern individual. The gospels were not just a collective, canonical ritual but an address by God to each individual (Gadamer, 1975: 427); individuals were thus thrown back on themselves to make sense of sacral truths in terms of their own inner understanding. Similarly, the breaking of the connection between divine and earthly rule gave the individual the right to withdraw assent from worldly power, helping constitute the individual as a centre of consciousness and judgement in their own right. These developments led up to the concept of individual conscience central to modern democracy and social movements; but they also led to the experiential focus of Romantic and postmodern understandings of nature.

Bearing these transformations in mind – the emergence of secular ideas of political rule, which themselves led to the biopolitical ordering of society, and the emergence of individual subjectivity due to the epistemological gap opened up by the Incarnation – the rest of this chapter will explore two clusters of ideas of nature that have been taken up into the modern conception of the environment, placing them against the social and historical context out of which they emerged, and against the larger background of the ongoing transformation of the sacred. Of course, concepts of nature have a far longer and more complex history than that sketched here (Collingwood, 1945; Glacken, 1967; Williams, 1980). Here the focus will be on ideas of nature that have provided some of the key elements for environmental discourse in the late twentieth century, ideas which draw on the Hebrew and Greek origins of Christian thought, and which can be linked to specific transformations in the sacred that have occurred in the last two millennia of Western religious history.

Nature as a System to be Protected

The first set of ideas present nature as a system to be managed or safeguarded. Ideas of nature's senescence – that it is becoming less fertile – have a long history. In the classical world, Democritus and Lucretius speculated that environmental change might explain the diminishing productivity of the earth, using an organic rather than technological analogy: Lucretius, for example, compared the earth to a mother who with age will no longer be able to bear children (Glacken, 1967: 70–2). But generally, pre-modern

notions of scarcity generally saw it simply as a regrettable episode of insufficiency, and one of particular things. Even the account of the expulsion
from the Garden of Eden in Genesis 3, where Adam is warned: 'cursed *is*
the ground for thy sake; in sorrow shalt thou eat *of* it all the days of thy
life', served as an aetiology of human labour rather than an exhortation to
manage resources. By contrast, in the modern period we see a growing
sense that problems in nature might be directly linked to technological
activity, and also that they can and must be brought under systematic and
rational human control as part of the Baconian project.

Ecological science, conceiving of nature as an interconnected living
system, played an important role in that development, both in terms of
identifying environmental problems and offering technical solutions. Its
authority, like that of other modern sciences, partly rested on its claim to
objectivity, its claim to understand nature's dynamics from an Archimedean
point outside worldly human interests (Arendt, 1958: 264). Although scientific forms of knowing have a close relationship with human beings'
instrumental interest in using and controlling nature, botanical science at
least arose partly as a reaction against approaches to plants based on their
direct usefulness. For example, until the mid-seventeenth century, all studies of wild plants in Britain had been oriented to their medicinal usefulness,
and it was only after this point, Keith Thomas suggests, that 'naturalists
had developed an interest in plants for their own sake' (See Sheail, 1976: 2;
Thomas, 1984: 271). But the rhetorical need to mark out their emerging
profession from other practices and institutions further shaped and refined
ecological-scientific conceptions of nature. In Britain scientific ecology
began in earnest in 1913 with the founding of the British Ecological Society, and the ecologists were quick to distinguish themselves from the pre-
servationists, for whom intervention in nature was always to be
discouraged. They were thus not above stressing the biopolitical usefulness
of ecology in understanding how marginal land could be made more productive, thus adopting the utilitarian approach of the progressive conservation movement in the United States, especially when government
funding was at stake (Lowe, 1983: 341). In the twentieth century ecological science presented itself as a form of knowledge capable of understanding and optimizing either nature's contribution to the ongoing
reproduction of society or simply nature's own self-reproduction, both of
which relied on the same, immanent conception of life as self-reproduction
and growth.[2]

Two particular ideas of nature as system became very significant in
twentieth-century environmental discourse – nature as exhaustible, and
nature as polluted. Let us explore each in turn in terms of its historical
and sacral origins. Firstly, the utilitarian, prudential concern for nature as a
collection of dwindling resources might seem a self-evident way of regarding

nature. Yet, while there are examples of attempts to protect forests from over-exploitation before the modern era, these were necessarily local in character, and generated more by conflicting sets of customary rights than by the managerialist approach of modern resource conservation (Glacken, 1967: 329). It is only in the nineteenth century that 'scarcity' was taken to refer to a general human condition, and its management seen as a plausible collective project (Xenos, 1989: 3). Xenos links the rise of this notion to that of the modern consumption-oriented character complex, for whom desires continually proliferate; but the step from that individual, quotidian experience of insufficiency to the idea that collective resources themselves should be stewarded is, as Samuel Hays has commented, not an obvious one (Hays, 1987: 207).

Indeed, the discourse of nature as exhaustible arose in its modern, coherent form in a particular institutional context, that of the emergence in the nineteenth and twentieth centuries of the biopolitical ordering of society. This radically new mode of social ordering merges two historically specific practices, those of industrial capitalism and the modern state – the first constructing the world as a set of resources to be used, and the second as something that can be brought under control through technology and rational planning. Although Foucault's account of biopolitics focuses almost solely on the administration of *human* life, the concept has been extended by others to help analyse the increasing management of non-human life that emerged at the same time (Rutherford, 1993, 1999; Darier, 1999; Clark, 2003). Like human beings, natural objects were progressively conceived in ways that stripped them of their old sacral ordering in terms of gift and reciprocity, and instead subjected them to new biopolitical orderings in service of a life conceived in immanent, biological terms. Initially, such a representation was applied to individual 'resources', such as timber or minerals, but as we saw in Chapter 4 it became increasingly generalized as a way of looking at the natural world (Heidegger, 2003).

Yet elements of the modern idea of the management of nature date back to the Reformation and early Enlightenment. Carolyn Merchant observes that a managerialist approach to nature first surfaced in Britain in the seventeenth century among latitudinarian divines (Merchant, 1980: 236 ff.), but became more widespread in the eighteenth century, manifesting that century's 'optimism over the technological progress of the human race as a rational species in control of its own environment' (1980: 251). Over this period, pre-millennialist preparations for the end of the world were partially displaced by a belief in the possibility of creating the kingdom of God in this world. There was a shift in the cultural function of counterfactual visions of how the world could be: rather than standing as divine judgements of human fallenness, for many groups in society they became goals for human endeavour; rather than signalling human limitation, they thematized the human power to transform the world. And even when overly optimistic predictions of technological mastery over the human condition were countered – as those of Condorcet were by Thomas Malthus – they were countered in technological terms, by arguing that the natural environment imposed limits on human technological achievements (Glacken, 1967: 623–54).

However, Merchant fails to emphasize that ideas of managing nature arose first within the context not of humanity but of nation. For example, by the 1660s Britain's forests had been declining for at least a century, due to population growth and the increase of industries using wood for fuel or materials. It was in that decade that John Evelyn, a founder of the Royal Society, undertook a survey of the 'Timber in His Majesty's Dominions', in part prompted by the concern felt by the navy that there was an increasing shortage of timber with which to build ships. Evelyn's study, published under the title of *Silva*, resulted in a stewardship policy for forestry in England. This involved the planting of seedlings over thousands of acres, the rational, sustainable exploitation of existing forests, the draining of land, the care of standing trees, and so on (Merchant, 1980: 238–40). Similar policies were also developed in France, about this time, by the natural philosopher Count Buffon (Glacken, 1967: 671).

But it is in the nineteenth and twentieth centuries that such practices began to be gathered together into an all-embracing idea of nature as something to be managed. We saw in Chapter 3 how monotheistic ideas of a transcendent creator laid the grounds for modern ideas of objective, scientific knowledge – the world seen not as by empirical beings but as if by God. In the context of the modern biopolitical state this Archimedean conception of knowledge was embraced not just in order to increase control over nature, but also to remove the basis of decision-making from the worldly context of plurality and disagreement.[3] For example, in the United States the conception of nature as a collection of national resources to be husbanded became not just the dominant conservation ideology but a whole paradigm for national planning at the beginning of the twentieth century. Theodore Roosevelt, president from 1901 to 1909, had a predilection for using scientific experts to generate policy, partly out of a fear of populist unrest and a belief in the existence of governmental techniques that could 'legislate that conflict out of existence' (Hays, 1969: 267). Under the influence of Gifford Pinchot, who was concerned to 'put resource development on a thoroughly rational and efficient base', Roosevelt in effect applied the tradition of rational, progressive agriculture to the management of public land (Ekirch, 1963: 89; Worster, 1977: 266). Pinchot's hand is particularly evident in the US Forest Service, which he helped shape in 1905. For Pinchot, 'the purpose of forestry ... is to make the forest produce the largest possible amount of whatever crop or service will be most useful, and keep on producing it for generation after generation of men and trees' (quoted by Worster, 1977: 267). While some of its more crudely utilitarian aspects became softened with a growing appreciation of the recreational value of nature, and of ecological interdependence, the resource-management approach to the American environment was extended in the inter-war New Deal era by the strengthening of federal government and an enthusiasm for national planning (Ekirch, 1963: 117–18; Nash, 1976: 97–8).

Ideas of nature as an exhaustible resource in need of stewarding, then, only arose in any comprehensive sense in the biopolitical context of modern nation states intervening in the life process in order to shape and optimize it according to technical criteria. Of course, colonialism and general economic interdependency meant that concern about resource depletion often spilled out of a strictly national context.[4] As we shall see in Chapter 11, it was only under specific historical conditions that awareness of the finitude of natural resources became framed as a *global* problem.

But in the late nineteenth and twentieth centuries the immanent sacrality of the modern sacred also generated another idea of nature as threatened, one which depended on the idea of nature as a self-reproducing organic whole which was being polluted by industrial activity. The conception of the pollution of nature as being of profound moral significance originated in the nineteenth-century Romantic movement. Both William Wordsworth and John Ruskin wrote eloquently about the effects that the rapid industrialization of their time was having on the English countryside, using pollution as a symbol of moral decline and alienation from authentic existence. Ruskin, for example, in his *Storm Cloud of the Nineteenth Century,* used the phenomenon of atmospheric pollution as the basis for a biblical, prophetic onslaught on modern, technological existence. Before we can purify the sky, he insists, we must purify ourselves (Ruskin, 1908; Bate, 1991: 83). The salience of ideas of nature as a polluted body was thus not only due to the existence of scientific evidence, but also to their resonance as cultural symbols which drew on a natural theology which itself fused biblical and neo-Platonic ideas of nature.

This resonance was particularly important in the second half of the twentieth century, when such representations achieved particular prominence. In the choice of the first main foci of such concern, atomic testing and pesticides (Hays, 1987: 174), cultural criteria were clearly significant – the invisibility of these pollutants only adding to their symbolic resonance. Even the construction of pollution as a risk to the individual depended on a cultural shift, experienced in many industrialized nations, in which the rise of a new, 'consumption-oriented social character' for whom even health has to be maximally consumed, combined with a marked decline of life-threatening diseases, allowing a 'turn to life' in which quality-of-life issues were given a new inherent sacrality (Freund and Fisher, 1982: 73–4; Hays, 1987: 24–6, 28). Nevertheless, although the *rise* of this representation of nature-as-polluted over the last few decades has relied crucially on its cultural resonance, the *form* that it now takes, in contrast to that of a century earlier, is one which is mediated through the language of science. Pollution no longer sacramentally signifies a deviation from right relation with a transcendent divine; instead, it is understood as a threat to an immanent life process, itself now the locus of the sacred. Scientific language, rather than the aesthetic and biblical language of Ruskin, has become the medium for apocalyptic judgements (Alexander and Smith, 1996). Rachel Carson's *Silent Spring*, first published in 1962, is perhaps the most significant example of this scientized but still intensely moral representation. In graphic, relentless detail Carson shows us a world once full of life, but fast becoming a 'sea of carcinogens' (1965: 211). The problem is presented not so much as the destruction of individual animals, or even of individual species, but as the contamination and disturbance of the delicate balance of nature, and thus the possible destruction of life itself. 'In the less than two decades of their use,' she laments, 'the synthetic pesticides have been so thoroughly distributed throughout the animate and inanimate world that they occur virtually everywhere' (1965: 31).

So we have seen that the modern sacred gave birth to two specific ideas of nature that would become highly significant elements in the twentieth-century conception of 'the environment'. Let us just rehearse how the general idea of nature as an immanent whole to be protected from exhaustion or pollution emerges as a particular contingent product of Western sacred history. In the context of the transition from the primal to the archaic sacred, interactions with nature had become personal in a new way; they were understood not simply as transactions with individual beings, but typically with a spirit who guarded over particular species or places. With the emergence of the monotheistic sacred, this was transformed into a relationship between creation and a creator no longer understood as a being among beings, but as transcendent, sublime, and as creator of all. Relations with nature became understood as primarily symbolic or educative, as natural truths mediated a personal relationship with the creator. As we saw earlier in this chapter, medieval and early modern ideas of divine kingship had positioned certain individuals at the fulcrum between earthly and divine power, preserving features of the archaic sacred. But when under the modern sacred the understanding of rulership changed from one of hierarchical dissimilarity to the management of relations in the social whole, an idea of the sacrality of life itself emerged, of nature not symbolically praising God but materially serving itself, a move which finally resulted in the immanent sacrality of biopolitical society ordered through technique.

Nature as a Collection of Beings

But these two ideas of nature as an immanent system were also joined by other understandings of nature as threatened which focused more on individual creatures, species and habitats. The first of these depended on a different construction of the personal in nature, one that generated a powerful current of humanitarianism in contemporary relations with the non-human. The emergence of the monotheistic sacred created a new understanding of the individual as standing before the transcendent divine. The very sameness of human beings before the transcendent divine made them different in a new way, unique subjects of unique lives. This implication of the monotheistic sacred was radicalized in the Protestant sacred, as the earthly and divine intermediaries between the individual and their God were stripped away. At the same time, the monotheistic notion of the disinterested love of God (in contrast with the 'interested' relations with divine powers characteristic of the archaic sacred) became more sharply realized. And just as God was increasingly seen as not useful to humanity, so too humanity was seen as not needed by a God made increasingly sublime and unconditioned. And as reason takes the place of God, in thinkers like Kant it is the human individual, the bearer of that reason, who takes on the characteristic of being worthy of regard above and beyond their usefulness, in what Durkheim would later approvingly call the 'cult of man' (Durkheim, 1969). This was a sacralization of the individual, which for some sections of society was extended to other species, constituting nature as a collection of subjects deserving of moral considerability.

There were precursors of such attitudes, of course, in the 'bloodless' tradition in Western thought identified by Eder (Eder, 1996; see also Chapter 7 below). Biblical thought, and particularly the doctrine of creation, had laid the grounds for ways of thinking about human relationships with animals that were not just magical, contractual or customary. All creatures – and not just all human beings – were made by the same creator. Human beings were created on the same day as the other animals (Genesis 1:24), and, like them, from the earth (Genesis 2:7–19). Although the covenant between Yahweh and his people, Israel, is central to the Old Testament, others, such as those of Noah (Genesis 9:12, 15, 17) and Hosea (2:18a), are with all of God's creatures. Human beings have much in common with the animals: 'death comes to both alike. They all draw the same breath. Men have no advantage over beasts; for everything is emptiness. All go to the same place: all came from the dust, and to the dust all return' (Ecclesiastes 3:19–20). Such sentiments were continued among the Greek Fathers. A prayer of Basil the Great founded concern for animals on the commonality of our plight: 'And for these also, O Lord, the humble beasts, who bear with us the heat and burden of the day, we beg thee to extend thy great kindness of heart, for thou hast promised to save both man and beast, and great is thy loving kindness, O Master' (Passmore, 1980: 198).

Yet if such concern was latent in the monotheistic sacred from the beginning, it was not really worked through until the modern period. And it is striking that the humanitarian attitude to animals seems to have most firmly taken root in those Western countries most influenced by the Reformation. Part of this is likely to be due to the puritan character ideal of northern European countries and countries colonized by northern Europeans: criticism of the mistreatment of animals is often motivated as much by moral disapproval at what are seen as lowly pleasures as by concern for the animal itself. But it seems also to be the case that before nature could be invested with modern, ethical understandings – those of rights and abstract, deontological ideas of moral respect – it was first necessary for older, symbolic and sacramental codings of nature to be stripped away. Ironically, then, in so far as nature has been disenchanted under modern conditions, it may be that this has helped rather than hindered the development of ideas of the moral considerability of non-human nature.

Such ideas certainly became a powerful social force in mid-nineteenth-century Britain. At the beginning of that century Britain had a reputation for exploiting animals quite ruthlessly, whether for food, clothing, labour or entertainment. By its close, compassion for animals had become a prominent and durable element in the British sense of self-identity. As early as the 1830s, as Harriet Ritvo reports, 'the English humane movement had begun to claim kindness to animals as a native trait and to associate cruelty to animals with foreigners' (Ritvo, 1990: 126–7). Much of this claim might be dismissed as sheer rhetoric; but the gap between rhetoric and practice might also be seen as indicating that the human–non-human relationship, like the body, was at least at this time a key site of contestation between different orderings of the sacred, with correspondingly different understandings of the relation between the individual, the social body and nature. One of the functions of the discourse of humanitarianism was certainly to make social distinctions between the 'genteel' upper classes and the 'cruel' lower orders. The Royal Society for the Prevention of Cruelty to Animals (RSPCA), founded in 1824, repeatedly showed a predilection for attempting to outlaw the cruel sports practised by the working classes, rather than those favoured by the elites (MacKenzie, 1988: 27; Ryder, 1989: 100–1; Ritvo, 1990: 134–5, 143). Another related function was clearly to sanction the imposition of moral discipline and social order on a supposedly degenerate population, a goal that the RSPCA shared with its offshoot, the National Society for the Prevention of Cruelty to Children (NSPCC) (Thomas, 1984: 186; Ritvo, 1990: 132–3).

Nevertheless, real changes took place over the century in the moral consideration given to animals in Britain. One historically contingent factor in this shift in sensibility was the development of anaesthetic technologies in medicine, which led to a less fatalistic attitude to suffering (Ryder, 1989: 157–8, 165). But perhaps more important was the arrival of industrialization, which largely removed animals from processes of production. The movement for animal welfare drew its supporters from the emerging middle classes, who saw animals mainly as pets, rather than from the working classes, for whom they were a source of labour, or from the aristocracy, whose country sports were a symbol of social dominance and related to military tradition (Thomas, 1984: 181–4). The difference between British and American attitudes to animals is partly due to certain ideas of nature that became enshrined in American self-understanding during the revolutionary period. Revolutionary thought reversed the European Utopian image of the city on the hill; virtue lay not in urban sophistication but in honest rural simplicity and vigour (Albanese, 1990: 51–3). Although Thoreau was led to cleanse his diet of flesh as unclean, the dominant strand of American thought in relation to nature was one that accepted the pastoral and hunting life as not just permissible but virtuous.

After the First World War interest in animal welfare did not feature prominently, even in British society, until the 1960s, which saw the rise of a more radical animal *rights* movement, concerned not just to minimize suffering, but to bring animals into the arena of full moral considerability, as ends in themselves. In 1963 the Hunt Saboteurs Association was formed, in 1978 the Animal Liberation Front, and in the 1970s the RSPCA itself came to take a more radical stance, in particular over the use of animals in pharmacological testing (Nash, 1989: 187; Ryder, 1989: 181). Since then the relationship between the animal rights movement and the rest of the environmental movement has been ambiguous, because of the tension between the very different ideas of nature involved, and the different implications they hold for the treatment of animals. On the one hand, ecological conceptions of nature represent particular animals as having only instrumental utility to the ecosystem of which they are a part. Such biopolitical understandings of the self-reproducing life process sacralize life, but not individual lives. Thus state agencies and NGOs, notably the World Wildlife Fund (WWF), have often pursued policies in support of the culling of wildlife populations for ecological reasons. On the other hand, the doctrine of creation set up relations between empirical beings and the divine which could be taken as implying the sacrality of individual beings, above and beyond their place in the self-reproduction of life itself. International NGOs like Greenpeace have pursued campaigns under the influence of this sacralization of nature, notably over whaling and seal hunting.

But there is a further important idea of nature as a collection of beings to be protected, one which displays continuities with the way that nature and society are connected together in the archaic sacred: namely, picking out certain species or habitats as of special significance. Rather than the protection of the whole of nature for the sake of the ongoing performance of life, only certain parts of nature, particularly the rare or endangered, are marked out as bearing intrinsic value, above and beyond their usefulness to the reproduction of the wider life process of nature or society.[5] Here contemporary meanings of nature come closest to the Durkheimian idea of the sacred.

In Britain a concern for the protection of rare and endangered species emerged in the nineteenth century. One of the main contexts for this emergence was the rise of the natural history movement. Fuelled by the Victorian obsession with travel and self-improvement, and enabled by increased affluence and better transport, the amateur collection and study of natural specimens soon became a pastime which was popular – and, importantly for the Victorian era, morally acceptable. The number of natural history societies grew considerably over the century, so that by the 1880s their combined membership reached around 100,000 (Lowe, 1983: 333). An interest in rare or unusual specimens made sense in the context of such a practice, and in a class-based culture with a fascination for taxonomy (Gold, 1984: 27; Katz and Kirby, 1991: 262), and for the exotic (Said, 1978: 51, 108; Ritvo, 1990: 205), however much scientific ecologists would at times problematize the importance of rarity as a basis for the understanding of nature. But the early period of natural history was by no means conducive to the *preservation* of the rare. Indeed, the practices engaged in often contributed to the rarity of species, due to the sheer numbers of people – including professional collectors – seeking to enlarge their collections of the rare or interesting.[6] However, a concern to prevent the rare becoming the extinct arose easily within the context of this practice, and, from the mid-century, naturalists' field clubs began to express a growing concern about the dangers of collecting. The growth of private and public natural history museums and collections accentuated this tendency for nature itself to be seen as a great museum, a common collection which should be preserved. Indeed, it was the activities of amateur naturalists, with their field clubs, which provided the first catalogue of that museum in Britain, against which later changes could be judged (Lowe, 1983: 335).

Another social context out of which a concern for the rare developed in the nineteenth century was that of hunting. In the era of imperial conquest the hunting of game in colonized territories had been an important source of tradable goods – skins, hides and feathers – and of meat for settlers and indigenous populations alike. However, as the nineteenth century progressed, hunting in the colonies became predominantly a ritual activity, the privilege of the dominant white male elites, and clearly served as a symbol of their social mastery (MacKenzie, 1988: 22–3). In a continuation of the ritual performance of social distinction that connected early modern monarchy with the archaic sacred, the sporting trophy became an important symbol of that dominance – and, of course, the rarer the species, the more highly prized was the trophy.[7] The displaying of hunting trophies emerged in the cultural milieu of early-nineteenth-century Romanticism, initially among aristocratic families who had members serving abroad. However, the practice soon became more widely adopted, creating a profitable but destructive trade in trophies by the end of the century (MacKenzie, 1988: 28–31).[8] This only accelerated further the dynamic whereby the rare became the most sought-after, and thus rarer.

In response to the rapid decline of animal populations in the colonies, the scheduling of animals was introduced. Species were assigned to one of up to five different categories, from 'fair game' to 'royal game', determining who could shoot them, and how many they were allowed to shoot, with rarity being the main consideration (MacKenzie, 1988: 210). It was from this context that many conservation practices developed – first as game preservation, and then, as the twentieth century progressed, as wildlife conservation (MacKenzie, 1988: 286). Using the American experience as a model, national parks were developed in both Africa and Asia, with a focus on the preservation of endangered species. The main threat to the animals was generally perceived to come from the hunting (or poaching, in the ruling class's terms) carried out by indigenous populations, who were not allowed to settle in the parks. The ideology of conservation is thus in many ways closely caught up with that of a colonialism which itself had roots in the archaic sacred's notions of continuity between earthly hierarchies and divine power.

The WWF in particular had its cultural roots in this post-colonial conservationism. The fund was founded in 1961 by Max Nicholson, director-general of the Nature Conservancy Council, as a campaigning and fund-raising counterpart to the scientifically inclined but underfunded International Union for the Conservation of Nature (IUCN) (Nicholson, 1972: 261–2; Pearce, 1991: 46), and its first report indicates the flavour of its concerns, concluding as it does with a 'preliminary list of rare animals and birds', each of the 516 species listed being categorized as to its rarity (Scott, 1965: 155–207). But a concern for the rare has also been strengthened in recent times by the practices of the mass media. The competition among both the broadcast and the print media for affecting but simple storylines has even further enhanced the appeal of narratives of extinction – either of particular species and habitats, or of nature as a whole (Porritt and Winner, 1988: 87; Burgess et al. 1990).[9] Particularly

since the campaigning phase in natural history television of the 1970s and
early 1980s, nature, often in the form of individual species or habitat types,
has increasingly been represented as 'finite, vulnerable and under immediate threat of total extinction' (Burgess, 1990; Burgess, 1993: 61; see also
Lowe, 1983: 347).[10]

From an anthropological perspective, the symbolic significance of
threatened species such as panda, whale and rhinoceros can be understood
as part of the history of animal totemism in modern society (Franklin,
2001: 92–131). Adrian Franklin draws on Phillipe Descola's (1992) distinction between two kinds of pre-modern societies. Totemic societies use
the visual dissimilarities between animal and plant species to symbolize a
similar differentiation of society and nature into distinct social and geographical units. Animic societies, by contrast, regard non-human beings as
persons with whom can be exchanged material and characteristics. As
Ingold puts it in his version of the distinction, '[t]he totemic world is
essential, the animic world dialogical' (Ingold, 2000: 114). Franklin uses
this distinction to argue against the idea that the emergence of modern
societies involved a break with the naturalistic understanding of social
forms. He describes the totemic use of animals, plants and types of nature
to naturalize social identities, at the levels of nation, institution and social
class.

The function of endangered species as emblematic, totemic signifiers
differs from Franklin's examples in a number of ways. Firstly, these totems
signify not the ascribed identities of nation and class but the elective identities of those involved in nature conservation. Secondly, they also partake
of animic characteristics, in the sense that they are regarded not just as
heraldic emblems but also as persons, with whom an exchange can occur:
material benefit and protection in exchange for moral merit on the part of
the human benefactor. In a sense, endangered species represent a reversal
of the archaic sacred: they function as tutelary spirits of certain habitats,
but not of the hunt; and it is they who receive protection from their
human supplicants.

At times, ecological scientists have been concerned to distance themselves from the archaic sacralization of nature involved in natural history,
instead aligning themselves with the modern sublimity of abstract universals (Sheail, 1976: 141; Lowe, 1983: 341). Because of pressures towards
professionalization induced by the need to be taken seriously as 'hard'
science, ecology, and biology in general, articulated a notion of 'scientific
interest', particularly in the area of scientific nature conservation, which
was presented in contrast to human utility on the one hand and human
aesthetic tastes on the other, opening up a secular discursive space where
the non-anthropocentric evaluation of nature made sense (Ashby, 1978:
82–4). No longer able to ground the value of beings in their direct

creaturely relation with a transcendent divinity, instead non-instrumental value could be grounded in the sacrality of the life process itself, in which each being could be seen as playing a part. Such moves contributed to the shift in attitudes towards carnivorous wildlife which occurred in America in the twentieth century, where increased knowledge of their role in the control of other animal populations helped people see them as having a value beyond their usefulness to humankind or their aesthetic qualities (Worster, 1977: 260–1). As we shall see in Part IV, practices in contemporary society that can be seen as attempts to find a more authentic and non-dominative relationship to the non-human world can also be seen as a rejection of residual archaic characteristics of the nature–society relationship in contemporary society.

Nature as a Moral Source

A third set of ideas important to the modern conception of the environment present nature as a realm of purity and moral power in contrast to the instrumental, technological world of modern society. From the late eighteenth century nature started to be seen in various ways as the unspoilt, as an Edenic arena of goodness and innocence, unsullied by the artifice, alienation and corruption of modern life – as 'what man has not made' (Williams, 1976: 223). Both in the United States and in Britain this notion of nature as a rejection of industrialism and modern technology was deepened and transformed in the nineteenth century. In America the earlier agrarian ideal of Thomas Jefferson, which saw nature as a 'perpetual garden', an escape from the corrupting influence of European civilization, gave way to the less artisanal and more aesthetic notion of harmony with nature which Emerson drew from his Unitarian and neo-Platonist roots (Ekirch, 1963: 10–21, 47–69; Stoll, 1997: 102). In various ways, nature came to take on new sacral meanings, as a counterpoint to the increased technologization of society.

Firstly, then, the modern experience of nature produced new uses of nature, including as a place for contemplative retreat, a practice with its roots in the monotheistic sacred. Once the rise of monotheism had more or less cleared the wild places of supernatural presences, they had become a place for the individual to commune with God himself (Stoll, 1997: 26). But with transformations in the sacred this practice changed, the contemplative communion with the transcendent divine being replaced first by a more distanced, aesthetic and visual appreciation of the handiwork of an absent God, and finally by a Romantic notion of the self encountering itself in sublime nature. Christianity had authorized the individual subject by banishing miracles and opening up a gap between the empirical and supernal worlds that could only be spanned by individual subjective acts of faith and conversion. In the Romantic contemplation of nature, by contrast, the individual subject completes not liturgical and scriptural meaning but the visual landscape, which is seen as revealing not divine majesty but the very profundity of the observer's soul.

The idea of nature as something to be appropriated visually, as a landscape, makes its appearance most decisively in the eighteenth century, and can be traced through a number of phases. Initially it was an elite phenomenon, depending as it did on a familiarity with classical literature, and with a style of European painting where representations of human beings and human labour were absent, or at most only part of the landscape (Barrell, 1980). Descriptions left by the cultivated individuals who travelled to gaze on the English Lake District or rural Hampshire are peppered with references to Rubens, Poussin and Claude. Indeed, it was often lamented that real landscapes fell short of the standard presented in paintings (Thomas, 1984: 265–6). But by the beginning of the nineteenth century the dominant taste in landscape had shifted its focus from the picturesque, cultivated scene to sublime, 'unimproved' scenery (Nicolson, 1959; Nash, 1973: 45–7). This Romanticist conception of nature went hand in hand with a growing sense of alienation from the increasingly crowded and noisy cities, and from the progressively enclosed and rectilinear agricultural landscape, and also paralleled a resurgence of the Renaissance cult of the individual (Thomas, 1984: 266–9). But however much this aesthetic left behind the pictorial confines of earlier times, it was still firmly embedded in the social practices of the educated classes.[11] It was only the twentieth century that saw a democratization of landscape aesthetics, due in part to the working classes having increased affluence and leisure, and thus the ability to travel. The development of mass tourism allowed people to experience, and thus develop discernment about, different kinds of landscapes (Urry, 1992a: 8–10). Advances in photographic techniques enhanced the tendency to travel to aesthetically pleasing locations (Urry, 1992b: 180–1), and helped to frame people's perceptions of landscapes which they had never actually visited.

However, visual representations of nature played very different roles in the life of nations, roles which owe more to the archaic than to the modern sacred. On both sides of the Atlantic aesthetic representations of nature were often used to invoke ideas of nation in a revival of modes of sacralization characteristic of the archaic sacred. In turn-of-the-century Britain landscape preservation was often cast in nationalistic terms – in 1899 Octavia Hill described National Trust property as 'a bit of England belonging to the English in a very special way' (Lowe, 1983: 340). In Britain journalistic photography of the inter-war years powerfully promoted a nostalgic notion of village life (Lowerson, 1980: 261), and during the Second World

War, the English landscape featured heavily in British national iconography. In the United States after the Second World War colour nature photography helped to raise concern among the population about particular threatened landscapes, such as deserts (Hays, 1987: 24, 37–8). Images of dramatic landscapes, both invoking and further articulating the nation's sense of itself, played a crucial role in the United States in generating support for the idea of national wilderness areas (Hays, 1987: 37). The distinctive character of the American landscape was used to make symbolic connections between the American nation and universal, sublime values, furthering the sense of America as a nation in a special historical relationship both with God and with universal reason.

Secondly, in the modern period nature became an arena not just for contemplation and visual consumption but for recreation, as a temporary respite from the stresses of modern life (Green, 1990: 6; Urry, 1992a: 2–3). This notion of nature as a place for recreation depends on the work–leisure dichotomy of modern industrial society for its force, and represents nature as a non-rationalized space in stark contrast to the disciplined character of the productive sphere. In the light of this it is not surprising that urban parks were all but coeval with industrial capitalism, as the direct encounter with nature was perceived as having exactly the restorative qualities that modern life lacked. For example, New York's Central Park was developed by Frederick Law Olmsted in the 1850s and 1860s in order, as he argued, to provide New York's working-class inhabitants with 'a specimen of God's handiwork that shall be to them, inexpensively, what a month or two in the White Mountains, or the Adirondacks is . . . to those in easier circumstances' (see Ekirch, 1963: 30–1; Strong, 1971: 23). The national parks too, initially developed in America largely for the preservation of game and water supplies, became increasingly seen, and used, as a leisure resource.

In Britain there was a rise in the importance of leisure and recreation in the early twentieth century (Katz and Kirby, 1991: 266–7). From around the turn of the century the shorter working week and the spread in ownership of bicycles and cars resulted in a rapid increase in the numbers of people visiting the countryside. This cultural change was reflected in the founding of the Co-operative Holidays Association in 1891 and the National Trust in 1893. But it was in the 1930s that what had always partly been a biopolitical project to maximize the health of the working population became politicized, and framed more clearly as a realm of freedom. In that decade rambling became a mass activity, with perhaps 10,000 hikers in the Peak District on a summer weekend. This decade was marked by the founding of the Youth Hostels Association in 1930, the Ramblers' Association in 1935, and the beginnings of mass social conflict over rights of access to enclosed land, which the latter helped to organize. With this development the representation of nature as a realm of freedom and restoration, often couched in the state-oriented discourse of public health, changed key into one of transgression (Sheail, 1976: 68; Lowerson, 1980: 268).

Thirdly, in the late nineteenth century there had been a widespread decline in confidence in the urban, industrialized, technological trajectory of Western society, and some had turned to nature for a more permanent escape from the ills of the modern world. In Britain, worsening economic performance brought a general social and economic pessimism, and a greater sensitivity to the negative consequences of modern technology and industrialization (Lowe, 1983: 338). Large parts of the bourgeoisie adopted the cultural values of the aristocracy, which in Britain retained a pronounced disdain for productivism (Wiener, 1985). Drawing powerfully on biblical ideas of Edenic harmony and on monastic traditions of communal living and manual work, nature came to stand for a rejection of faith in social progress by human endeavour, and of the city – and, for many, for a rejection of Victorian convention itself.

In response to this, groups and individuals attempted to establish Utopian communities, many of them rural and agrarian in character, representing nature as offering not just a temporary but a permanent escape from the modern, transplanting not just production but the social itself into a nature conceived as a realm of freedom and harmony (Hardy, 1979: 14). While the social and moral benefits of working the land had some importance for the Utopian socialist communities founded by Robert Owen, and for many nineteenth-century sectarian communities, it was the agrarian socialists who most systematically represented the return to the land as a way to restore what was seen as a lost social harmony. In the 1840s the radical Chartist Feargus O'Connor envisaged a Britain transformed into a peasants' republic, where the land had been returned to the people as 4-acre smallholdings. His Chartist Land Company purchased five estates, where he built almost 280 cottages, allocated by lottery (Darley, 1978: 170–1; Hardy, 1979: 76–8). Later in the century John Ruskin was also to found several agrarian communities, this time along medievalist lines, but with little success. At the same time many anarchist communes, influenced by the ideas of Peter Kropotkin and Leo Tolstoy, offered a largely agrarian social vision which attempted to harmonize individual autonomy and communal solidarity, manual and intellectual labour, and society and nature (Hardy, 1979: 78–80). This broad back-to-the-land movement strengthened the idea of nature as offering a realm which could offer not just a temporary respite but a permanent solution to the alienation of modern urban life, and laid the ground for the revival of the rural commune in the late twentieth century (Pepper, 1991).

In summary, Part III has examined two important areas and traced in them the dynamics described in Part II, those of the emergence of

scientific nature, and of modern technology, within the ongoing transformation of the sacred. Chapter 5 explored the changing meanings and practices surrounding the body and healing in the last two millennia, which I
argued has always been a key site of struggle over the sacred. Through
trying to assert and sustain one form of embodiment over another, both
institutions and more informal sociations have been engaged in contestation over the ordering of the sacred – over how individuals are constituted
in terms of their relationship to society, to nature, and to transcendent and
immanent divinity. I argued that the Christian era had seen the introduction of a new model of healing that involved setting up a 'vertical' dependency on human or sacramental vehicles for transcendent spiritual power, in
contrast to the traditional pagan model of healing in terms of the
strengthening of 'horizontal' ties into the social and natural environment.
Then in the sixteenth century Protestantism rejected the cult of the saints
and sacramentalism, and also set itself more firmly against folk medicine,
emphasizing instead an individualized, cognitive monitoring of the self.
But the nineteenth century saw both the birth of modern, professionalized,
biologically based medicine, and a resurgence of a folk medicine now hybridized with Enlightenment belief in reason and revivalist religion.
I argued that healthcare practices in modern societies still exhibited a tension
between these last two models, with many individuals drawn to forms of
embodiment which escape a narrowly technological orientation to health
and well-being. I closed by exploring the reasons why alternative therapies
might be growing in the context of a postmodern sacred in which the
immanent sacrality of modernity has been fragmented by the elevation of
subjective experience as the origin and guarantor of reality and truth.

In the current chapter I briefly surveyed a number of ideas of nature that
help constitute the contemporary notion of the environment, in terms of
how they have taken shape in the context of the transformation of the
sacred in Western societies. Christian ways of thinking about nature drew
on two traditions of thought – Hebrew ideas of *creatio ex nihilo* and *imago
dei*, and Greek, neo-Platonic ideas of nature as organism and as emanation
of God. These traditions of thought were combined and transformed in
various ways over the last two millennia, resulting in a number of ideas of
nature, each of them with different roots in the ongoing transformation of
the sacred, which have informed the modern understanding of the environment. The first cluster I explored involved ideas strongly embedded in the
modern sacred, and particularly in the biopolitical understanding of life as
an immanent self-reproducing process, and involved seeing nature as a
system under threat from depletion or pollution. The second set of ideas
both constituted nature as a collection of individual beings: the first of
these, with its roots in the monotheistic and Protestant sacred, was a humanitarian discourse of the moral considerability of individual beings; the

second, more archaic in nature, singled out rare or aesthetically pleasing animals for concern and protection. The third cluster of ideas presented nature as a moral source, as a locus of meaning and sacral value in contrast with the technological life – as a place of contemplation or aesthetic experience, of recreation, or of communality and virtue.

What the chapters of Part III should have made clear is the coexistence of multiple sacralizations of nature and technology in modern society. The schema set up in Part I, and embellished in Part II, was necessarily simplified in order to clarify the main categories and narrative being used in the analysis. However, despite the pervasiveness of the immanent sacralization of life itself in Western societies, it is not the case that it is totally hegemonic. As we saw in relation to the body in Chapter 5, and the environment in Chapter 6, transformations in the sacred are not sudden and uncontested. But also, as shown in Chapter 2, the collapse of the transcendent axis in the modern age, the end of the dominance of transcendent religion, can be seen as allowing a greater proliferation of forms of the sacred, as sacral meaning escapes from a long period of institutional confinement. Indeed, it is constitutive of what I called the postmodern sacred that in the general context of a sacralization of individual subjectivity, multiple subjective forms of the sacred coexist.

But the significance of this complexification for the next three chapters is the way that competing forms of the sacred help to organize the cultural forms taken by attempts to refuse the technological mastery of non-human nature. For in Part IV we will be turning to the question of how individuals and groups in contemporary society find ways in their private and public lives of taking up critical positions in relation to the technological rendering of nature, and the way these attempts draw on different orderings of the sacred. As we shall see, cultural resources with their roots in the Protestant sacred are prominent in such attempts; but at a more general level, movements concerned to escape or critique the technological condition of modernity can be seen as engaged in a continuation of the monotheistic tradition's struggle against the archaic sacred's rendering of continuities between social, natural and supernatural orders.

Part IV

Against the Technological Condition

Chapter Seven

The Politicization of Nature

The end of the 1960s saw the emergence of a new phenomenon, as a distinctive group of political associations and movements sprang up almost simultaneously in a number of industrialized countries. Both Friends of the Earth (FoE), founded in the USA in 1969, and Greenpeace, founded in Canada as the Don't Make a Wave Committee in the same year, but re-named Greenpeace in 1971, were independently brought into being by members of the Sierra Club, one of the foremost American conservation organizations, who wanted to bring something of the radicalism of the student movement to the politics of environmental protection and technology critique. In Britain the Conservation Society, now disbanded, was founded in 1967, FoE (UK) in 1970, and Greenpeace (UK) in 1977 (Lowe and Goyder, 1983: 124; Pearce, 1991). All brought the dramatic, moralizing political praxis of the 1960s to bear on the issues of environmental protection discussed in the last chapter, but in doing so they also transformed the meaning of the environment and became a vehicle for critical debate about the technological character of modern society. By the end of the 1980s environmental movements and NGOs were an influential and seemingly permanent feature of technologically advanced societies.

Is there any evidence that the phenomenon of environmentalism is part of the Western religious tradition, and predominantly a Christian and post-Christian one? It would not be accurate, for example, to say that Christians are more likely to be environmentally concerned than non-Christians. Attempts to find a statistical correlation between the religious beliefs and environmental concern of individuals have been inconclusive (see Proctor and Berry (forthcoming) for an overview of this research). But it seems clear that, although religiously active churchgoers may be more than twice as likely to have religious experiences concerning nature (Opinion Research Business, 2000: 79–80), they seem no more likely to be involved in environmental politics. Indeed, some studies have indicated that American environmentalists are less likely than the general population to be involved in mainstream religion (Shaiko, 1987), and that American Christians and Jews are more likely to favour mastery over nature, and thus be less sympathetic to environmental politics, than other Americans (Hand and Van Liere, 1984). No, to find evidence of this shaping we have to look for less direct influences, influences which can be usefully divided into two kinds.

Firstly, at the most general level, the modern concept of the environment, with all the complex of attitudes and practices Western societies have towards it, could only have arisen because of what I described in Chapter 2 as the long arc of transcendental religion. The very ways of thinking about nature that we take for granted in contemporary society were only made possible by changes in thought which occurred during the long period in which the world was seen as ontologically dependent on a transcendental divinity beyond the empirical world. This of course raises the question of how understandings of nature might be different in areas of the world which have had quite a different religious history.

Generally, the evidence seems to support the idea that 'the environment' as it is conceived in the contemporary West is the product of a quite specific cultural history. There is a burgeoning literature on how forms of environmentalist beliefs and values might be discernible in the different world religions (e.g. Callicott, 1994; Gottlieb, 1996; Taylor and Kaplan, forthcoming), demonstrating that an ethics or politics of nature can in principle be grounded in very different cosmologies. Yet much of this literature takes an apologetic form, assuming a Western model of environmental concern and then claiming to find this implicitly or explicitly present in the religious tradition under consideration. For example, although the protection of sacred groves in India appears to be a similar phenomenon to the protection of forest habitats in Western societies, the purpose of their conservation is not to protect an abstract 'nature', but to serve a particular deity (Freeman, 1994; Tomalin, 2000). Using the terms developed by David Mandelbaum (1966), in Western society the emphasis is on the transcendental dimension of religion, concerned with the long-term welfare of society and questions of ultimate significance. By contrast, Indian religion focuses on Mandelbaum's pragmatic dimension, on the local and the particular. In Hinduism, transcendental matters are left to the brahmin; popular religion is pragmatic in focus, concerned with the specific needs of individuals (Tomalin, 2000). In such a context it should not be surprising that Indian environmentalism, like that of the developing world generally, is usually pragmatic (Guha and Martinez-Alier, 1997).[1] Societies outside the Western world have not passed along the Western path from the archaic sacred to the modern sacred, with the resulting emphasis on the sublime, and thus on the indifference of the divinity to particular human interests. The kind of environmentalism that emerges in such contexts thus typically focuses on what Roy Rappaport calls the indexical rather than the canonical dimension of religious action – on present needs and situations rather than abstract, impersonal ideas of cosmic order (Rappaport, 1993).

Secondly, in more specific and contingent ways, the character of modern environmentalism is heir to particular ideas, practices, ways of speaking and models of community that developed during the West's religious history, particularly since the Reformation. If this is indeed the case, then one might expect the geography of environmentalism to follow that of religion. And indeed, David Vogel argues that it is overwhelmingly historically Protestant societies that have developed dark green approaches to nature (Vogel, 2002). Vogel starts his argument by defining dark green countries as those in which environmental concerns have a durable presence on political agendas, affect the behaviour of individuals and institutions in a greater way, result in greater levels of regulation, and are more oriented to protecting nature for its own sake. Vogel acknowledges that other factors seem to be at play here: dark green countries are likely to be wealthy, to have more natural resources, to be more urban, and to have stronger democratic traditions. But he argues that religious heritage also plays a part – all but one (Austria) of the societies he defines as being dominated by dark green attitudes to nature have been historically Protestant. Where concern for environmental protection has developed in non-Protestant (including non-Christian) societies, Vogel argues, this has focused on the solution of specific environmental problems injurious to human well-being, and to wax and wane on political agendas according to their perceived urgency – in the terminology of Mandelbaum and Rappaport, it has been pragmatic and indexical.

Vogel explains this by pointing to an elective affinity between Protestantism and environmental thought, grounded in a number of shared features: a pessimism about human beings; a valorization of asceticism and self-discipline; moralism and an emphasis on consistency between principles and actions; an egalitarianism that in political ecology is extended to the non-human; and a concern for the empirical, material world. In effect, he argues that dark green environmentalism is a secularized version of Protestantism. So in attitudes to the environment as well as in relation to the rest of culture, Europe once again 'divides along the line of the olive trees' (Weinstein and Bell, 1982: 183).

It is also true, however, that environmentalists have taken ideas of nature from non-Western cultures, especially from the major religions of Asia and from small-scale societies. Yet in most cases these have been grafted onto the Judeo-Christian rootstock of the Western idea of nature. And the importance of Protestantism lies not just in ethical principles and concerns; environmentalism also inherits from it certain practices of action, speech and community. Recall for example that the focus of this chapter is environmental *activism* – the deliberate, conscious performance of public actions in defence of nature. So what we need to explore here is not just the religious roots of concern for nature, but the religious roots of how this concern for nature becomes *public*. Consequently, in Part IV we will be examining the ideals of moral excellence, traditions of public speaking, narrative forms, and models of sociality that environmentalism draws from its religious history.

But just because environmentalism has been deeply shaped by Protestant Christianity this does not necessarily mean that it is bereft of ritual. Indeed contemporary radical environmentalism, despite having an anti-ritualistic character due to its reaction against more formal, institutionalized forms, has itself developed distinctive ritualized forms of action which play various roles in the sacralization of nature. Like the wider 'cultic milieu' of which Bron Taylor argues it is a part, radical environmentalism engages in a postmodern religious and cultural *bricolage* which goes beyond conventional religious syncretism (Taylor, 2001a: 178–9), and can be seen as a highly creative 'laboratory of the sacred'. Environmentalism mounts a prophetic critique of the Enlightenment pretension to know and control nature. In doing so it draws not only on Romanticist ideas of nature as a moral source, but also on core ideas and values of the Enlightenment itself to thematize the way modernity endangers nature and itself through technology.

Through the twentieth century, and particularly during its middle decades, the idea of a rational, planned society organized through biopower became more prominent, partly as a reaction against the unplanned development produced by liberal capitalism. Modern nature conservation and landscape preservation owed much to the idea, dominant at the time of their origins, that human activities could and should be increasingly brought under centralized, rational control. Environmentalism, with its own internal theology of the immanent life process, can partly be seen as an extension of that biopolitical project, a reflexive supplement to industrial modernity which sought to correct its self-endangering properties.

However, as we shall see in the next two chapters, it is the way that environmentalism draws on *other* forms of the sacred, particularly those of Protestantism, that prevents it from being wholly identifiable as a corrective, adaptive extension to simple industrial modernity. But first it is necessary to explore environmentalism's more proximate roots in the turbulent events of the 1960s. The globalizing processes that have transformed world societies in the modern era intensified during the twentieth century, creating a trans-national institutional and communicational context where universalizing notions of a threat to nature itself, rather than simply to (often nationally) specific examples of nature, had a growing plausibility. And cultural changes in the second half of the twentieth century led to a grow-

ing postmodernization of society, which eroded particularist understandings of identity and paved the way for a growing cultural resonance of
ideas of 'global citizenship' or even 'oneness with nature'. So while contemporary environmentalism retains a paradoxical link with the increasingly
rationalized character of Western societies, it was also shaped by the 1960s,
during which the sacred underwent further transformations.

The 1960s – the Counter-culture and the New Left

From the middle of the 1960s to the early 1970s Western societies experienced an explosion of cultural and political experimentation, largely among
the young middle classes. A number of elements were brought together in
numerous and varied combinations: an explosion of interest in oriental
mysticism; the widespread use of psychoactive drugs; the creation of new
social spaces in which to explore personal experiences and new forms of
social relationship (pop festivals, 'happenings' and communes); and a new,
prefigurative style of political radicalism, exemplified by the student movement in America, France and Germany. While it is possible to separate this
mixture for analytical convenience into those elements which attempted to
change the institutions of mainstream society (the new left) and those
which tried to enact new forms of life in subcultural enclaves (the counter-
culture), the reality was far more complex (Robbins, 1988).[2]

But common to all of these elements was a reaction against the prosper-
ous complacency of post-war society, a society which seemed to the young
to lack any motivating ideology beyond material consumption and con-
formity. Many post-war societies seemed to adopt a new civil religion of
conspicuous consumption, surrendering any sense of the transcendent in
favour of the immanent sacrality of consumer capitalism. Nineteen-fifties
America in particular seemed to epitomize the emphasis on normalization
that Foucault had identified in modern societies (Foucault, 1977). Against
this conformist, instrumentalized, bureaucratized world, the 1960s generation sought to mobilize a vague but powerful notion of liberation – the
liberation of oppressed minorities both at home and in the third world, but
also the liberation of aspects of human existence which were felt to be
suppressed in contemporary industrialized societies. More than a simply
secular project, this constituted a kind of this-worldly salvation, as the
baby-boom generation increasingly turned to politics and culture as a
domain in which to perform prophetic denunciations, and to find answers
to what had previously been seen as *religious* questions about human existence (Lee and Ackerman, 2002).

Several factors seem to have contributed to this cultural revolution.
Firstly, the deep division between the private and public realms in modern

society had set up pronounced strains between the role-ideals proper to each realm – between the values of intimacy, openness, self-expression and care held appropriate to the private sphere, and those of rational, disciplined behaviour and competitive striving which operated in the public sphere (Bell, 1979).[3] Changes in the patterns of bringing up children, particularly among the middle classes, were encouraging a heightened sense of the individual as an end in himself or herself and consensual rather than authoritarian styles of decision making (Inglehart, 1971). And the rise of a consumer-led capitalism had also generated a kind of self which was oriented to the proliferation of inner desire, rather than to a productivist discipline (Campbell, 1987). The post-war baby-boom generation took these values out into the public world and found it wanting (Tipton, 1982: 26).

Secondly, a number of other social changes encouraged the development of these private values, and their generalization into areas of public life. Post-war affluence made it possible for ever more individuals to expect greater fulfilment in their lives than merely material security (Inglehart, 1971). The huge expansion in education led to a generalization of critical thought and liberal values (Gouldner, 1979). The reduction in working hours and subsequent increase in leisure time increased the importance of the private sphere. And the rise of the 'expressive professions' of the service sector (such as welfare professionals and university lecturers) increased the value put on sensitivity, and facility in interpersonal relations (Martin, 1981: 185 ff.; Tipton, 1982: 24–6).

Thirdly, the cultural globalization of the late twentieth century, encouraged particularly by developments in the mass media and tourism, tended to erode particularist and localist understandings of identity, and to encourage the development of what Emile Durkheim called the 'cult of man' – the sacralization of an abstract humanity understood to underlie the differences between individual human beings. This global moral perspective can be seen in both the quietist and activist modes of 1960s praxis. On one level it manifested itself in expressive understandings of the self as being of sacral significance, and of cosmic union, while on the other it encouraged a concern for universalistic ethico-political issues such as human rights and, eventually, the global environment (Durkheim, 1969; Heelas, 1996).[4]

Fourthly, the mass media and information technology have come to enjoy an increasingly important position in modern societies since the Second World War, resulting in a growing centrality of the processes whereby information, images and messages are produced and circulated. Social power has increasingly come to reside with those who are in a position to shape and control this flow, and thus to influence the codes and frames within which reality is constituted. Consequently, social conflicts in the late twentieth and early twenty-first centuries have been displaced more and more away from issues of material distribution and into the area of representation and cultural reproduction (Melucci, 1989, 1996). The praxis of the 1960s, in both its counter-cultural and political manifestations, reflected this displacement to the cultural in its emphasis on slogan, image, symbol and drama. The counter-cultural movements attempted to open up new social spaces for the generation of alternative codes, while the new left attempted to intervene in the reproduction of the codes dominant in the institutions of wider society.

These innovations of the 1960s both manifested and intensified a growing postmodernization of culture. The culture of contentment of the 1950s had appeared as the end of the Enlightenment in both senses of 'end' – as the final arrival of Kant's 'perpetual peace' (albeit one held in tension by the cold war), yet at the same time as the abandonment of critical public reason in favour of the idolatry of consumer capitalism. Yet by the 1960s that very culture had given birth to a dramatic process of cultural fragmentation, in which the highly individuated selves of the baby-boom generation revived the Enlightenment traditions of public reason but now in a new register, one that validated public speech in terms as much in reference to the inner nature of the heart and its sentiments as to the outer nature of fact and argumentation. Existential and religious questions received renewed attention; but instead of individuals turning to the established religions for answers to these questions, they turned to a range of cultural resources – music, literature and events of collective effervescence – all of which helped shape a sense of the sacrality of inner, private subjectivity (Bellah, 1970: 39–44; Gauchet, 1997: 200–7).

Many changes wrought by the 1960s were crucial for the development of environmentalism. On the institutional level many developments – including mass demonstrations, consensual decision-making practices, and a regenerated notion of the rural commune – had provided forms of social organization which the environmental movement was to make its own (Eyerman and Jamison, 1991: 91). But at the level of ideas, the 1960s also saw the articulation of a Utopian moral sensibility which combined Enlightenment ideas of a just and peaceful social order with Romanticist notions of inner authenticity and naturalness. The environmental movement has set about filling both of these discursive spaces with a greater degree of determinate content, by deploying and further articulating ideas of nature which were by now firmly embedded in Western culture.

But the environmental movement did not begin to make its appearance until the closing years of the 1960s. The intense period of professionalization that the ecological sciences had enjoyed since the early 1950s, reinforced by the rapid expansion of higher education in the 1960s and a renewed interest in nature from the mass media, had hugely increased the currency of ecological ideas among the population. From the beginning of the 1960s, writers like Rachel Carson and Barry Commoner had started presenting prophetic critiques of contemporary industrial practices from within the academic establishment, framing these practices as perilously threatening the natural order (Commoner, 1963; Carson, 1965). However, recognizably environmental concerns had little prominence on the agenda of the 1960s student movement – the environment had yet to generate its own representatives, its own movement intellectuals.

But by the end of the decade the 1960s movement had fragmented into a number of distinct, but more determinate, social movements, including the peace movement and second-wave feminism. Environmentalism, too, took form, as the earlier representations of nature as threatened, and of nature as a moral source, given contemporary resonance by critical writings from within the scientific mainstream and by dramatic media images of accidents such as the sinking of the *Torrey Canyon* oil tanker in 1967, were articulated and developed within the discursive and institutional space opened up by the events of the 1960s. These ideas were fused with both the Romantic, interiorized individualism of the 1960s and the this-worldly, purposive asceticism inherited from the modern sacred. Placed in a newly postmodernized cultural context suspicious of metanarratives of techno-logical progress, this complex *bricolage* constituted a powerful new force in developed societies.

The 1970s – the Emergence of the Environmental Movement

The new environmental organizations of the late sixties and early seventies were different from the older, more established conservation bodies such as America's Sierra Club and Britain's Council for the Protection of Rural England (CPRE) and Royal Society for the Protection of Birds (RSPB), and even from the more recently formed WWF, in a number of ways. Firstly, the older organizations' main orientation had been towards the protection of specific examples of nature, such as scenic landscapes and wildlife habitats, from human encroachment. In this way they signified their connection with the archaic sacred, with its marking out of particular objects, places and people as joining worldly and sacred hierarchies. Their approach had tended to dualistically define nature as something that did not include the human, as the sacred must always exclude the profane. But also, from the emerging new perspective, the approach of the older groups appeared extremely piecemeal.[5] The approach of the newer groups was more systemic, seeing the destruction of nature as symptomatic of deeper problems in modern industrial culture which needed to be addressed at source. For the new environmentalism, it was not *particular* nature that was sacred, but the ongoing life process itself. As such, their campaigns were aimed less at individual sites and species, more at certain practices of contemporary society which were seen systematically to damage the environment, such as the use of non-returnable drinks containers, or a car-oriented transport policy. Of FoE (UK)'s first ten national demonstrations, for example, three concerned whaling, two non-returnable bottles, two transport policy, one paper, one packaging, and one thermal insulation (Lowe and Goyder, 1983: 131).

These issues were not self-evidently 'environmental'. It was the task of the movement to further develop an emerging discourse of 'the environment' to which a growing portfolio of issues, shaped by political opportunity and public resonance, could be linked. A framework for this had been supplied by the new left, which had further developed the prophetic modes of social critique which the traditional left had taken from its Christian and Jewish roots and developed in a this-worldly direction. Society – 'the system' – was sick, and it needed a radical reorientation if it was to survive, let alone offer its members a fulfilling future. What the environmental movement did was to insert within this framework the ideas of nature as threatened and as moral source explored in Chapter 6. By now, these ideas of nature were firmly embedded in industrialized societies, but had not been as thoroughly incorporated into ideological systems as had other cultural symbols, such as those of class, individual, and nation, and so provided fertile ground for discursive innovation (Lowe and Morrison, 1984: 79). On the one hand, they could be appropriated by an emerging and overarching discourse of 'the environment'. On the other, they could provide symbolic resonance to the issues which the new environmental campaigners, with increasing facility, were inventing and pursuing.

The newer groups took full advantage of the growing power of the mass media as a conveyor of messages and images. The 1960s had seen a further extending of the reach of both the press and the broadcast media. The resulting intensification and acceleration of the circulation of visual and textual messages presented an opportunity for smaller and more marginal groups to assert their presence in the public arena. As Robert Hunter said of the early days of Greenpeace, 'we saw it as a media war – we'd all studied Marshall McLuhan' (Pearce, 1991: 19; see also Dale, 1996). The mass demonstrations, televisual direct actions, and powerful condensing symbols characteristic of 1970s environmentalism all attest to this awareness of the new importance of the media. Creative use of dramatic protest events enabled environmentalists to draw on the power of ritual and iconography to set up synecdochal relationships between particular examples of nature (such a threatened species or habitat) or technology (such as a nuclear reactor or oil platform) and the more general critique of modern technological society to which they were trying to draw attention (Szerszynski, 2002a).

This orientation to the media was itself made easier by the different institutional form of the new groups. The older organizations tended to be highly institutionalized, imposing certain legal and cultural limitations on their style of operation. The new environmental groups, by contrast, were initiated or at least quickly dominated by the generation who had come of age in the 1960s, and had a corresponding informality and flexibility which helped them to take far better advantage of the opportunities presented by such institutions as the media and the public inquiry system. Many remained as highly informal local social movements, with a sect-like core of committed individuals and a wider dispersed network which could emerge into the public sphere around the focus of a specific environmental controversy before submerging again into civil society (Melucci, 1989: 45). Even those, like FoE and Greenpeace, who were to become further institutionalized, did so in the form of limited companies with professional campaigners. They were thus able to react with growing acumen to the political and symbolic opportunities open to them, unrestrained by restrictions which might have been imposed had they adopted available institutional models or developed unwieldy democratic structures. As they selectively absorbed the campaigning tactics developed effectively by the older groups such as WWF and CPRE in Britain and the Sierra Club in the United States, the latter also learnt from their new colleagues and rivals, adopting many of their organizational and tactical innovations during the 1980s.

At least in the early years of this new environmentalism, representations of nature as threatened and representations of nature as a moral source were combined in one and the same movement. The early movement was apocalyptic – messages of imminent ecological and social collapse proliferated, from the influential reports *Limits to Growth* and *Blueprint for Survival* to the television drama series *Doomwatch* – but it was also Utopian, in its articulation of a social vision based on ecological interdependence and harmony with nature. The movement in this phase was as much concerned with prefigurative social practices such as participatory democracy as it was with saving the planet, and as much engaged in articulating ecological world-views as it was in influencing political decisions (Jamison et al., 1990: 9–10).

But as the various strands of this movement started to harden, the early sense of unity soon gave way to division. Specialization of environmental campaigning occurred across the Western world, but was particularly pronounced in Britain because its centralized political culture encourages the formation of 'policy communities' clustered around the decision-making elite (Szerszynski, 1991: 12). From the mid-1980s the rapid growth of the main environmental NGOs in Britain and elsewhere has tended to produce a Church-like division of labour between, on the one hand, a professional and increasingly specialized group of campaigners focused on pursuing close lobbying tactics with decision-makers and running media-oriented campaigns and, on the other, a supportive, but rarely directly mobilized, 'attentive public' (Szerszynski, 1997). At the same time, in order to gain resonance with the increasingly technocratic style in which environmental issues have been taken up by Western states since 1970, NGOs have consequently tended to mobilize representations of nature as threatened – and particularly realist versions of these – in preference to those of nature as a moral source, in contrast to the early movement when both representations coexisted (Grove-White, 1991).

To varying degrees, all Western countries seem to have witnessed this fragmentation of the cognitive praxis of environmentalism (Eyerman and Jamison, 1991: 69, 77–8). During the late 1970s and 1980s the Utopian strand of the new environmentalism, which structured itself around representations of nature as a moral source, was led to find its main expression outside the mainstream of the environmental campaign movement – in the communes movement and rural retreats, in deep ecology and eco-spirituality groups, and in movements for natural food such as permaculture. In the 1990s, however, a number of informal activist groups and networks emerged in Britain and the United States – Earth First!, the Environmental Liberation Front and so on – engaged primarily in direct action, who could be said to have revived the more unified cognitive praxis of early 1970s environmentalism in that they deployed both apocalyptic and Utopian representations of nature within a broadly new left framework of social activism and prefigurative political praxis (McKay, 1996; Seel et al., 2000). Nevertheless, the general trend has been towards a divergence of these discourses into quite separate practices.

Environmentalism and the Critique of the Archaic Sacred

We have seen, then, that in the late twentieth century conditions of progressive economic and cultural globalization laid the foundations for an increasing universalization of representations of nature as threatened and as a moral source, within an overarching discourse of 'the environment'. This discourse crystallized in the 1970s when both sets of representations were reworked within the institutional and discursive space opened up by the counter-culture and the new left of the 1960s, as elements of the cognitive praxis of a new environmental movement with a systemic critique of modern, technological society. Ideas of nature that had originated in specific social contexts, and that drew on various moments in the transformation of the sacred, became rendered as universalized representations of humanity's relationship with nature. Attached to a powerful Utopian strand within modern thought, they seemed to offer almost a mirror image of the modern Baconian project – a promise of this-worldly salvation, an over-coming of the alienation between humans and nature and a solution to the ecological contradictions of modern society. However, this movement rapidly fragmented into a powerful and progressively professionalized and specialized NGO sector on the one hand, deploying increasingly technocratic representations of nature as threatened, and a marginalized but culturally innovative set of prefigurative social practices on the other, deploying representations of nature predominantly as a moral source.

Prominent in the discourse of almost all sections of the environmental movement since the 1960s has been an immanentist discourse of life and its self-reproduction as the locus of sacral value. In the more spiritual wing of the movement this has often been overtly neo-Platonic in character, regarding life as an interconnected emergent whole, and itself divine (e.g. Seed et al., 1988; see also Taylor, 2001a).[6] But as we have seen, even the scientific ecological discourse of nature, which is drawn upon by formal environmental groups such as Greenpeace, relies on an immanentist understanding of life as a self-enclosed, autotelic process, an understanding which has its roots in the emergence of the modern sacred after the collapse of the transcendent axis. However, the events of the 1960s also signalled the growing importance of an alternative cultural code in shaping human relations with non-human nature. Eder (1996, ch. 4) identifies two cultural codes as having organized European culture in the last two millennia. The dominant one has been the carnivorous one characteristic of archaic cultures, where solidarity between human and human, and between humans and the gods, was secured through the sacrificial feast. This 'bloody' cultural code uses sacrifice and eating to affirm the social order; participation in the meal signifies membership of the community, and the eating of clean or unclean meat defines one's position in the social hierarchy. Underlying the elitist, exclusionary forms of republicanism characteristic of the Greek polis (Detienne and Vernant, 1989; Brunkhorst, 2000), this code also runs through much of European history (Elias, 1978).

Eder rightly points out the tension between this 'bloody' cultural code and environmentalism's emphasis on peaceful coexistence between humans and nature. However, he also identifies an alternative, 'bloodless' cultural code that weaves through Western culture, usually surviving in religious minorities such as the Jews and the Pythagoreans. From the latter group onwards, the practice of vegetarianism has been used to negate the carnivorous code underlying the social order. Eating neither unclean nor clean meat, religious groups (and many social movements in the nineteenth and twentieth centuries) have used vegetarianism to ground sociality outside the dominant social order – in relation to a transcendent reality, or to an Edenic state of nature. Hebrew thought has played an important role in this counter-tradition. The notion of Eden as an originary myth of peace

(Genesis 1:5–25) has also served as a prophetic and eschatological image – for example in Isaiah's image of the wolf and the kid, the leopard and the sheep living in peace (Isaiah 11:6). But perhaps more significant was the slowly emerging prohibition against killing in Hebrew and in later Christian society, as prefigured in the non-sacrifice of Abraham's son Isaac. Eder sees this as the emergence of a form of consensus based on discourse and agreement rather than power. Eder's claim that the discursive co-ordination of society, and hence democracy, have roots that are more Hebrew than Greek is a complex one that cannot be fully explored here. Yet the shift towards the word rather than blood and *de facto* might as the mediator of divine and social power is a development that can be traced in both Jewish and Christian religious history. This development leads away from the tribal deity and towards a more universal, transcendent divine – and towards a recognition of the power of language to secure uncoerced agreement without the prior existence of customary tribal solidarities.

So even when environmentalism reaches to Greek thought, or indeed to other forms of paganism, these are usually 'unbloodied' by being hybrid-ized with elements of biblical thought. There are exceptions; Taylor, for example, reports the custom of 'amoebas' at Earth First! campfires – circles of activists with linked arms chanting 'eat, excrete and die' (Taylor, 2001b: 227). But political ecology is dominated by the Edenic, vegetarian image as a determining ideal, whether in anthropocentric notions of stewardship or more biocentric ideas of peaceful coexistence. And this idea of a peaceful, egalitarian relationship with nature depends to a great extent on changes in the conception of the social bond – and the idea of and relationship with nature that symbolically underwrote that bond – that occurred in the Christian era. The elitism of the Greek republican tradition, where freedom is the possession of equal, male, property-owning members of a political community, was symbolized by the violent appropriation and exploitation of nature (whether animal or slave). This was softened by the Augustinian notion of the abstract and universal human being, inherently possessing freedom in its God-like capacity to create new beginnings *ex nihilo* (Brun-khorst, 2000), and by a model of the social bonds between humans and with God as being mediated primarily by the word rather than predation and power.

In the next two chapters I will explore the way the cultural codes of this bloodless tradition are drawn upon in both the private lives and public speech of those who are trying to find an 'authentic', non-technological relationship with nature. I want to suggest that immanentist neo-Platonic or biopolitical construals of nature do not by themselves seem to provide the cultural resources necessary to provide a non-dominative orientation to nature. It does not seem enough, therefore, to 're-enchant nature'. Nature, as I have been arguing all along, is already enchanted; indeed, the emergence of nature in the modern sense was made possible by the theological understanding of nature associated with a particular ordering of the sacred. The only question is that of *which* enchantment of nature might offer a genuine alternative to the domination of nature and humanity by modern technology. Of course, we should not assume a priori that historical or existing movements and lifestyles have actually been successful in attempting to provide such an alternative. But as I indicate in the following chapters, movements against the domination of non-human nature in the modern period have drawn powerfully on the monotheistic and Protestant sacred. Furthermore, in doing so, they can be seen as engaging in an extension of the repeated struggle between the monotheistic and archaic sacred, withdrawing from or actively opposing the repeated eruptions of the archaic intertwining of divine and worldly power, in defence of an image of peace grounded in a fundamentally Christian idea of the suspension between natural and spiritual power. Perhaps, without the transcendent axis, without the idea of a divinity beyond the empirical world, nature would have remained conceived as a cyclical realm of violence seen as symbolically underwriting a conservative social order, rather than as capable of peaceable coexistence with a human social order constituted though relations of gift and speech. I will return to this question in the chapters of Part V.

Chapter Eight

Nature, Virtue and Everyday Life

Chapter 7 traced the development of the environmental movement in the 1970s, and the emergence of a political discourse of 'the environment'. But the shift in people's relationship with nature and technology during that period did not simply consist in changes in public discourse; with roots in cultural changes in the 1960s, it also involved a new demand that individuals should change their own behaviour in radical ways. It is a truism that it is difficult if not impossible to discuss ideas about nature without also examining the ideas about humanity and society that they both imply and assume (see Douglas, 1975). But from the 1970s this close relationship between discourses of nature and humanity became intensified and politicized. In the context of a postmodernized sacred in which individuals turned to a wide range of cultural resources to answer their religious needs and questions, a new discourse of human identity opened up, one which involved the rethinking of the dominant technological relationship with nature that had emerged since the scientific and industrial revolutions.

One area of environmental thought and practice that has laid the most explicit emphasis on human identity is deep ecology. Deep ecology as a philosophical and political movement was initiated in a 1972 lecture by the Norwegian philosopher Arne Naess, 'The Shallow and the Deep, Long-range Ecology Movement' (Naess, 1973). Naess's point was to make a distinction between types of environmental concern which value nature simply in terms of its utility (or necessity) for human beings, and those which value it for its own sake. But from that modest starting-point Naess and others after him have tried to articulate a more prescriptive deep ecology, which has been adopted (and transformed) by diverse sections of the environmental movement, particularly by wilderness protection activists in the US Midwest and Australia, and by those working in the area of ecological education and psychotherapy (e.g. Seed et al., 1988).

Deep ecology could be described as what Beyer (1994: 217) calls an eco-spirituality – a form of contemporary religion which does not just concern itself with environmental matters, but is completely structured around ideas of ecological interdependence, indeed, around the monistic desire for a fusion between self and cosmos. Deep ecology echoes Zen Buddhism's claim to provide an unmediated access to truth, grounded in experience rather than dogma and ritual (see Faure, 1991). As Jim Cheney (1989) argues, as a philosophy it echoes the Stoicism that emerged in an Alexandria at the collapse of Hellenic culture, and possibly represents a similar move of stoic resignation at a moment of social fragmentation; unable to feel at home in a postmodern culture of diversity, the deep ecologist, like the Stoic, seeks to identify with a unitary principle beyond worldly difference.[1]

The kind of monistic fusion offered by deep ecology has found a certain social location in contemporary society (Luke, 1988). But as a cultural phenomenon it is also significant for its symbolization of a wider mood for a reconfiguration of individual identity in relation to the natural world, a mood which has manifest itself in a wide range of cultural phenomena, including movements for organic products and wholefoods, vegetarianism and veganism, green and ethical consumerism. Alternative diets such as organic, health food and wholefoods are pursued in a quest not just for health but for this-worldly salvation (Hamilton et al., 1995). Consumption has become politicized, as individuals and groups use boycotts and ethical labelling schemes to engage in what Micheletti (2003: 25) calls 'individualized collective action'. In different ways, many individuals in Western societies are seeking forms of life which might bring them into a different relationship with nature and with human power over it. For the rest of this chapter I will focus primarily on one such practice – vegetarianism.

Meat and Moral Virtue

Between 1994 and 1997 I carried out social research with ethical vegetarians and animal rights activists as part of a larger study of social movements and voluntary associations. The vegetarians were recruited on the basis that their primary motivation concerned ethical, rather than health-related reasons for a meat-free diet. The activists belonged to a local group involved in on-street campaigning, but the individual members had also been involved in hunt saboteur work and other direct action activities. The study used individual biographical interviews, and focus-group discussions held with each group separately, in order to explore individuals' motivations for becoming and remaining engaged with that particular practice.[2]

Despite deliberately screening out any activists from the vegetarian group, the research found that the core motivations of both sets of respondents were very similar. For both groups, a powerful concern for animals and for the wider environment was, unsurprisingly, their primary reason for being involved with the practice in question. However, as other research would lead us to expect (Beardsworth and Keil, 1992, 1993), both groups also described a number of secondary motivations as playing an important role in keeping them involved. Both referred to social relationships as a significant factor – the fact that their way of life and their friendships had been structured around their being vegetarian or activists respectively. But the emotional or psychological reasons cited by the two groups were very different. The vegetarians referred to habit, to the fact that their palates had become used to vegetarian food, and to their desire to avoid feelings of guilt. The activists, by contrast, described emotions of anger, a powerful sense of personal agency gained through activism, and a strong sense that the world was such that social activism was needed.

How are we to understand this difference? How do we understand the fact that, for some, conversion to vegetarianism remains at the level of a personal, if often highly committed, lifestyle choice, whereas for others the same conversion propels them into a life of activism? Let us consider a number of possible interpretations and explanations in turn.

Life politics and emancipatory politics

The first possible interpretation rests on the distinction made by Anthony Giddens between 'life politics' and 'emancipatory politics'. Giddens's work in the 1990s was focused on developing an account of contemporary life not as postmodernity but as high modernity – as the full realization of the post-traditional order promised by modernity. Such a society, Giddens suggests, is one in which the individual has no option but to choose, since 'the signposts established by tradition now are blank'. For those of us who have become 'freed from the hold of traditional contexts of activity, a plurality of lifestyle choices exist'. A person's life narrative is no longer set out in its main features by inherited tradition, but is a reflexive project carried out by the self. Indeed, for Giddens, modernity's essence is the principle of reflexivity, whereby 'social practices are constantly examined and reformed in the light of incoming information about those very practices, thus constitutively altering their character' (Giddens, 1990: 38). In high modernity we thus have an obligation to choose by what codes and through what patterns we live our life; even those who remain in traditional lifeways cannot avoid knowing that this, too, is a choice – one that they either have made or are prevented by circumstances from making (1991: 82–4).

For Giddens, the rise of life politics, as exemplified in contemporary feminist and ecological politics, results from this permeation of lifestyle by reflexivity. Whereas politics in earlier phases of modernity was dominated by a justice-based emancipatory politics concerned with the liberation of groups and individuals from tradition, inequality and oppression, contemporary politics is at least as much concerned with questions of how one should live. Life politics is a politics of self-realization, concerned with extending and deepening the reflexive development of the self in a situation where a certain level of emancipation is already assumed. It is thus also a 'politics of life decisions', in that it thematizes how people can choose responsibly in a post-traditional order where we are able – indeed obliged – to choose (1991: 214–26).

Giddens's formulation of life politics represents a useful contribution to our understanding of the contemporary political condition, if one that takes a very partial reading of its character. Giddens's analysis depends on a Kantian sacralization of persons as ends in themselves, and a spiritualized sublime reason that can be a universal grounding for valid ethical judgements. However, this distinction has limitations for understanding the distinction between vegetarianism as a private lifestyle option and animal rights activism as a purposive political orientation. Despite its many life-political elements, animal rights activism has many of the features that Giddens ascribes to emancipatory politics – most graphically in its covert animal rescue work. Although following an alternative lifestyle is an integral feature of contemporary direct action, integral to the protest lifestyle is a purposive orientation, which also marks it out from – or at least has to mark it as a distinctive variant of – life politics as described by Giddens. Individual self-realization is indeed a feature of animal rights activism, but this is a self-realization which is achieved through a sense of political effectiveness. Constant self-monitoring in the name of individual responsibility is also characteristic of this protest subculture, but this is not simply felt as the demand to respond reflexively and responsibly to the choices that life lays before its members, but as a call actively to pursue a project of societal transformation. If Giddens's distinction does apply to the ethics and politics of meat, then vegetarians are pursuing life politics and animal rights activists, emancipatory politics.

But, for Giddens, life politics characteristically takes over as the most appropriate form of political movement when emancipatory politics has done its liberative work. Given the intensifying industrial exploitation of animals in Western societies, the problem for Giddens would not be to explain why the politics of animal rights sometimes takes the form of emancipatory politics, but why it ever takes the form of life politics, as it does in the case of vegetarianism and veganism. How can both the emancipatory project of animal rights activism and the life-political choice of vegetarianism, feel to their adherents like adequate expressions of personal moral responsibility in relation to the suffering of animals?

Commitment and ethical development

A second approach would be to see these different options – lifestyle and activism – as simply reflecting different levels of commitment and moral consistency. These and other ways of life could thus be placed on a continuum, according to a hierarchical, developmental understanding of ethical reasoning as having an immanent drive towards universality and consistency (see Kohlberg, 1981; Habermas, 1984). Certainly such scales of consistency and levels of dietary exclusion are often used to understand the varieties of vegetarian lifestyles (Beardsworth and Keil, 1992: 264). At one end might be those who eat meat and perceive no moral problem in this; close to them might be placed those whose meat consumption is accompanied at least occasionally by twinges of guilt; next to them might be those who have stopped eating flesh to one degree or another; then would come total vegans; and then those whose convictions are so strong they feel compelled to act – to take up animal protection as a life project (see Castells, 1997: 356–8).

Some vegetarians certainly do see vegetarianism as the first step in a wider personal transformation, and this in a number of different ways. Firstly, they may locate themselves on a path which leads, ultimately and logically, to veganism. In this sense, they fit Julia Twigg's account of vegetarianism as being symbolically structured around a reversal of the dominant symbolic food hierarchy which places meat at the top (1983). In the reversed, vegetarian hierarchy, the more intense exclusions of the vegan lifestyle would place *it* at the top, as being the most morally desirable; all other forms of vegetarianism would be considered mere compromises with practicality or with human weakness.[3] Non-vegans who accept this hierarchy, such as the ones quoted below from the vegetarian focus group, will characteristically apologize for not being vegans themselves:

And so for some people there seems to be something in them which is questioning what's going on with what they're eating. I don't have to have that – apart from the fact that I also would like to have the will power in a way to be vegan, I think I'm just a bit weak willed.

I don't feel particularly proud because I'm a vegetarian, like I'm doing something brilliant in the world. It just seems really, really natural. Now if I was vegan, I might feel different about it.

It annoys me, you know, because I'd love to be a vegan and, you know, I think being a vegetarian is probably a progression to becoming a vegan or something for me.

Secondly, vegetarians may also see their own conversion to vegetarianism as their first symbolic break with conventional mores, which over time has become merely an element in a wider ethic of responsibility and social questioning:

> I think it makes me think quite a lot about it. I've got an allotment at the moment and I grow my own vegetables organically. Before I was a vegetarian I wouldn't have given a damn about what I was eating basically, it just all went in. Now I'm aware about pesticides and chemicals and things in food. Vegetarian foods aren't necessarily all that good a lot of the time so there's that issue as well. So yes, I certainly think more about it.

Such an account is consistent with quantitative research carried out in the USA, which found that vegetarianism was negatively correlated with a generally traditional outlook to life and a resistance to change, and was positively correlated with more generally altruistic values (Dietz et al., 1995: 539–40). The specific interpretation of the conversion to vegetarianism as a symbolic act of individual moral self-definition also finds indirect confirmation in Jasper and Poulsen's work, which found that animal rights activists, unlike some other kinds of social activists, are more likely to be recruited by 'moral shocks' from strangers than through established social networks of family or friends (1995). Certainly my own respondents tended to narrate their conversion to vegetarianism as a private, personal act – not only done without any external prompting from known others but also often in the face of incredulity or resistance. Twigg describes modern vegetarianism as correlating with a 'highly individuated sense of the self', involving as it does the stepping outside of culturally dominant forms of eating, inverting traditional hierarchies of which foods are desirable and undesirable (1983: 19, 27). The sense of having stepped out of a traditional form of life, of having chosen another for oneself, is an important source of identity *above and beyond* the actual choice made.

> It's the first time I actually decided to do something moral, I suppose. I was now using my moral code rather than the one I'd been brought up with and it meant that then having done that I realized that I might not be able to change anyone else's life but I could change my life and I could run it like I wanted . . . Yes, it was the first step.

> It's like making a stand, you know, like you're not going to tell me what to do anymore, I'm going to live my life how I want to live it and this is one way I'm going to do that.

The above examples illustrate that, in many ways, vegetarians can indeed see their vegetarianism as not by itself constituting an adequate and fully formed life of moral responsibility, but perhaps as an element in, or preparation for, something more morally demanding, comprehensive and consistent. The refusal of meat can be seen as in part a symbolic act which refuses the archaic, 'bloody' naturalization of social codes, in favour of the socially distanced mode of existence characteristic of the Christian, held in tension between two worlds due to the continuous deferral of the eschaton (see Chapter 6).[4]

However, this does not mean that vegetarians necessarily see the life of activism as the ultimate and logical expression of concern for animals. Whereas for Giddens life politics characteristically only takes over as the most appropriate form of political movement when emancipatory politics has done its liberative work, for many people the life-political response seems to feel like an adequate moral response to forms of oppression in its own right. Vegetarians do not seem characteristically to feel that they have to apologize for not being involved in political activism on behalf of animals. The experience of this calling as an inescapable moral demand resulting from the recognition of the moral status of animals seems not to be a part of the moral phenomenology of lifestyle vegetarianism. So even if we place vegetarianism on a scale of moral consistency, this is not necessarily one that has in its higher reaches a life of activism.[5] If we want to explain these two very different practical relationships to non-human nature, this does not seem a fruitful way of doing it.

The virtues

A third approach to understanding the activist/lifestyle distinction in ethico-political responses to nature is to see it in terms of different accounts of the virtues. Virtue theory is a distinctive approach to moral philosophy that focuses neither on acts nor consequences but on character as the primary locus for moral judgement (see Kruschwitz and Roberts, 1987; French et al., 1988). Could it be that our vegetarians and activists are operating with distinct accounts of the virtues? An article by Lawrence A. Blum is instructive here. Blum explores the contested notion of moral excellence using examples of morally exemplary action in the face of the Holocaust in continental Europe, citing figures such as Oskar Schindler and André and Magda Trocme (Blum, 1988). The distinctions that Blum makes between different types of moral excellence can be used to tease apart the different moral phenomenologies of different approaches to the sacrality of nature.

The primary distinction that Blum makes is between the 'moral hero' and the 'moral saint'. According to Blum's account, these notions of moral virtue have much in common, in that in order to be candidates for either label individuals have to be primarily animated by morally worthy motives rooted in deep levels of their character. However, beyond this point the two kinds of moral excellence diverge. For our purposes, the salient differences that Blum identifies are:

- while moral heroes have a great moral project, saints generally do not;
- while heroism can be confined to a limited period in someone's life without disqualifying them from the label, sainthood has to be more enduring;
- sainthood generally involves more consistency and purity of action and motive than heroism;
- the saint does not have to be particularly concerned with a wider community;
- heroes, to a greater degree than saints, have to endure risk or adversity (Blum, 1988: 204–8).

It should be noted that both of these are modern figures – even the saints discussed by Blum are more like Calvinist than Catholic saints. As David Matzko argues, saints in the Catholic Church 'must be noticed; their virtue must have a place within a community of saints; they cannot be saintly as individuals'. The Catholic saint serves to constitute a community, and their identity is the product as much of the cultural work by that wider community as of their own discipline and virtue (Matzko, 1993: 30). Modern saintliness, by contrast, is private and inward, consisting of an inner moral consistency.

Blum also introduces a second distinction, one cross-cutting that between saint and hero – that between 'idealist' and 'responder'. The idealist is someone who consciously chooses their ideals, guides their life according to them, looks for ways to implement them, and tries to bring the world into line with them. The responder, however, while having character traits which lead them to respond to situations in a morally excellent way, has no clearly articulated principles (Blum, 1988: 208–9). Blum illustrates this distinction by the contrast between Oskar Schindler and André Trocmé, who both took great risks to rescue Jews from the Nazi Holocaust, in Poland and France respectively. Whereas the idealist hero Trocmé actively sought out ways to live out his principles of resistance to evil, turning the town where he was pastor into a haven for Jewish refugees, the responder hero Schindler simply responded at the time in a morally excellent way to what he saw was happening to the Polish Jews. By using these two independent dimensions of moral excellence, including hybrid versions between the four 'pure' ideal types, Blum tries to lay the foundation for a 'psychology of moral excellence' which does not automatically privilege one version of what it is to be morally excellent over another.

How do these distinctions apply to vegetarians and animal rights activists? Both of my research groups were predominantly idealists in Blum's sense. For many vegetarians, conversion to vegetarianism seems to take the form of a moral *responding*, rather than the working out of pre-formed principles, which only over time – and then only for some vegetarians – becomes the beginning of what Blum would call an idealistic moral position (Beardsworth and Keil, 1992: 226–8). But all of the activists and all but a few of the vegetarians I talked with could clearly articulate the principles behind their actions. However, whereas the vegetarians were oriented to the ideal of the idealist saint, the activists could be seen as more oriented to that of the idealist hero. Vegetarianism simply involves living according to one's principles, perhaps to an unusual degree, and ordering one's own life in a morally excellent way in relation to them. Animal rights activism is also characterized by a strong adherence to principles, such as veganism. But as a practice it is more centrally focused on pursuing a project of societal transformation to *implement* one's ideals, putting oneself at risk in order to maximize the good. As such, the activists can best be described as hybrid saint–heroes.[6]

Many writers have seen such exemplariness as a form of moral perfectionism which inflates the importance of extreme virtue and demeans the more ordinary goodness of the unexceptional person (see Wolf, 1982; Sherman, 1988). However, according to Blum, the moral exemplar – whether responder or idealist – does not characteristically see their responses, or the ideals which shape and are shaped by them, as noble or heroic, but 'merely "right" or necessary, even in a sense ordinary' (Blum, 1988: 213–14). This echoes some of the work of feminist ethicists, who have tried to shift attention away from the emphasis that mainstream moral philosophy places on the dramatic moral choice, advocating instead a wider exploration of the less dramatic, ongoing work of moral attention, and the way that situations, when attended to, can be felt to *demand* a particular response (Scaltsas, 1992: 22–3). Nechama Tec's interviews with less famous people who saved Jews in occupied Poland all show these responders as viewing their actions in very matter-of-fact terms – not as heroic, nor even as undertaken after the careful weighing up of conflicting considerations, but as the simple, undramatic response to a particular situation. 'It never occurred to me that one could behave in a different way', said one rescuer. 'I just had to help people who needed help and that was that' (Tec, 1986: 167). In a different context, Iris Murdoch quotes Sartre to try to capture this quality of moral experience, of knowing *already* what one must do: 'Quand je délibère les jeux sont faits... When I deliberate the die is already cast. Forces within me which are dark to me have already made the decision' (Murdoch, 1970: 36).

Members of both focus groups – both the lifestyle vegetarians and the animal rights activists – echoed this emphasis on what might be called the mundanity of moral responses. Both talked about the way that their respective moral responses seemed natural, unexceptional, just simply what was required of them:[7]

> I'm a vegetarian because it just feels totally natural; it doesn't feel different, it just feels like it's always been.

> It just seemed like the most natural thing in the world and I don't find it hard at all.

However, there were differences in the way that this perceived mundanity and ordinariness of the moral demand seemed to shape the way that the two groups regarded those who did not share their moral response. Blum, pointing out that self-righteousness is, after all, a vice, suggests that moral exemplars are in fact *less* likely to think of their own standards as being binding on others (Blum, 1988: 214–15). This appeared to be true of the vegetarians, who seemed willing to proclaim their beliefs to strangers – or even to some friends and colleagues – only in exceptional or unavoidable circumstances:

> I sometimes find myself, you know if somebody's eating meat next to me I sometimes find myself looking at it and I just have this look of disgust on my face and that isn't really good, you know, because that's being judgemental and stuff.

However, the hybrid saint–hero is more likely than other kinds of moral exemplar to expect others to live up to the same ideals. The saint pursues a moral consistency as a personal project, in terms consistent with Giddens's account of life politics, and may have little or no interest in converting others to the principles by which they seek to live. The hero, for their part, is less concerned with character and more with consequences – with realizing their moral project. The saint–hero, however, seems more likely to expect others to live up to their own – what they, after all, see as unexceptional – standards, as the following example illustrates:

> It's for me a kind of setting of standards . . . a word I use quite consciously is the word 'appropriate'. Because I think to do anything with this kind of aim is only a matter of appropriateness . . . There's no kudos about it – there's none of that. It's just, 'this is what I expect of people', on a common standards level. And that anything less than that is, for me, isn't good enough.

While not all of the animal rights activists in the focus group were so forthright in their condemnation of those who do not take up the activist way of life, nevertheless it seemed as if, in *this* form of the living out of a life of moral responsibility, the very ordinariness and self-evident quality of the moral demand to be, for example, concerned for animals, tended to translate into an impatience with those who did not seem to recognize that moral demand.

Nature, Ethics and Forms of Life

We have seen that the virtue theory approach can help us understand the life-political character of many responses to the politicization of nature. Rather than activist, emancipatory forms of politics, on the one hand, and models of private moral consistency, on the other, simply being rational forms of politics appropriate to different stages of societal evolution, they can be seen to rely on different substantive accounts of moral virtue. This insight helps us to understand the coexistence of public and private forms of response in contemporary society. In the next chapter I will return to this coexistence, locating it more systematically within the transformations of the sacred in Western history.

However, another problem with Giddens's account remains unaddressed. An understanding of contemporary life politics based solely on individual cognitive reflexivity would imply that the specific way that any given individual conducts their life in late modernity is, ideally at least, assembled out of discrete elements, each of which is reflexively appraised. Giddens's life politics is fundamentally Kantian in character; the individual and consumer is as a citizen in a republican city, autonomously choosing according to the demands of universal justice, and treating humans – and possibly nature too – as ends in themselves. But as Giddens himself recognizes, in reality life choices cohere into 'lifestyles', clusterings of 'habits and orientations' (1991: 82). How can Giddens explain this? Why has the ever-deepening and broadening of reflexivity not resulted in a situation where each pursues their own, private lifestyle, suited solely to them?

Part of the story here has to involve *habitus*. Pierre Bourdieu developed this concept to show how ways of thinking are absorbed as habits into the body, but are also socially located (Bourdieu, 1977, 1984). For Bourdieu, forms of *habitus* represent, crudely speaking, ways that different social groups try to reorder the moral hierarchies of society in order to ensure they are higher than other groups. Thus, green and ethical lifestyles can be seen as cultural ensembles which have embedded within them forms of evaluation which mark out their members as morally superior to those of a different *habitus*. Dave Horton has produced illuminating analyses of green lifestyles using this approach (Horton, 2003). Thus life politics is carried out not by autonomous, self-legislating individuals, but by individuals embedded in social groups pursuing a given form of life.

Such a socially grounded *habitus* seems to resolve the tension between the reflexive monitoring required in modern, normatively regulated lifestyles and the routine character of everyday life. As Bente Halkier (2001) argues, 'a common assumption in the research field of such reflexivity is that either consumers' practices are greened as a result of reflection or they are not greened as a result of the routine character of consumers' practices'. Halkier uses her qualitative research with consumers in Denmark to offer an alternative – that consumers find different strategies for mediating the demand to be reflexive with the pressure towards routine inherent in everyday life.

When the environmental movement first engaged with consumerism as an arena of political action in the 1970s and early 1980s it was in the form of the renunciation of worldly goods in order to live more fully (e.g. Hollyman, 1971). Environmentalism values a simplicity of lifestyle: the reduction of consumption, the buying of second-hand clothes and articles, and repairing and reusing as much as possible (Pepper, 1984: 23–4). Prophetic calls like John Button's *How to be Green* (1989) summoned the reader to withdraw consent and support for an ecocidal industrial system, and also invoke the notion that withdrawal from consumerism is itself a path to improving one's soul. Ecological communes, such as those explored in David Pepper's *Communes and the Green Vision* (1991) and catalogued in the directory *Diggers and Dreamers* (Ansell et al., 1989), facilitated a greater withdrawal from the anti-ecological dynamics of mainstream life. Practices of self-sufficiency such as the growing and baking of food, the sharing of consumer durables, the pursuit of low-energy lifestyles, the withdrawal from employment and participation in what is seen as an ecocidal social system – all of these were facilitated by the life held in common (Pepper, 1984: 132–9). This strategy had clear echoes of the Christian tradition of *anachoresis*, or withdrawal (Burton-Christie, 1993: 40). In Christian history this tradition ranged from the individualistic eremitism of the Desert Fathers to the coenobitic life of communal self-sufficiency prescribed by St Benedict (Lawrence, 1984: 20). In all cases it was a piety of self-renunciation, the giving up of self-serving desires, or the surrendering of the individual to the collective, of turning 'away from things to their Creator, in order...[to] receive them back, restored, transformed' (Montefiore, 1975: 50).

But by the late 1980s this anti-consumerist vision had largely been displaced by a form of piety much closer to the Protestant self-monitoring described in Chapter 5. In harmony with the contemporary elevation of consumer sovereignty to the driving force of society (Keat et al., 1994), the green consumerism advocated by John Elkington and others was one which told us not that we should withdraw from consumption but that we should engage with it more fully – with our political and moral identities, and not just in order to meet our preferences and desires. The act of consumption thus became a purposive political act, one judged in terms of its effects on the ecological integrity of the planet (Elkington and Burke, 1987; Elkington et al., 1988; Elkington and Hailes, 1988). In so far as there was an asceticism here it was not the monastic asceticism of self-denial. Elkington was saying that we could have capitalism, consumerism, high standards of living *and* ecological sustainability, as new, ecological markets stimulated a round of industrial innovation which enhanced environmental protection (Hajer, 1996). If we did not consume at all, we could not send market messages to producers in order to reward or punish their ecological behaviour. The asceticism of green consumerism was more akin to the this-worldly asceticism of constant self-monitoring and self-examination, because of the requirement that all our actions – buying, investing, disposing and so on – be examined in terms of its social, and thence ecological, effects.

But there is a further, third stage of this narrative. People's consuming and recycling activity could never fully be underwritten by the calculative intent to improve the world through consumer choices. Such an intent relied on trust in suppliers' information – trust which was soon all but undermined by competing and contested claims about the ecological virtues of different products, such as those exposed by FoE's Green Con awards, launched in September 1989 (Ehrlichman, 1989). It also relied on the consumer possessing extraordinary degrees of information and powers of calculation about the relative environmental effects of different options – of washing greasy dishes using lots of hot water, versus using less hot water but more detergent, for example. It relied on trust in those exhorting energy reduction or operating recycling schemes: how could you be sure where your old newspapers actually ended up? As the green consumer movement came up against problems like this in the early 1990s its significance as a self-conscious political movement started to wane.

And yet people do still continue to recycle their waste and to shop using ecological criteria. How should the persistence of these practices in the face of all the ambivalences that people feel about their effectiveness be understood? I am suggesting that we regard such practices as a form of folk piety – as a specific form of ritual activity. Our point of reference here is the religion of the peasant majority of late medieval and early modern Europe, which was dismantled by the forces of the Reformation and Counter-Reformation in the sixteenth century (see Chapter 3). This form of piety invested the rounds of everyday life with religious significance. Each kind of action, from sweeping out the hearth to urination, was surrounded by elaborate taboos and rituals. Women were at the heart of this culture, partly because of their importance in its transmission, but also because of their centrality in the rhythms of the domestic sphere and in negotiating the boundaries between nature and culture. The world was full of souls and spirits, ambivalent in character, which had to be navigated around through taboo and ritual. The dead played an active role in this, being regarded not as segregated from daily life, but as integrated into it at every turn, offering protection from beyond the grave in exchange for the prayers and intercessions of the living. The whole of this popular religion was characterized by an inextricable mixture of the sacred and the profane, the spiritual and the bodily, faith and prosaic self-interest (Muchembled, 1985).

What has all this got to do with green consumerism? Firstly, like the popular religion of the early modern period, green consumerism is a kind of ritualization of the everyday, both in the sense of investing everyday actions – shopping, cooking, discarding – with sacral significance, and in terms of involving a certain habituation of bodily action, the going through of formulaic movements in given contexts. As research into green domestic practices has suggested, recycling and green consumerism are less to do with a constant purposive process of self-questioning than with the development of habits of hand and eye – the sorting of rubbish into different bins, the orientation towards iconic brands such as Ecover and Suma, and so on (Harrison et al., 1994: 10–11). To paraphrase the historian James Obelkevich on popular religion, they are 'more a matter of feeling and doing and of taking for granted than of abstract subscription to theological [or ecological] doctrines' (Obelkevich, 1979: 6).

Secondly, like popular religion, this kind of ecological piety helps to stabilize self and society in a world understood as permeated with risk and hazard. The world of the early modern peasant was seen as full of threatening forces which had to be avoided through the observance of taboos or warded off through propitiatory rituals (Muchembled, 1985: 28–9). Similarly, for the modern green consumer everyday domestic practices are fraught with hazards to both body and soul which have to be negotiated – pesticides in food which threaten one's health, for example, or chlorine in paper which threatens the environment and thus the ecological conscience of the shopper.[8] The rituals of a green lifestyle allow the individual to pass safely through such moments of decision and danger.

Thirdly, like those of early modern popular religion, the rituals and taboos of green consumerism can be seen as expressive as much as instrumental, as serving to affirm the identity of the individual and their social bonds with others, as much as to navigate around a risky world. To purchase green alternatives, to recycle glass and paper, is to assert the kind of person one is – and to stop doing so would be to jeopardize that self-identity. Maintaining the rituals of green consumerism thus binds the individual in a relationship of moral solidarity with both proximate and imagined communities of like-minded others.

In this chapter we have explored some of the ways in which individuals in contemporary society are seeking in their everyday lives to reorder their relationship with non-human nature. Giddens's notion of life politics has been useful for articulating the extent to which such quests for a new, non-dominating relationship with nature are shaped by the Reformation tradition of self-monitoring and individual narrative. Yet we have seen that this current within contemporary culture is also shaped by substantive ideals of moral character and virtue, ideals which produce and authorize very different social practices – some based on private purity, some on public excellence (Arendt, 1958: 74). We have also seen that these under-standings of virtue become embedded in distinct, socially located forms of life which temper the demands of continuous self-monitoring with habits, routines, and relations of trust.

Such processes hybridize Protestant self-monitoring with more Catholic forms of corporate embodiment. As such, they suggest a eucharistic charac-ter to contemporary alternative lifestyles. Choices of consumption and non-consumption can be seen to symbolize a disaffiliation from worldly power, just as the eucharistic communities of early Christianity signalled their dual membership of the city of God and the earthly city. The avoid-ance of meat and other symbols of dominance over nature have long been used in what Eder calls the bloodless tradition within Western culture, a tradition which refuses the symbols of earthly social power that are grounded in the totemism of the archaic sacred (Eder, 1996; see also Hamilton, 2000). However, at the same time such refusals also become embodied in individual and corporate *habitus*, within individual routines and collective subcultural milieux, in constant tension with the demand for reflexivity and social distancing. In the next chapter we will focus on the activist variant of this tradition, one which sees the sacrality of nature as requiring not just private consistency but public speech and action on behalf of nature.

Chapter Nine

Nature and Public Speech

In this chapter I will be arguing that the practice of making public testimony in defence of nature can be seen as partly rooted in ideas of moral excellence developed and passed down in specific religious traditions. Consider, for example, two great figures in the history of environmental protection in America, Muir and Leopold. John Muir (1838–1914) was a tireless campaigner for nature conservation, the first president of the Sierra Club and one of the chief architects of the American national parks. Aldo Leopold (1887–1948) developed not only the principles of what would later become wildlife ecology, but also the influential 'land ethic', set out in *A Sand County Almanac* (Leopold, 1966). Both men were animated by a profound sense of the spiritual significance of wild places, having honed their sensibilities towards nature during years spent exploring the forests and other wild places of America, and both were led to distance themselves from the prevailing social codes concerned with the domination of nature. Both in their later years abandoned the orthodox Christianity of their upbringing for Transcendentalist and neo-Platonic ideas of nature as interconnected and filled with divinity. Yet while Muir felt called to militancy in defence of nature, Leopold was convinced that environmental protection could only come through an inner change within individuals, the adoption of an ethic that saw human beings as 'plain' members of the community called land.

So, of those who experience the sacrality of nature in terms of a moral demand in tension with established, worldly customs and power, not all experience it in the same way. For some, it is experienced as a demand to appear in public in defence of nature with the clear aim of political effectiveness; for others it is felt as requiring them to aspire to a private moral consistency, to a life lived in accordance with clear moral principles. This divergence is rarely absolute, but it is one that has repeatedly manifest itself in the history of environmentalism – for example in the debate between social and deep ecology in the United States, and in that between 'Realos' and 'Fundis' in the German Green Party. But why was Muir drawn one way and Leopold the other? As Stoll points out, these different trajectories make more sense when we look closely at the religious origins of these two conservationists. Muir was born to a Campbellite preacher – the Campbellites being a radical, zealous offshoot of Calvinist Presbyterianism. His later move towards neo-Platonic and Transcendentalist ideas about nature were simply grafted onto the evangelical, prophetic militancy of his Calvinist origins. Leopold, by contrast, came from Lutheran stock, and was drawn not to evangelism and preaching but to the development of a personal, contemplative ethic (Stoll, 1997: 143–7, 184–5).

Such biographical details present a vivid illustration of the way that environmentalist practice, as well as environmentalist ideas, have both been woven out of existing elements in Western religious tradition. But also it reinforces the sense, gained in the last chapter, that it would be a mistake to see the difference between Leopold and Muir in quantitative terms – as if Muir's public evangelism indicated a greater commitment to nature's sacrality than that exhibited by Leopold. Rather, these different responses to the sacredness of animals draw on different understandings of the moral life, both of which have been reinforced and given more definition by specific theological traditions. This distinction is closely related to that made by Manuel Castells between resistance and project identities in the politics of the contemporary 'network' society – between those forms of identity which are oriented around resistance to the emerging global order and those organized in terms of a positive project of societal transformation (Castells, 1997). However, what I am focusing on here is how these are both *moral* identities, identities that are not just examples of cultural disaffiliation from dominant social codes, but ones that are accompanied by a strong sense of being grounded in a universally valid ethic. The very idea of a universally binding ethic – one that is not simply custom, or a collection of duties owed to specific others – is one that can only have arisen after the transcendental axis had opened up. The historic religions of the axial age, with their distinction between the empirical world and the transcendent realm, made it possible to think of a source of moral obligation that transcended the specific solidarities, interests and loyalties of empirical society. The heroes discussed in the last chapter are thus radically different to the heroes of Homeric myth and legend, for example. But the later radicalization of the transcendent axis that occurred with the Reformation's rejection of the medieval cosmos also played a crucial role in laying the foundations for the purposive politics of contemporary social movements. In medieval and early modern society the dominant idea of politics was conservative, concerned with the 'preservation and health of the body politic' (Walzer,

1968: 182). Even peasant revolts in early modern Europe were typically conceived as attempts to restore traditional moral relations, rather than trying to overturn them. The Reformation played a crucial role in the dismantling of the traditional organic bonds between individual members of medieval society, thus making it possible to think of a new, methodical form of politics.

But their rejection of the medieval cosmos not only freed Protestants from their organic bonds; it also bound them into a newly individualized sense of personal responsibility to fulfil God's wishes. For the Protestant the only mediator of this dependency was Christ, as revealed in the word of the Bible – not the hierarchy of the Church, nor tradition, nor the sacraments. The Protestant faithful were to be a 'priesthood of all believers', rather than relying on the priesthood of others; their moral lives were thus predicated on self-reliance and self-discipline (Troeltsch, 1931: 470). One result of this was a change in the concept of sainthood: the saint was no longer an *other* – to whom one had a relationship of companionship, emulation or supplication – but *oneself*. Similarly, the Reformation changed the meaning of asceticism: no longer an other-worldly high-water mark of religious achievement, which assumed a contrast with average, worldly morality, it became a straightforward refusal of worldly pleasures – a refusal demanded of all – in favour of purposive conduct within the world (Troeltsch, 1931: 332; Weber, 1985: 118–19).

Moral activism in contemporary culture, then, has important roots in Calvinism, however much it was later detached from its Calvinist moorings and attached to immanentist ideas of a 'higher law' (Stoll, 1997: 50–1). Yet Stoll points out that, whereas Calvinism emphasizes the need for righteous action to indicate salvation, in Lutheranism this was softened by a greater confidence in the active, saving grace of God (Stoll, 1997: 185). This meant that, although it places great emphasis on individualism and interiority, Lutheranism does not quite share in Calvinism's intense emphasis on the need for individual action; instead, it shares with Catholicism a basic confidence that, as long as the individual does not actively pursue evil, good relations with God can be maintained. So although the Reformation in general, with its radicalization of the vertical dualism between world and God, encouraged an understanding of the righteous life in terms of moral consistency and the following of inner conscience, it was Calvinism in particular that provided a source for many of the ideas and practices drawn on by environmental activism.

Counterintuitively, then, we can conclude that activist environmental movements (as opposed to the private adoption of environmentally friendly lifestyles) are more likely to emerge in a culture which emphasizes active rather than contemplative relations with nature. The very same cultural trajectory which resulted in the industrial domination of nature thus also seems to be responsible for the emergence of the very movement to resist that domination. Eder makes this point, drawing contrasts both between and within religions – between Christian and Taoist cultures, where the latter's contemplative concern for nature has not historically predisposed them to environmental activism; and among the different Christian traditions, singling out Protestant cultures as fostering environmental movements because of their assumption that right relations with God have to be demonstrated rather than assumed (Eder, 1996: 188). To this latter contrast we can now add one within Protestantism itself – between Lutheranism and Calvinism. This further nuance helps us understand why, although Arne Naess's deep ecology emerged in Lutheran Norway, it was only when it was transplanted to America under the influence of Dave Foreman, founder of Earth First!, who like Muir a century earlier grew up among the Campbellites (by then called the Churches of Christ), that it became an evangelically confrontational movement (Stoll, 1997: 196).[1]

But the contrast between the ethical and the political, between private and public action, should not be drawn too sharply in our account of the contemporary politics of nature. Of Blum's 'idealists' – those who have clearly articulated principles that guide their life choices – some are 'saints' and some are 'heroes'. And in many cases, such as the animal rights group discussed in the last chapter, the 'heroic' calling to effective political action is also coloured by the 'saintly' demand for moral consistency in all areas of life – here, for example, manifest in the vegan renunciation of animal products. And when we consider the widespread adoption by environmental movements of non-violent direct action (NVDA), a 'saintly' emphasis on moral consistency is at least as important as a 'heroic' concern for political effectiveness.

Consider, for example, the wave of direct-action protests against the British road-building programme in the 1990s (Doherty, 2000; Szerszynski, 2002a). The first of these protests was at Twyford Down in 1992, which protest saw the emergence of the Dongas tribe, but over the next few years similar protests took place at dozens of rural and also some urban sites across the country. Protesters at these events were typically drawn from two distinct social groupings: local residents, often quite 'establishment' in background and outlook, and young, unemployed and geographically mobile eco-warriors, living in squats or in on-site protest camps (Doherty, 1996; McKay, 1996; Seel, 1996). Typically, such protests took place at a chosen site on the route of a planned bypass or motorway – generally rural and wooded – which was first occupied through the setting up of a protest camp made of home-made shelters called benders. During eviction by the construction company's security guards and police, the protesters would move to tunnels, tree houses or rope walkways, locking themselves on using handcuffs or bicycle 'D-locks' (Doherty, 1997, 2000).

After eviction, during the construction process, tactics involved harrying construction workers and the occupation or 'monkey-wrenching' of construction plant such as earth-movers.

A striking feature of these protests is that a passionate concern for political effectiveness was fused with an equally strong commitment to moral consistency. For such activists, moral consistency required them, at least sometimes, to take action in opposition to worldly power; but the taking of action had to be in a form consistent with their moral principles. As we shall see below, this is a praxis whose orientation to the future is not merely instrumental but also prefigurative; it does not seek just to influence a desired future, but also to foreshadow it in the present. Non-violent direct action as a praxis is thus on the cusp between private principle and public action, as is starkly evident from the lives of three prominent men who, although not considered environmentalists, have been hugely influential in the development of politically principled non-violent direct action – Henry Thoreau (1817–62), Leo Tolstoy (1828–1910) and Mohandas Gandhi (1869–1948). While all of them were at some time in their lives drawn to establish a monastic, rural retreat where lives of moral consistency would be possible, all three were also led to develop philosophies of non- violent resistance to unjust laws.

Thoreau is of course more famous for his contemplative sojourn at Walden Pond; yet his Transcendentalist views also meant that he regarded the individual's inner conscience as the surest guide to spiritual and moral truths. His following of this principle led to a jail sentence in 1846 because of his refusal to pay the poll tax supporting the Mexican War. In his 1849 essay 'Civil Disobedience' he set out his justification for the refusal:

> Can there not be a government in which the majorities do not virtually decide right and wrong, but conscience? – in which majorities decide only those questions to which the rule of expediency is applicable? Must the citizen ever for a moment, or in the least degree, resign his conscience to the legislator? Why has every man a conscience then? I think that we should be men first, and subjects afterward. It is not desirable to cultivate a respect for the law, so much as for the right. The only obligation which I have a right to assume is to do at any time what I think right.[2]

In Blum's terms, and like the vegetarians discussed in the last chapter, Thoreau was more of a responder than an activist: 'It is not a man's duty, as a matter of course,' he wrote, 'to devote himself to the eradication of any, even to most enormous, wrong; he may still properly have other concerns to engage him; but it is his duty, at least, to wash his hands of it, and, if he gives it no thought longer, not to give it practically his support.'

The Russian writer Leo Tolstoy abandoned the privilege of his titled estate in later life, adopting a simple, peasant existence. He was harshly critical of organized religion, feeling that it was a barrier against the consistent Christian moral life, for which quasi-Protestant sentiments he was excommunicated by the Russian Orthodox Church (Leon, 1944). His advocacy of an absolute consistency between principles and conduct led not only to the voluntary simplicity of propertylessness, manual labour and the meeting of only basic needs, but also a philosophy of passive resistance, for example defending the rights of conscientious objectors to resist conscription (Green, 1986).

Mahatma Gandhi is best-known for his use of passive resistance in the struggle against British rule in India, but he first advocated its use in 1906, while working as a lawyer in South Africa, in response to a proposed law requiring the registration of all Indians in the country. In developing his political philosophy, Gandhi combined Hindu ideals of asceticism with ideas he encountered in Jesus's sermon on the mount and in the lives of Thoreau and Tolstoy.[3] However, not satisfied by either Thoreau's or Tolstoy's terms, Gandhi and his second cousin Maganlal Gandhi coined the term *satyagraha* to denote his political philosophy of truth- or love-force – *satya* meaning truth or love, *graha*, firmness or force (Fischer, 1951: 102). Like those earlier figures who had influenced him, Gandhi was drawn to a 'saintly' life of moral consistency. Gandhi had undergone a moral conversion in which he resolved to renounce the carnality and pleasure-seeking of his earlier life and pursue an ascetic life consistent with spiritual values; he himself describes his turning-point as occurring in 1903 when he read John Ruskin's *Unto this Last*. But in the mission to secure home rule for India he also found the moral project around which to organize a 'heroic' life narrative.

As well as exhibiting the subtle shadings between private saintliness and public heroism, the lives of Thoreau, Tolstoy and Gandhi provide concrete examples of the way that ideals of radical moral consistency can be traced not just to religion in general, but to specific kinds of religious idea, one described by Catherine Albanese (1990) as a form of nature religion. All three men were committed to a direct relationship with God, one unmediated by organized religion. All three believed in a God who was at once discernible in the order and lawfulness of the universe and also in a transformation wrought in the hearts of individuals. This is not the capricious and distant God of the Hebrew Old Testament, but a God who is at once rational and natural, who is available to the senses, the reason and to moral intuitions. This is a divinity who, as a source for a natural, universally binding, rational ethic is radically other to the *de facto*, material world. But at the same time it is an immanent deity, who can be found in nature and in the heart.

Time and the Sacred in Environmental Politics

If environmentalist practice is informed by ideas of nature and of the moral life which have been shaped and honed by religious history, it also draws on temporal ways of thinking and talking inherited from that same history (Szerszynski, 2002b). Firstly, environmentalists often use metanarratives as interpretive schema for specific historical events; by locating events within a larger narrative whole, they are given shape and meaning (Szerszynski, 1993). The dominant metanarrative of the modern era has been one of continuous progress towards a possible rational Utopia – a narrative that itself has been seen as a secularization of the Christian salvation story (Lowith, 1949). Some forms of environmentalism – such as ecological modernization – replicate this kind of narrative structure, seeing environmental problems as the product of an incomplete modernization and rationalization of society. Against a background narrative which sees history as the increasing realization of reason in the world, environmental problems such as pollution, habitat loss and resource depletion are seen as the product of ignorance and market distortions, to be corrected by the application of more rationality (Sonnenfeld and Mol, 2000; Mol, 2001).

Whereas proponents of the New Age are likely to share this upward narrative of modernity (in their case simply replacing rational enlightenment by spiritual enlightenment), radical environmentalists are more likely to invoke a 'fall' narrative, in which present ills are seen as the result of a historic fall from a primal state of harmony with nature (Taylor, 2001a: 186). Taylor describes the dominant metanarrative in American radical environmentalism as one that looks back to an original primal harmony with nature, followed by a fall into social oppression, first by agriculturalists and then by industrialists (Taylor, 2001b: 228).[4] According to such a view, what is needed is not more but less rationality; instead of humans saving nature through science and technology, which is grounded in their transcendence of the natural world, humans need to become more natural. This places emphasis on the healing power of nature as a moral source rather than on the ability of human beings to improve nature, or even to undo the damage they have already done to it. It is through allowing nature to be – through a more natural, sensuous existence, through natural healing techniques, through living in natural surroundings, and through growing food in natural ways – that human beings' alienation from nature will be reversed, and their original harmony restored.

But it is not only at the level of doctrine and cosmology that temporal forms of thinking structure environmentalism's relationship with the sacred. Human beings use the language of time and tense not just to structure and express succession and ordering, but also to orient themselves in relation to value, whether in terms of a past that should be preserved, a present that needs to be responded to appropriately, or a future that has to be anticipated or controlled (Reiss, 1981). Traditional societies typically favour an orientation towards the past; talk of earlier times is used aetiologically, to explain and justify present social arrangements, and actions carried out in the present are understood as mimetically recapitulating paradigmatic events that occurred in mythic time (Eliade, 1954). Contemporary society has its own manifestation of such a past orientation in the imperative to preserve natural and cultural objects that are seen as imbued with glacial or enduring time (Urry, 2000). A future orientation, by contrast, renders present action temporally meaningful by relating it to events that have not yet happened. But there are variants of this future orientation, variants that organize ideas of apocalypse, millennium and prophecy in the environmental movement.

The first is a consequentialist orientation, which organizes present activity around the intention of influencing the future. Sometimes this orientation is predicated on a sense of productive agency – on the potentiality of individuals and groups to make a difference in the world. The post-Reformation secularization and immanentization of eschatology in the form of liberal and socialist Utopias takes this post millennial orientation, which insists that by human endeavour the millennium, the kingdom of God, can be realized on earth. We saw in Chapter 4 that this has been an important religious theme in Western culture since Francis Bacon. Its adoption by parts of the environmental movement is one of the key ways in which environmentalism departs from Calvinism in its otherwise similar orientation to the world (Nelson, 1993: 239; Stoll, 1997: 176).

A second version of this consequentialist orientation to the future is associated not with a sense of agency and control but with a lack of control, and with uncertainty about the future. Among Christians, such an orientation is generally more characteristic of conservative evangelicals than liberals, the former being concerned to prepare themselves for the apocalypse and for judgement, rather than actively to build the kingdom of God. Taylor suggests that among radical greens this kind of orientation dominates; unlike New Agers they are generally pessimistic about the future, to the point of expecting an impending apocalypse (Taylor, 2001a: 186). Both survivalist movements, which prepare to be self-sufficient in the event of the future collapse of society, and consumer movements that have grown up around concerns about risks in the domains of the environment, food and health, take this pre-millennial, apocalyptic orientation to the future, more concerned with the relative avoidance of risks or 'bads' rather than the more positive securing of individual or collective 'goods' (Beck, 1992; Alexander and Smith, 1996; Lash, 2000).

A third, quite different kind of future orientation is based less on an attitude of *control*, or of *expectation*, and more on one of *hope*. This is a politics of prefiguration, anticipating in the here and now a different and better world, through Utopian moments which stand as partial glimpses of another way of being (Kershaw, 1997: 264–5). Unlike traditional societies, this future orientation sees actions in the present not as mimetically repeating a mythic past but as prefiguring a future Utopia. However, rather than working instrumentally towards a different, green society, the ideal is to be lived out directly in the present. As a political concept, 'prefiguration' originated in the debate between anarchists and communists in the nineteenth and early twentieth centuries over 'the question of means and ends'. Whereas orthodox communists worked instrumentally for the liberated society, using whatever means seemed most effective in the given circumstances, anarchists were more likely to argue that the means used in the present should in some way prefigure the desired social goal (Boggs, 1986: 150).

In the radical tradition, such arguments for prefigurative politics have generally taken one of two forms, both of which in fact attempt to reduce the prefigurative orientation to a consequentialist strategy. The first one argues that prefiguration is a *necessary* condition for achieving the good society, because of the disastrous effects of pursuing a 'politics of deferment'. Either because of the corrupting effects of using instrumental strategies on those pursuing them, or because they might negatively affect public support for their cause, prefigurative movements like the early German Greens insist that 'humane goals cannot be achieved by inhumane means' (Boggs, 1986: 185).[5] The other type of consequentialist argument for prefigurative politics is that it is a *sufficient* condition for desirable social change. From this perspective, simply living the green Utopia in the present will, through 'propaganda by the deed', bring about social change, as the new and desirable form of life is taken up by more and more people. David Pepper, in his study of ecologically motivated communes, interprets prefiguration completely within the framework of 'social change through example' (1991: 32, 46, 56–9). It thus stands or falls as a worthwhile ethico-political orientation by the efficacy or otherwise of exemplary action.[6]

However, as we have seen above in our discussion of figures such as Thoreau, Tolstoy and Gandhi, a political orientation which we would now call prefigurative was historically more likely to have been described in the deontological terms of 'duty' and 'higher law', suggesting that such political and moral identities were grounded not in the instrumentalities of this world, but in a higher moral law derived from another world. Yet in the case of movements of societal transformation such as radical environmental movements, this law is not simply eternal but has a directionality in time, a futurity focused on the desired Utopia. Forms of protest organization such as the camp of occupation can be oriented to the future in a kind of ritual, eucharistic anticipation (Szerszynski and Deane-Drummond, 2003). In such an ordering of the sacred, what links present, empirical political acts with future, possible states of affairs is not so much chains of causal relations, but typological homologies such as those sought in traditional hermeneutic interpretations of scripture; the meaning of individuals and their actions are to be found not simply by reference to their immediate goals and intentions, or to some atemporal 'law', but in the way that they have relationships of similitude with past or future such actions. In the most intense moments of protest, the time of concrete human actions can be felt to be linked with the sacred, abstract time of 'world-historical trans-formation' (Jasper, 1997: 22). Protesters can feel that they are acting out almost mythic roles, like the peoples of the primal sacred (see Chapter 2).

Finally, a fourth orientation to time in environmentalist praxis is different again – that of *prophecy*. Rather than relating to the future in an attitude of control, expectation or hope, prophetic speech and action uses future talk to express critical judgements of the present. According to Richard Fenn, prophetic talk is 'serious' or 'operative' speech that has in some sense 'leaked out' from its usual liturgical setting into wider social life (Fenn, 1982: 104). Unlike apocalyptic speech, prophetic speech typically refrains from making specific predictions about future events, instead using 'future talk' as a way of bringing out the urgent demands of and judgements on the present.[7] Environmentalism draws on such speech acts and cadences; it is not just about disseminating certain beliefs and values, it is also an *evangelical* movement, and as such has to persuade others of the urgency of action, using both speech and symbolic action to bear prophetic messages (see Szerszynski, 1997, 1999). Like the gospels, environmentalism thus frequently employs what Paddy Scannell, in his analysis of contemporary mass media, calls a 'for-anyone-as-someone' mode of address (Scannell, 2000). 'For-someone' messages are personal, intended for one recipient; 'for-anyone' ones are by contrast impersonal. A for-anyone-as-someone message is broadcast to many but is received as if personally intended, as addressing the individual directly.

Stoll cites many key figures in the American preservationist and environ-mental movements, all of whom had an evangelical background, as evi-dence of the importance of this religious tradition for developing the cadences of speech of environmental politics – from John Muir, through Howard Zahniser (a key architect of the 1964 Wilderness Act), to Dave Brower and Dave Foreman, founders of Friends of the Earth and Earth First! respectively (Stoll, 1997: 176). Foreman, however, combined the evangelical Christian form of speech with very different content, particu-larly referencing neo-paganism. Foreman's use of pagan Celtic symbols on the *Earth First!* journal masthead, which presented EF! as a forum for 'earth religion in whatever guise' was criticized by another co-founder of

EF!, Howie Wolke. Wolke privately professed a deeply spiritual motivation for conservation, but nevertheless felt uncomfortable with the evangelical cadences. For Wolke, spirituality was interior and private, not something to be shared publicly and used to persuade. Wolke preferred to express his 'deep spiritual feelings for wild places ... with ordinary words and gestures' (Taylor, 2001a: 185).

Polytheism and Contemporary Environmental Politics

Contemporary environmentalism thus received and transformed a rich vocabulary of ideas of nature, combining these ideas with particular forms of moral existence and public speech from the Christian tradition to produce a political force capable of challenging the dominant technological trajectories of modern society. Yet one vital element in the late-twentieth-century politicization of nature consisted neither of a new idea of nature, nor a transformation of an existing one. This consisted of a postmodernization which opened up a more radical plurality in the way that nature was conceived (Lyotard, 1986). Nature was politicized not just by being conceived in terms of new concepts; it also became contested (Macnaghten and Urry, 1998). From the 1960s onwards the monopoly of science was increasingly challenged, in the kind of return to polytheism that Weber predicted, a polytheism rooted less in forces outside ourselves and more in the irreconcilable nature of different societal subsystems and different subjective points of view (Weber, 1989: 22–3). The monotheistic roots of modern science have bequeathed to it the idea of a singular truth, holding in check the proliferation of alternative understandings of nature. But in the late twentieth century the single vision of modern science was increasingly displaced by the polytheistic plurality characteristic of the Greek polis, as nature was taken out of the hidden semi-private realm of scientific institutions and brought into public view. A different model of scientific objectivity started to take shape, positing not that the pre-social singularity of nature guarantees agreement, but that out of social disagreement a more adequate understanding of nature may emerge (Arendt, 1958: 57).

However, as we saw above, from the 1980s there was an increasing tendency – however strategic – for the more institutionalized parts of the environmental movement to deploy realist, scientized understandings of nature. And outside the world of the environmental pressure groups, there have been many attempts to articulate a unified green cosmology as a basis for environmentalism, a system of thought that would short-circuit the need for public contestation of claims about nature. Such projects rarely draw solely on empirical ecology and biology for their metaphysical basis. The practical biological sciences were never subjected to the levels of reductionism experienced in physics, instead retaining closer links to their roots in direct experience, amateur natural history and natural theology (Stoll, 1997: 25). However, their concern with the particular has not made them a very fertile soil for ecotheological systems; instead, where they have been given religious interpretations, these tend to be highly personalized spiritual meanings (Taylor, 2001b: 235). But less experiential, more abstract ideas from quantum physics, cosmology and evolutionary biology figure prominently in the work of Fritjof Capra (1975, 1983), Thomas Berry and Brian Swimme (Berry, 1990; Swimme and Berry, 1992), writers who seek to identify a unifying, scientifically validated vision on the basis of which an ecologically sustainable society can be developed. This style of sacralized science writing was an important influence on the Earth Charter, a global attempt to agree 'a declaration of fundamental principles for building a just, sustainable, and peaceful global society in the twenty-first century'.[8] Taylor describes the charter as 'the consecration of scientific narratives in an ambitious effort to inculcate nations in reverence for life on earth' (Taylor, 2001b: 237).

But the monolithic character of such ideas is in tension with the increasingly contested nature of scientific and ethical ideas about nature. Indeed, projects like the Earth Charter could be seen as a hangover from earlier periods in Western history, when the unifying effects of the vertical, transcendent axis still made ideas like the unified Christian hegemon of Christendom appear not just plausible but sometimes inevitable. But today, as some environmentalists seek to raise scientific metanarratives to sacred status, others are levelling science, attempting to strip it of any pretensions to divine authority it may have had, instead presenting it as human, interested and fallible. In a related development, advocates of various forms of environmental pragmatism seek to respond to the *de facto* plurality of normative descriptions of nature by finding ways in which co-ordinated action need not depend on agreement about foundational, ontological matters (Light and Katz, 1996). These initiatives can be seen as attempting to go with the grain of the contemporary situation. We no longer live in the Middle Ages, when the inherent instability of an interpretative approach to nature was contained within an overarching hermeneutic framework. But society has also all but lost faith in the existence of modern nature, in the idea of knowledge production ever coming to a halt as science finally stabilized its object (Szerszynski, 1996); such a timeless finite object was always only the mirror of a timeless infinite deity. Now that that deity has all but disappeared from the horizon of modern society, nature appears as irredeemably multiple.

Some European social theorists of the environment, such as Ulrich Beck and Klaus Eder, take from this that the existence of substantive ideas and ethics of nature are less a positive resource than a handicap to be overcome

(Beck, 1992; Eder, 1996). To be more accurate, what they feel needs to be overcome is the idea that achieving an environmentally sustainable future depends on arriving at a substantive descriptive and normative agreement about the environment – an agreement about whether and how nature might be being damaged by human intervention, and about whether and which ethical imperatives flow from this. In this, they are to one extent or another embracing a postmodern nature; they are starting from the premise that in contemporary society there are multiple, socially situated views of nature, with no agreed, neutral way of deciding which can claim to be the privileged truth. The social authority of the institutions of religion, science and government can no longer command automatic assent; the power to define what is true is thus increasingly dispersed across society – and above all is seen to reside in the subjectivity of each individual.

Given such a background, both argue in different ways that traditional environmental ethics and environmental theology are mistaken in their characterization of the environmental problematic. Such traditional approaches – including those examples given in the second paragraph of this section – assume that what is needed is the identification of the one, true, philosophically, theologically or scientifically grounded account of what is happening to nature and how we should respond, an account which is so persuasive that it ought to command the assent of all. In contrast, Beck and Eder argue that environmental learning is maximized when no one perspective on nature has automatic authority; instead, we should embrace as both inevitable and desirable the coexistence of a plurality of perspectives about nature. Rather than seeking to determine in advance which perspective is true, we should focus on identifying the kind of features society should have if we are to maximize the chances of this pluralism resulting in both beneficial mutual critique and pragmatic compromise.

Beck associates environmentalism with what he calls reflexive modernity. Beck, like Giddens, insists that industrial or 'simple' modernity was never completely modern. Industrial society was always a transitional but ultimately unstable hybrid between traditional and modern social forms – part feudal, part industrial. The liberating effects of the labour market of industrial modernity always operated in tension with the solidity of traditional gender roles and class cultures, and the development of cognitive reflexivity was held in check by the concentration of epistemic authority in the new priesthood of expert institutions. The feudal aspects of industrial society were thus not a survival from pre-modern times, but a product of and precondition for industrial society itself. However, the working through of these contradictions, not least through the continuing pressures of the labour market, are progressively eroding the last vestiges of traditionality in modern society (1992: 89). For Beck this emergence of 'reflexive' modernity constitutes nothing less than a second Reformation, as processes of individualization free up individuals from their embedding in institutions. 'People are *set free* from the certainties and modes of living of the industrial epoch – just as they were "freed" from the arms of the Church into society during the age of the Reformation' (1992: 14). Under such conditions, all ideas of nature are contested; for Beck the core of environmentalist thought is not to be found in particular dogmatic claims about nature but the *freeing up* from dogmatic claims.

Although like myself Beck makes conceptual and historical links between the Reformation and environmentalism, our emphasis is different. Put crudely (though of course the contrast can only be relative), whereas I am presenting environmentalism as being religion dressed up as Enlightenment, Beck presents the Reformation as Enlightenment dressed up as religion. Where I see environmentalism as coloured by its cultural past, and thus as not wholly modern (see Latour, 1993), Beck invites us to see the Reformation as prefiguring its modern, reflexive future. Yet even if Beck's account were true it itself draws on a fundamentally religious image. In the twelfth century Joachim of Fiore propounded a view of salvation history which divided time into the ages of the Father (the law), of the Son (the gospel), and of the Spirit, an age of freedom in which humanity would have direct, inner access to knowledge of God (Burrell, 1983: 257). In the final epoch people will be released into Spirit, and know divine truth without the need for any intermediaries, even Christ. This spiritualized eschatology – one also recognizable in Hegel's idea of Absolute Spirit (Hegel, 1977) and in Habermas's account of the ideal speech situation (Habermas, 1987b) – seems also to inform the more chiliastic moments in Beck's reading of environmentalism, as people are delivered from the revealed religion of industrial, scientific modernity into the immediacy of reflexive modernity.

Klaus Eder (1996) offers a broadly consistent theoretical analysis of contemporary environmentalism; however, he recognizes that any plausible account of ecological morality has to acknowledge an irreducibly symbolic, cultural element to ideas and ethics of nature. Eder too makes links between what he calls contemporary 'ecological reason' and the Protestant tradition. For Eder, ecological reason is still ultimately rooted in a utilitarian approach to nature, but one now 'enlightened' by an ecological awareness of the prudential reasons to protect nature for human benefit. It is thus a further rationalization of the instrumental relation to nature promoted by Protestantism. However, he also acknowledges a disjunction between ecological *reason* and ecological *morality* – the traditions and customs which actually shape people's dealings with nature. Underlying this are the hidden cultural codes that shape our practical relations with nature. So Eder acknowledges that there is always an unthematizable symbolic basis to society – in practice we operate in accordance not with an abstract ecological rationality but with a concrete ecological morality informed by unexamined symbols and metaphors.

Yet at the same time Eder does not want to lapse into a Burkean conservatism by wholly abandoning the modernist hope of finding moral principles transcending *de facto* social mores (Burke, 1968). Instead he wants to suggest that the very awareness of the ineradicable plurality of truth claims in modern society can itself bring a kind of reflexivity. If Eder's 'ecological enlightenment' is emerging, as he claims it is, there will not be any agreed *substantive* ethic which will tell us how to act in relation to nature, but there will be an agreed *procedural* ethic which will tell us how competing visions can most productively engage with each other (Eder, 1996: 183–4). Eder describes this as 'post-environmentalism', a form of environmentalism that has become 'political' in the specific sense of being aware of the contingency of its own claims, and identifies two main preconditions for its institutionalization in modern societies. Firstly, a new environmentalist 'master frame', a set of background assumptions and symbolic meanings, has to displace the industrialist one that has organized public discourse for the last two centuries (Eder argues that this is indeed occurring (1996: 190ff.)). Secondly, a growing awareness of the contested character of postmodern nature means that society has to develop institutions and procedures for dealing with competing claims about the common good (1996: 203–4).

Eder has an approach to orderings of the sacred which locate them as cultural phenomena within society, rather than seeing the social itself as constituted through an ordering of the sacred. Because of this, he ends up with a postmodern social ontology of competing world-views, to which the only solution seems to be an agonistic version of environmental pragmatism, where a basically market model of co-ordination is relied upon to generate societal ecological virtue from the self-interest of individuals and corporations. Nevertheless, he usefully encourages us not only to acknowledge the irreducibly plural character of modern nature, but also to look at environmentalism not as a simple freeing up from tradition but as being woven out of transmitted cultural elements. Detraditionalization – like individualization – is not a simple one-way process, where individuals are freed up from ideological structures into a pure, unmediated existence. Instead, it is simply a more active kind of working with those elements, altering and recombining them in new ways. Environmentalism, and other critical responses to the modern technological relationship with non-human nature, fashion cultural resources to promote new relations with nature and technology out of the elements of Western sacral history, located within a distanced relationship to the social order with its roots in the monotheistic ordering of the sacred.

At the end of the next chapter I will return to the question of how to conceive of societal reflexivity in relation to specific orderings of the sacred.

But first I will consider an emergent form of the sacred – that constituted in terms of the unity and sacrality of the earth itself. The very ambiguity of the sacral meaning of the image of the globe can provide some clues about the future of the sacred, and the possibility of a critical politics of nature and technology.

Part V

The Future of the Sacred

Chapter Ten

The Global Sacred

On 7 December 1972 the Apollo 17 mission lifted off from Cape Canaveral, Florida, and was on its way to the moon. Shortly after the separation of the final stage of the Saturn V rocket, the astronauts took a sequence of 11 photographs. One of these photographs, NASA image AS17-148-22727, or 22727 for short, became an almost ubiquitous image.[1] Perhaps one of the reasons why this particular photograph has been so popular is because it appears to show the whole globe, not crossed by the terminator (the line between day and night), and because of the political implications of the fact it is Africa, rather than continents of the affluent North, whose outline is clearly visible in the upper part of the disc. As a signifier of the earth, this mimetic image has partially displaced the cartographically conventional globe in many places it might otherwise have appeared (Cosgrove, 1994). Compared with such conventional representations of the globe, there are certain key features of images such as 22727: the earth is seen as a whole, defined against the darkness of space behind and around it; there are no lines or political colouring, so it is an apolitical, asocial view of 'our common world'; the photographs freeze a moment in time, with change suggested by the moving clouds and, in most cases, the terminator. The overall effect has a persuasive mimetic force, one that seems to speak a universal truth that transcends individual ideological perspectives.[2]

Four years earlier, around Christmas 1968, William Anders had taken another photograph, as the Apollo 8 craft completed the first manned circuit around the far side of the moon. NASA image AS08-14-2383, commonly referred to as Earthrise, was not the first full-earth image; a few had been obtained from unmanned craft in the previous two years, such as the one reproduced by Goldberg (1991: 55). However, these images had generally been of low quality, and were not widely circulated. Earthrise, by contrast, was taken on a 70 mm Hasselblad hand-held camera, and was startlingly clear. When the image was circulated after the astronauts had returned to earth, it had an immediate impact, not least because the television images sent back live during the mission had been black and white and of very low definition, showing the earth as a wobbling, melon-like white shape. Anders, the astronaut who took the photograph, says that he prefers to hang the picture as he experienced it – as if he were once again coming around the side of the moon, with vertiginous infinite blackness 'below' him, and catching a welcoming sight of the earth again. However, as Cosgrove points out, Earthrise is usually reproduced as a conventional nocturnal landscape with a half moon, except for the reversal of landscape and celestial object – all colour is in the celestial sphere, not the landscape – and the lack of any stars in the image, which seems to emphasize the isolation of terrestrial life (Cosgrove, 1994: 275).

Earthrise quickly achieved classic status. A few weeks after the flight, someone sent a telegram to Apollo 8 commander, Frank Borman, that just said, 'You saved 1968.' The image was used as a backdrop for news and current affairs programmes and on the cover of *The Whole Earth Catalogue*. It has been widely cited as playing a key role in inspiring the first Earth Day, held in 1970, and in galvanizing the then still emergent environmental movement (Goldberg, 1991: 57).[3] Cosgrove quotes at length the essay by the American poet Archibald MacLeish that appeared in the *New York Times* on Christmas Day 1968.[4] It was reprinted alongside the Earthrise image in the May 1969 issue of *National Geographic*. 'For the first time in all of time', McLeish wrote,

> men have seen [the earth] not as continents or oceans from the little distance of a hundred miles or two or three, but seen it from the depth of space; seen it whole and round and beautiful and small ... To see the Earth as it truly is, small and blue and beautiful in that eternal silence where it floats, is to see ourselves as riders on the Earth together, brothers on that bright loveliness in the eternal cold – brothers who know now that they are truly brothers. (MacLeish, 1968)

Here, for once, we seemed to have the perfect icon for the sacrality of the earth. In a way, the real icon was the globe of the earth itself, and the NASA images were simply copies of it. The earth was the perfect image of itself. Just as its horizon curved around and joined up in perfect self-identity, so did its semiosis; the sign was its own referent. Here surely was a religious image for the contemporary sacred, for the 'unlimited finitude' of the earth, and for the 'panhumanity' which dwelt upon it (Franklin et al., 2000). The opening up of the transcendent axis between an empirical world and a transcendent monotheistic deity had made it possible to think of the physical world and the humanity that dwelt in it as a united whole, united in its creaturely ontological dependence on the same transcendent source. The idea of a transcendent God had provided a vantage point outside the empirical world, an Archimedean point at which science would seek to stand to gain objective knowledge of the world, knowledge untainted by the perspectivism suffered by empirical beings dwelling in the world. And now that human beings stood – in fact, floated – at that vantage point, and gazed back at their world, what they saw was something in the face of which 'the only valid human responses were awe, wonder and humility' (Cosgrove, 1994: 286–7).

Such a reading of the images suggest a new way of relating to the sublime characteristic of the modern sacred. Those who had made the pilgrimage to Cape Canaveral to watch the great Saturn V rocket lift off may have had 'a sublime experience that renewed faith in America and in the ultimate beneficence of advanced industrialization' (Nye, 1994: 256). But for the astronauts on that rocket, the act of gazing back at the earth provoked a very different, even pre-Kantian sublime, one that was experienced in terms not of human rational and technological mastery but of fragility and humility. William Anders himself described the earth as perceived from the moon in more homely, tactile terms than MacLeish, as looking like 'a fragile Christmas-tree ball which we should handle with care'. Similarly, the Apollo 11 astronaut Michael Collins described the earth as seeming as small as a pea, 'so small I could blot it out of the universe simply by holding up my thumb ... I didn't feel like a giant. I felt very, very small' (Cosgrove, 1994: 284–6). Like the ancient Greek *theoria*, the functionary who would travel to other cities and return to report on their customs, or like Siberian shamans who travel to the spirit worlds and back, the astronauts seemed to return from space with an important universal spiritual truth. The very sublimity and power of human technology, it seemed, did not raise humanity to universal mastery; instead, through self-endangerment, it shrank humanity to a tiny speck in the vastness of space. Such responses to the earth from space seem to presage the years between 1968 and 1972, which saw the growth of a pessimistic futurology described in *The Limits to Growth* and 'Blueprint for Survival' (Goldsmith et al., 1972; Meadows et al., 1972), as well as the beginnings of a range of 'nature religions' in opposition to the structures of global instrumental power (Beyer, 1998).

Global Mastery

However, Tim Ingold argues that images of the world as a globe always bear subtle meanings of technological mastery over nature (Ingold, 2000, ch. 12, also published as Ingold 1993). Distinguishing two ways of conceiving of the environment, in terms of globes (perceived from without) and spheres (experienced and engaged with from within), he suggests that 'the movement from spherical to global imagery is also one in which "the world", as we are taught it exists, is drawn ever further from the matrix of our lived experience' (2000: 211). He describes the shift from the pre-modern to the modern as one from sphere to globe, from cosmology to technology, and from a practical, sensory engagement to detachment and control (Ingold, 2000: 216). Although Ingold does not talk in detail about the photographs from space, he implies that such images must necessarily distort our relationship with nature, positioning us outside a world conceived as pure matter, on the outer surface of which meaning is actively inscribed by the perceiver (Ingold, 2000: 213). Thus, as *icons*, images such as 22727 may be representations of the fragile, bounded earth; as *indexes*, however, they can be seen as signs and symptoms of the technological power that both makes them possible and which they serve. From this perspective, such images can be seen as bearing meanings not of humanistic humility in the face of the boundless universe but of technological mastery over the earth.

Ideas of global environmental management have certainly been a significant current in the history of environmentalism, at least since the colonial era started to generalize the biopolitical orientation of nation states to a wider awareness of global environmental dependency. In Chapter 6, I touched on the role that colonialism played in the evolution of conservation policies and concern for rare and exotic species. The control of game populations also led many, such as the legendary Anglo-Indian hunter Jim Corbett, to an awareness of ecological relationships.[5] Concern about anthropogenic climate change was generated by the experience of rapid deforestation on islands such as Mauritius. Scientists, for a while, came to play a key role in the formation of government policy (Grove, 1990: 23–4, 29–30).

The colonial era also facilitated the emergence of a nascent global discourse. The relationship of economic interdependence in which the rapidly industrializing colonial states ironically found themselves with the colonized territories led to the representation of the finitude of resources and the possible alteration of the climate as *global* problems, which might yet threaten human survival. For example, it was the scientists employed by the East India Company who, in 1852, published the first report on the dangers posed by global deforestation (Grove, 1990: 27–8, 31–2, 37). It was against this colonialist background that Thomas Malthus produced his population theory, based on the tragic incompatibility between a geometrically increasing population and an arithmetically increasing food supply, framed in strikingly global terms (Glacken, 1967: 639, 654; Pepper, 1984:

91–8). Furthermore, the experience that the imperial powers had in administering their colonies was crucial to the germination in the twentieth century of the idea of supra-national planning bodies (Bramwell, 1989: 89–90).

After the Second World War the notion of a rational, planned society, which had advanced conservationist ideology in both the USA and Britain in the inter-war period, came into its own, particularly in the context of post-war reconstruction in Europe. Science had improved its status in policy terms during the war, particularly through large research schemes such as the Manhattan project. On both sides of the Atlantic, conservationists and ecologists came to be held up as examples of the kind of technical expert who could be trusted to guide the planning of society, and thus came to have even greater policy influence (Nicholson, 1987: 93–5; Bramwell, 1989: 88–91). The internationalization of capitalism in the late twentieth century also meant that concerns about resources took on a global character. In the USA awareness of global interdependence had increased with the growth of its imperialist ambitions after 1900. Nevertheless, resource conservation was still seen largely as a matter of nationalistic concern, as a matter of patriotism (Ekirch, 1963: 98–9).

In the 1950s, however, as America rapidly became aware of its new hegemonic position in global politics, it started to see itself as having an obligation to steward the world's resources, partly out of an awareness of its own massive role in their depletion. American concern for natural resources came to be framed in global terms, a change evident in the 1952 report of the President's Materials Policy Commission; in the conservation group Resources for the Future, founded in the same year; and in the Princeton symposium, 'Man's Role in Changing the Face of the Earth', in 1955 (Ekirch, 1963: 131–4). At the same time, famines in India and elsewhere prompted global media concern and calls for supra-national organizations which might respond to, or even avert, such catastrophes, while also reviving the idea of population as a global problem. With the founding of the United Nations, the World Bank and other international bodies the idea of a planned world society had come to seem increasingly realizable, and a global, universalized notion of 'the environment' was taking shape in policy discourse.

Ecological science was itself changing under these conditions. Since the 1920s and 1930s, because of the pressure to seem more relevant to the biopolitical reorganization of nation states, it had moved in a decidedly positivistic direction, modelling itself on physics and economics. Under the influence of the British biologists Charles Elton and A. G. Tansley, in particular, its dominant scientific paradigm had become one which described nature in mechanistic terms, as flows of energy and nutrients (Worster, 1977: 294–304). But there was also a sense abroad among ecologists in both Britain and the USA that, despite the horrors of Nazism, global society, like nature, was moving towards a state of greater and greater integration and harmony. In Britain the plant biologist Sir George Stapledon felt that the post-war world order would become as integrated as a single organism through the intervention of supra-national organizations (Bramwell, 1989: 90). In America a group of ecologists at the University of Chicago, who became known as the Chicago organicists, declared that nature was guiding societal evolution towards 'an interdependent world unity' (Worster, 1977: 329).

As Cosgrove himself points out, representations of the globe have always played a role in the iconography of worldly power – in terms of monarchical rule, bourgeois intellectual and worldly ambition, and the commercial ambitions of corporations today. He suggests that Earthrise and 22727 had a similar function in American iconography, in terms of an alternative, 'One World' interpretation, very different to the 'Whole Earth' reading discussed in the last section. 'One World' interpretations draw on a modernist project of the expansion of US power and influence, and stress the incorporation of all nations and peoples into a single peaceful entity united in universal humanism. He argues that such readings of the images underscore a distinctively American vision of global harmony, rooted in the axial conception of universal Christendom, and expressed using the conventions of missionary cartography. Even the MacLeish essay, he suggests, hides an American missionary ideology, which the poet had expressed more unequivocally elsewhere (Cosgrove, 1994: 281–2, 285).

The images with which I opened this chapter, photographic images of the earth suspended in space, seemed at first to have a single, clear message. Their mimetic character – even down to the way that the clouds (and in Earthrise the terminator) signify that this image was taken on a particular day, at a particular time – seemed to make them above perspectivism and ideology. Yet, as we have seen, such images have already delivered up at least two separate readings at odds with each other over the place of humanity in the world: one places humanity inside a bounded and finite nature, and signals the limits of technology to transcend the human condition; the other places humanity outside of nature by knowing and mastering it (see Arendt, 1958: 1–6). In terms of the narrative of this book, within the struggle over the meanings of these very images we can see a struggle between two different orderings of the sacred. These are not wholly opposed: both sacralize life itself, rather than seeing life as a preparation for eternal life. But for the first, 'Whole Earth', reading, life is the ongoing self-reproduction of the biosphere, one guided by its own homeostatic processes – but one which can be threatened by excessive technological intervention (Lovelock, 1987). The lack of visible boundaries on the earth from space signifies the artificiality of political boundaries for a human race radically dependent on a common natural world. In the second, 'One World', reading, by contrast, technological society is the life process made reflexive, life shaping and optimizing itself. Here, the lack of boundaries signifies not the social solidarity of the peoples and environments of the earth, but the mimetic realism of a universal scientific truth which maps and catalogues the earth.

Banal Globalism

Between 1996 and 1999 I and others at Lancaster carried out a study of the production, circulation and reception of such global images.[6] Using interviews with communications professionals, a survey of broadcast television output and a series of focus-group discussions we sought to understand the dynamics through which global imagery, narratives and appeals are produced and circulated within the mass media, and the effect this might be having on people's sense of themselves as bearers of rights and responsibilities in an increasingly globalized world (for a summary, see Szerszynski et al., 2000). One way of describing what we were doing in the project is that we were trying to identify the cultural conditions for a putative post-national, global or cosmopolitan citizenship (Bauman, 1993; Tomlinson, 1999, ch. 6; Beck, 2000). In relation to the emergence in earlier centuries of *national* citizenship, Benedict Anderson has brought attention to the crucial cultural work that needed to be done before people could begin to feel themselves to be part of such large political and civic units. Printed books and newspapers, radio and public service television, flags and civic rituals all played important roles in this process – not just by making possible the circulation of information about the life of the nation, but also by providing ways in which people could feel part of an 'imagined community' made up of people they would never meet in places they would never visit (Anderson, 1983). We argued that the formation of anything like global citizenship in the twenty-first century would require a comparable amount of cultural work, and that the global media may be functioning as a vehicle for the production and circulation of cultural materials out of which globalist identities, sensibilities and values might be being fashioned (Szerszynski and Toogood, 2000).

We found numerous examples of global images over a 24-hour period of broadcast content:[7] images of the earth, including the mimetic blue earth; long, often aerial images of generic global environments; images of wildlife that index the overall state of the environment; images of the family of man sharing a global product; images of relatively exotic places that suggest the endless possibilities of global mobility; images of global players famous in and through the world's media; images of iconic exemplars who demonstrate global responsibility; images of those engaging in actions ultimately on behalf of the global community; images of corporate actions; and images of global reportage shown to be present, live and staffed by iconic figures able to speak, comment and interpret the globe.

On the basis of this research we suggested that global imagery was starting to constitute an unremarked, all-pervasive background to people's lives, one with the potential to reshape their sense of belonging. Michael Billig (1995) had argued that perhaps the most important symbols of national belonging are those of what he calls 'banal nationalism' – the almost unnoticed symbols of nationhood that pepper our everyday lives, from coins and maps to the very use of the word 'we'. In a similar way, we suggested that televisual images and narratives were developing a global equivalent, a 'banal globalism' which might help create a sensibility conducive to the cosmopolitan rights and duties of being a global citizen. The contemplation of the earth from space – or, for most people, that of a photographic image of it – constitutes a kind of high mass for the religion of global modernity, comparable with other global media events such as the Olympic games and the release of Nelson Mandela. For Dayan and Katz, the Apollo missions together constituted a *transformative* media event, after which 'society's members are as if reborn to a different world', in this case by translating the awareness of the boundless universe beyond the earth and the earth's smallness and unity in relation to that wider universe, into an experience (Dayan and Katz, 1992: 165). But once the image of the globe from space becomes routine and repetitive, we are no longer in the vicinity of such transformative events; instead, we experience a profusion of minor icons and rituals which in less highly charged ways reinforce a sense of global belonging, but which may be more effective in reorienting people towards the global sacred.

Some evidence that such a sense is growing was found by *Soul of Britain*, a survey conducted in the UK in 2000. Respondents were provided with a list of geographical entities, ranging in size from their neighbourhood or community up to 'the world as a whole', and asked to say which of them they belonged to 'first of all'.[8] Of the respondents, 33 per cent chose England, Wales, Scotland or Northern Ireland as their primary source of belonging, 20 per cent chose the locality or town where they lived, 13 per cent chose their 'neighbourhood or community', 9 per cent chose Great Britain and 9 per cent chose the UK. But 11 per cent chose the world as a whole. The survey found that age, religious affiliation (or lack of it) and voting intention were among the most significant factors that seemed to shape the distribution of a sense of global belonging. For example, whereas 19 per cent of 18- to 24-year-olds chose the world as their primary locus of belonging, this figure dropped to 11 per cent of 25- to 34-year-olds, and dropped further to 9 per cent among those over 65. In terms of religion,

14 per cent of Roman Catholics and 'other' religionists and 13 per cent of those with 'no religion' chose the world, compared with 9 per cent of 'convinced atheists' and only 6 per cent of Protestants. Similarly, 12 per cent of Labour voters identified with the world, compared with 6 per cent of Conservative voters (Opinion Research Business, 2000).

As well as the global having a different *salience* for different social groups, our own research indicated that it is also given particular *meanings* within specific cultural worlds. Ideas of global connectedness, belonging and responsibility may be as ubiquitous, banal and taken for granted among the public as they are in the media, but they are interpreted in different ways. Very few of our respondents interpreted global belonging in terms of the imperatives of ecological responsibility and concern for the global unfortunates. Among younger and more mobile groups, ideas of globality took the form of a cosmopolitan openness to the new and the culturally different (although this too had its limits).[9] For older groups, ideas of responsibility and intervention beyond national boundaries were sometimes interpreted in relation to received notions of British character and the fulfilment of duty, familiar from the days of empire and the world wars. Also, although we never raised issues of immigration, some groups, who otherwise engaged in much localized care, expressed considerable cultural hostility to various categories of immigrant. As one respondent said, 'they don't have the right to come here and insist that they can do whatever they like'.

The global sacred thus does not seem to escape the fate of other forms of religion in the postmodern age – a fragmentation and subjectivization that allows the signs to mean what people want them to mean (Roof, 1999). Rather than being 'full', a self-enclosed sign, the globe seems to be an empty signifier, one that has to be filled arbitrarily with meaning by the observer. Modern consumer culture exploits this ambiguity of global images, completing the sign with its own, brand-specific signifiers. Many of the advertisements we collected used 'family of man' iconography, typically in the form of a collage of ethnically marked individuals engaged in a biologically universal activity, such as laughing, weeping or loving. 'The Family of Man' was a photographic exhibition held in New York in 1957 (Steichen, 1983). Roland Barthes saw the exhibition when it came to Paris, and analysed its 'ambiguous myth of the human "community"' in terms of the way it held together its insistence on diversity and difference, on the one hand, and a unity that it magically produced out of this diversity, on the other. Each person is marked as being different in clothing, appearance, and setting from the others; in being juxtaposed with each other, however, they suggest a common humanity (1973: 107). By linking this essential humanity to soft drinks, clothes or life insurance, global signifiers are filled with a determinate meaning which authorizes consumer choice.

Towards a New Global Sacred

At the moment when the ancient Hebrews first identified their tribal god with the creator of the world, a path was opened up from the archaic sacred to the image of the earth from space. Until then, supernatural agency had been local, particular, and within the world; any sense of a cosmic creator was as a distant immaterial speculation, of no significance to the world and experience of human beings. Judaism brought about a profound transformation by bringing these two religious ideas together, thus investing the foreground of religious life with cosmic significance. Christianity worked the logic of this move out in a particular direction by insisting in a more thoroughgoing way that the God of the Jews must be the God of all peoples. Rome found the new, universalized religion more fitting than its local gods to its experience as an imperial power (Gauchet, 1997: 128–9). Medieval Christianity took all too seriously the idea that their religion was *catholicus* – a universal religion, a faith that all should be made to embrace. From the sixteenth century, Protestantism's rejection of Rome encouraged a new emphasis on national identity – one still apparent in the *Soul of Britain* survey results reported above. But by pushing the divine further away from involvement in the everyday world, the Reformation did not effect a return to the remote creator god of the archaic sacred, however much the absent God of deism might resemble him. In time, the public world did indeed fill up again with the lesser gods of old, as the market encouraged the proliferation of individual desires and gave them absolute authority within their domain. In the heart and mind of the individual, however, God loomed larger than ever.

But the Reformation prepared the ground for the further sublimation and naturalization of religion as reason, in a shift which moves even closer to today's global sacred. This shift reversed the traditional estimation of nature as a lesser source of religious truth than revelation, instead elevating nature, reason and individual conscience as the source of wisdom and virtue. With this natural religion, Enlightenment thought was able to conceive of global commonness not in the sense of all peoples accepting the same revealed religion, but in terms of the shared reason that people shared by virtue of being rational beings. Modern science further developed this natural religion – the Copernican revolution even dethroning empirical, earth-bound humankind from the centre of the universe. Not humanity but reason itself was the *imago Dei*, the contact point between the natural and transcendent realms; speculation about sentient, even unfallen life on other worlds by Giordano Bruno and others was an inevitable corollary of this further abandonment of the empirical in favour of the sublime. Religion had finally became genuinely universal.

While the image of the globe seems a celebration of the panhumanity implied by the monotheistic sacred, the situation is more complex. In both its Enlightenment and Romantic forms, modern culture saw an introjection of the sublime into the empirical world, itself thereby made sublime. Whereas on one level the Reformation ushered in a modern sacred purged of the magical links between supernatural and earthly power characteristic of the archaic sacred, the rise of the biopolitical ordering of society – at first at the national, and finally at the global level – effects a reinstatement of the archaic sacred at the level *of society and nature as a whole*. Where once tutelary spirits watched over particular forests or particular species, now it is nature as a whole which is sacralized. For the critics of the technological domination of nature, nature is guided and guarded by its own immanent teleology, sometimes personified as Gaia (Lovelock, 1987). For the proponents of global environmental management, by contrast, the environment is under the protection of the abstract 'no-man' ruler of democratic society, who shapes and optimizes it for his own interests, interests rendered sublime and universal through the language of technical reason (Arendt, 1958: 40). In both, the sacrality of nature brooks no argument; the ritual demands of the tutelary god of nature are absolute and non-negotiable.

The limits of contemporary immanentist construals of nature thus become clearer when we see their links with the archaic sacred. But there is a third reading of the sacrality of the globe, one that seems more accommodating to the need for a critical politics of technology and nature than the discourses either of eco-spirituality or environmental management. The path of the modern sublimation of religion, rejecting the particular and local in favour of absolute unconditionedness, only led us back to the unforgiving gods of the archaic sacred. The love for nature (Milton, 2002) need not involve such a totalizing vision. Instead of seeing the globalization of society in terms of the infinite sublime, we need to understand it as the sheer multiplication of finite particulars. Let me try to explain what this would mean for the ethics and politics of nature and technology.

If Ingold is right, that we should dwell inside the environment, as a sphere around us, rather than regard the globe from outside, then what happens when that environment becomes global, becomes expanded to the point where there is no longer an outside, becomes an example of what Bataille calls 'unlimited finitude'? As Ulrich Beck (1998) puts it, the global society is a *Democracy without Enemies*; there is no boundary between inside and outside, between Christendom and the pagans, between capitalism and communism. Yet this does not make society unified – far from it. This is not a society made infinite, sublime, guided perfectly by reason. It is a society without an outside, but it is still finite; its members can still only know and act from within the world, not as God from outside. Their vision is still multiple, partial and divided, and problems such as poverty and environmental degradation will never wholly be overcome. Yet now, more than ever, such problems have to be embraced, since global society has no 'outside or deferred future on to which the rejected, the unwanted, the disowned effects of progress can be displaced' (Franklin et al., 2000: 28–32). With no division between inside and outside, the divisions are now *within* the social body.

Beck suggests that the division is between those committed to the bio-political project of simple modernity, that of the technological mastery of nature, and those committed to making our relations with nature more reflexive (Beck, 1998). But this is to turn reflexivity into a competing position *within* the social body, rather than, as Beck himself insists else-where, a property *of* a social body organized in such a way that social authority is not centralized but distributed (Beck, 1996). The kind of re-flexivity needed is one that cannot be claimed by any one actor within the social body, as if a kind of enlightenment. It has to emerge in the inter-actions that take place *between* actors in society. But neither can this reflex-ivity be provided for by institutional forms; the institutional reorganization of society in terms of deliberative democracy, whether along the lines argued for by Beck (1995), Eder (1996) or Latour (2004), can only help by opening up the epistemological and legislative organs of society to con-testatory voices. But such changes can never by themselves guarantee the free flow of speech necessary for a societal co-ordination that transcends archaic power, something which must sometimes move outside institu-tional forms to flourish.

As we saw in the previous chapter, for Eder, societal reflexivity is a pro-cedural rationality that rises above the substantive rationalities embedded in competing sacralizations of nature (Eder, 1996: 205). Yet the reflexive society is itself an ordering of the sacred, one which combines the polythe-ism of ancient Greek democracy with the idea of harmonious agreement promised by the tradition of monotheistic religions. If we are to have a genuine pluralist politics of nature and technology, we need a better under-standing of *this* form of the sacred, which is at best struggling to establish itself in contemporary society.

Chapter Eleven

Nature, Technology and the Sacred: a Postscript

Let us return to the poem by Matthew Arnold with which this book began. If the sea of faith has indeed retreated, what has it left behind? As I look out from my window I see the great tidal mudflats of Morecambe Bay, which appears by name on the maps of Europe drawn by Ptolemy of Alexandria in the second century AD.[1] At first glance, the twice-daily retreat of the tide, a treacherous tide that can fall back and advance as far as 12 kilometres, seems to leave a desert of mud, bereft of life and beauty. Yet on closer inspection the intertidal mud and sand teem with marine and avian life of an extraordinary richness and variety. Perhaps, similarly, the general retreat or fragmentation of hegemonic, organized religion in many Western societies is resulting not in a secular wasteland, devoid of sacral meaning, but rather in a huge diversity of forms of enchantment. As Weber himself put it in a different context, under conditions of modernity '[t]he many gods of old, without their magic and therefore in the form of impersonal forces, rise up from their graves, strive for power over our lives and begin once more their eternal struggle amongst themselves' (Weber, 1989: 22–3). I have been similarly suggesting in this book that in contemporary society we can see not a decline but a *profusion* of the sacred; dispersed across the social, natural and technological landscape, the sacred becomes feral.

But the contemporary sacred is not thereby without order and pattern. I have been arguing that our contemporary understandings of nature and technology have been profoundly shaped by the long arc of institutional monotheism, the emergence, radicalization and collapse of a transcendent axis between natural and supernatural realms. The very idea of nature as a self-sufficient material order obeying immanent causal laws came into existence through this trajectory. So too did the idea of technology, of the wedding of the productive arts to knowledge of *physis* and *aiton*, nature and cause – to the extent that it was thought that the arts could be made as certain as reason, and thus deliver humanity from the necessity and uncertainty associated with finite existence. But with the collapse of the transcendent axis in modernity, a profoundly immanent form of the sacred took over, the sacrality of life itself, whether the subjective life of the Romantics and postmodernity, or the biological construal of life that lies at the heart of biopolitical society. And it is with the biopolitical ordering of the modern state that technology becomes not simply the soteriological project it was in the Reformation period; as the goal of technology comes to be rendered in technical terms, technology starts to order the ends of life in its own terms. And finally a postmodern sacred, constituted by a plurality of meanings grounded in individual subjectivities, further overlays this modern biopolitical ordering of society.

Given this historical embeddedness of the contemporary technological condition, what possibility is there for effective technological and environmental critique? If I am right – if nature is not, sacrally speaking, a vacuum – then the task of those who would seek to establish an alternative relationship with nature by resacralizing it certainly has to be entirely rethought. Nature is not a blank slate that can simply have a theology and liturgy inscribed on it. For it is already under an enchantment, one reproduced by the institutionally rooted *habitus* of modernity. And technology, far from being an instrument of desacralization that strips meaning from nature, itself serves ceremonial functions in maintaining a particular sacral ordering of nature. The goal of achieving a right relation to nature and to technology is thus only possible if we engage at the level of the sacral meanings – both benign and malign – that inform our current relationships with them.

But what should be our guide in such a process? I have suggested that the characteristic form of the sacred in contemporary culture is a postmodern sacred where the ultimate ground of value and meaning has been drawn into human subjectivity itself. This ordering of the sacred is not without its distinctive modes of truth. Yet it seems unable to provide either a place outside the social and technological world, or an inherent rationality within it, on which could be grounded a critique of modern society. It thus seems only able to generate either celebrations of the contemporary extension of consumer choice that simply sacralize the modern technological condition, or at best offer purely symbolic escapes from that condition that ultimately leave it unchallenged (Roberts, 2004). And, as I argued in Part IV, movements critical of the technological domination of nature seem to have found the immanent sacrality of modern or postmodern thought inadequate to their task, and instead have drawn extensively on resources from other, transcendental orderings of the sacred in order to support critical positions in both private and public life.

However, technological thinking has a grip on the modern mind that is hard to shake off, radically shaping the thinking even of critics of modern technology. In the nineteenth century, for example, there arose movements which criticized new technological practices because they alienated humanity from 'a certain order and more of being which is timeless and universal' (Massingham, 1945: 10). In this kind of argument they manifest a continuity with the classical critique of *techne* (see Chapter 4). But nineteenth-century critics went further, also criticizing technologies in areas such as medicine and agriculture for failing efficiently to produce what they offered – and in this they were unmistakably modern. Jerry Weinberger argues that it is in the nature of the productive arts that each will regard social problems such as poverty and deprivation as simply due to 'the mere scarcity of what it alone knows how to produce', and thus make the implicit claim to be able to do what it does perfectly (Weinberger, 1985: 24). However, premodern ideas of technology were much more restrained in their claims to be able to produce predictable and certain outcomes. It was not until the Reformation and Enlightenment periods that technology in the modern, sublime sense emerged, that is, a technology promising an overcoming of contingency and finitude. And it is in this very same context that counter-technological discourses emerged which claimed that it is not technology but its *withdrawal* that can offer the certainty characteristic of reason. Whereas classical scepticism about technology had assumed that uncertainty was inherent in human affairs, and simply cautioned against technology diverting proper attention from spiritual and moral matters, this new discourse on technology argued that a rejection of technology in favour of nature could provide the very certainty promised, but not delivered, by technology.

For example, critics of existing agriculture called for practices which conformed more to our understanding of the natural order. In early-nineteenth-century America John Lorain criticized American farming techniques for interfering with natural cycles and thus exhausting the soil, and called for more rational husbandry (Glacken, 1967: 696–8; Worster, 1977: 268). Such critics typically claimed that more natural, rational food-growing practices would not only overcome the increasing alienation between humans and the natural order, but also produce more food for less labour, and food that was more nutritious (Oyler, 1945: 77; Hardy, 1979: 169). Similarly, as we saw in Chapter 5, nineteenth-century alternative healers castigated conventional medicine for producing the illnesses it claimed to cure. They represented health as a natural property of the body, and illness as a disturbance caused by living unnaturally, and invoked a 'state of nature' account of a pre-civilized state where illness was unknown. The movement, which included homeopaths, chiropractors and osteopaths, combined revivalist notions of sin and grace with an Enlightenment concept of nature, producing an individualized millennialism which offered perfect bodily harmony (Albanese, 1990: 128–9).[2] The contemporary natural health movement, too, insists that healing is a natural process, so the role of the therapies is not to heal, merely to allow healing to occur. The natural condition of the human body is presumed to be a state of perfect health. 'If the body can be helped on its way to true well-being, or real health, it will employ its own mechanisms of healing' (Coward, 1989: 47). It was the very emergence of modern technology that laid the conditions for such 'utopian technologies'. By 'granting to art the apparent certainty of reason', modern technology opened up a space which could be occupied by counter-technological discourses, in which the technology itself was blamed for producing the scarcity it promised to banish. Utopian technologies were thus inscribed within the discourse of the very practice against which they set themselves up in opposition.[3]

Yet this ironic intimacy between the discourses of technology and anti-technology should not, at this stage, surprise us. After all, just as in Part II I argued that modern science and technology were profoundly conditioned products of Western sacred history, in parts III and IV I suggested that movements resisting the technological domination of nature were also very much shaped by that same history. Taken as a whole, then, the book could be read as saying that the confrontation between modern technology and its critics is a confrontation that is very much internal to Western sacral history, and one in which opposing positions turn out to be internally related in complex ways. So the task of technology critique cannot be to escape historical conditioning; this indeed would be once again to reproduce the promise of modern technology to overcome finitude. Instead, the very embracing of our historical conditionedness, and ultimately of our embeddedness in the ongoing transformation of the sacred, can itself be seen as an anti-technological move, a negation of the negation of finitude. Such an embracing must involve a greater awareness of the way we are constituted by our past. And the point of such awareness cannot be to overcome our conditionedness, to refuse what is handed us by the past; such is the impossible dream of Enlightenment. Instead, the task must be to receive that past more consciously and responsibly.

But this is not to say that in order to resist the modern technological mindset we should simply be looking backwards along the trajectory of the Western sacred. Historicity involves a relationship not only to the past, but also to the future. Of course, it is integral to the approach I have taken in this book that we cannot predict the future of the sacred. I have been arguing all along that the path taken by the sacred in the West, with its product of secular (post)modernity, has been radically contingent, representing one possible branching route from the primal sacred where it started. There have been times when this route has been partly determined by internal tensions and contradictions within a particular ordering of the sacred. And, although this has not been a focus of the book, there have been many times when material social and natural events have also played an important determining role. And if the past has been contingent, so too will be the future.

Nevertheless, might it not be the case that new orderings of the sacred are emerging, orderings which offer new challenges and possibilities for our relationship with nature and technology? In the previous chapter I started to speculate about the future of the sacred by considering the globe as an icon for the contemporary sacrality of nature. While acknowledging the growing importance of the global as a significant framing of the contemporary Western sacred, I argued that the globe remains an ambiguous icon, one capable of simply reinstating the limitations of the archaic sacred at the planetary level by subordinating individual life to the self-reproduction of the globe. I ended the chapter by suggesting that only a version of globality that could accommodate the intrinsic plurality of perspectives characteristic of the post-monotheistic, postmodern sacred would be adequate to the critically important task of escaping the technological domination of humans and nature. Although there is no space here to develop the idea fully, I hinted that such an ordering of the sacred, one in which a conception of the transcendent axis was experienced as making possible rather than annihilating the multiple perspectives of empirical reality, could serve as the foundation for a viable technological democracy. Such a move would avoid the Enlightenment fiction of a secular polity that was not grounded in its own, disguised ordering of the sacred.

But any attempt to affirm and nurture such an emergent ordering of the sacred would also have to be sensitive to important developments in the area of science and technology. It is possible to identify a few related trends, all of which involve the blurring of boundaries that were crucial to what Latour (1993) calls the 'modern constitution'. The first involves the increasing interpenetration of science, technology and society. The worry for some earlier critical observers of modernity was that scientific rationality might constitute an 'iron cage' which diminished human agency and the meaningfulness of the world (Weber, 1930; Adorno and Horkheimer, 1997). To the extent that the modes of truth of experimental science displace those of public debate, it was feared democracy would be inappropriately 'scientized', losing its distinctive mode of truth and its character as a realm of freedom (Habermas, 1971b). Technology critique under such conditions rightly consisted in finding spaces outside the technological, spaces within and from which one could assert humanistic values (see Borgmann, 1984). Yet the situation today is arguably radically different; the increasing hybridization of scientific investigation with technical application, commercial exploitation and government regulation has meant that the cool detachment of 'science' has given way to the warm, risky, engagement of 'research' (Latour, 1998). It seems likely that under such conditions technology critique will consist less in acts of 'purification', which attempt to insulate politics as a realm of judgement and freedom distinct from that of scientific objectivity and necessity, and more in acts of 'hybridization' which creatively and reflexively merge science and politics (Latour, 1993, 2004).

A second trend involves the blurring of boundaries between humans, technology and nature (see Graham, 2002). Biotechnology in particular represents a site in which these boundaries are becoming particularly difficult to sustain. The molecularization of the biological sciences and industries, and the consequent rendering of life in terms of genetic information, suggests we may be going through a further reordering of the sacred. As we saw in chapters 3 and 4, with the emergence of modern understanding of technology in the context of the biopolitical ordering of society, the idea of the determinate object known by a sovereign subject was problematized; nature became constituted less as a set of objects known to an observer, and more as a collection of resources available to a technological system for transformation and distribution – as part of the self-reproduction of a life process now understood to include technology as its pinnacle and *telos*. But with the biotechnological revolution even life becomes problematized as a concept, as it becomes subsumed into information and code. This move seems to combine biopolitical ideas of life with earlier sacral orderings of nature – with medieval nature as text and sign, and early modern nature as analysed into its constituent parts – but it also seems to indicate a more fundamental shift in the ontology of nature (Szerszynski, 2003c).

A third notable trend consists of the breaking down of boundaries between the experiment and the real world. In the scientific revolution the boundary of the laboratory was essential to the emergence of the experimental method. The classical seventeenth-century scientist sought to know nature through *making*, by re-creating nature within the experiment. The walled laboratory thus operated as a space of fabrication, one which provided the conditions for the creation of knowable phenomena. By 'making' nature, the experimental scientist sought to glimpse the 'model' by which it was made, to know as well as its creator the natural law governing nature (Arendt, 1958: 282–3). But also the experimental scientific method was made possible by the way that the laboratory structure granted exemption from the material and social consequences of 'error'. This exemption operated as long as both material effects and scientific truth claims could easily be recalled, ending their circulation in society. But under contemporary circumstances these conditions are less and less applicable, as experiment and application are merged into 'real-life experiments', which produce unrecallable effects at the level of both materiality and discourse (Krohn and

Weyer, 1994: 174). New technologies are thus capable of setting off chains of irreversible and unpredictable material and social consequences, no longer insulated from society by the boundary of the laboratory. As such they exhibit a shift from *fabrication* to *action* as the dominant way of interacting with and knowing nature (Arendt, 1958). Rather than creating durable objects on the basis of a pre-existing model or idea, they rely on the human capacity to 'act', to create radically new elements, organisms or life processes. What would have been 'data' in the context of the classical laboratory experiment, become instead real-world 'risk events', emergencies, in which nature responds to our actions and to which in turn we have to respond. Knowing nature thus becomes much more provisional: nature comes to be known not as a fabricated object is known, but as we know a participant in a dialogue.

Cumulatively, these trends may indicate the resurgence of a more animic relationship with nature, one characterized by a greater sense of agency in non-human nature, and a more porous understanding of the human–non-human boundary (Ingold, 2000: 114). For example, there may be conditions under which the experience of technology as *in* control, as an autonomous system driven by its own self-grounding rationality rather than being subservient to human projects and happiness, gives way to the experience of technology as *out* of control, as proliferating unintended consequences which confront us as hostile forces. At such times the sublimity of a technology simply indifferent to human happiness could be displaced by a capriciously hostile *numen*, as human action – whether directly through biotechnology or indirectly through global warming – incites nature itself into action-hood. It must be the task of any new sacral ordering of nature to help us make sense of such experiences, experiences which are already within our horizon. To do this may involve us learning from the way that primal cultures understand their dealings with non-human nature (Descola and Pálsson, 1996); but it will doubtless also involve grasping and shaping radically new ideas and ways of thinking.

Above all, what I have been at pains to stress in this book is that the history of the West is not the triumphal emergence of universal reason and Enlightenment out of the darkness of tradition and superstition. There are things to applaud about the modern world, and things to lament; but we cannot simply appeal to an idealized account of Western history in order to ground such judgements. For that, we will have to find a more nuanced understanding of the relationship between reason, history and the sacred. Furthermore, human finitude is always historical, a passing on from past to future. Modern scientific and political secularism represents a theoretical denial of that finitude and historicity, just as modern technology is a practical denial of it. Thus the embracing of finitude is likely to involve a humbling of science as only one way of knowing nature, and of technology as only one way of dealing with it. And recognizing the historical embedd-edness of technology means that engaging with technology simply on its own, technological terms, through evaluating specific technical effects and consequences, will not be enough. And neither will it suffice solely to find spaces of human experience not yet colonized by technical thinking (Borg-mann, 1984). Instead, technologies need to be engaged with more fully, to be 'read' in a far richer way: in terms of what relationships they bear to our past trajectory, how they might be harnessed to non-technological goals in the present, and upon what future trajectory they might set us. Under-standing the embeddedness of our ideas of nature and technology in the ongoing transformation of the Western sacred is an essential component of that task.

Notes

Chapter 1   The disenchantment of the world

1   For a compressed but very useful summary, see Roberts (1998: 66–9).
2   For the sake of establishing the broad sweep of my argument I have omitted here any reference to Habermas's important distinction between instrumental rationality and communicative rationality (Habermas, 1979, 1984). Habermas shares the worries that Weber, Adorno and Horkheimer express about the extension of instrumental, technical rationality into more and more areas of life. However, he deflects their melancholic conclusions about the emancipatory power of reason by (a) characterizing a broader form of rationality he calls communicative action, oriented not merely to success or failure, but to understanding between human actors; (b) identifying a valid sphere for instrumental rationality, in terms of the relations between humans and nature; and (c) explaining the dystopian features of modernity in terms of the invasion of instrumental rationality into areas of life properly co-ordinated through communicative action. He thus preserves an Enlightenment belief in reason's power and beneficence in a way which more or less banishes technical reasoning from the social sphere, but at the same time leaves technology and science as the only legitimate way to deal with nature.

Chapter 2   Nature, secularization and the transformation of the sacred

1   Elsewhere I use the example of Greenpeace's occupation of Shell's Brent Spar oil platform to argue that ritual can be seen as creating the sacred as well as being an appropriate response to it (Szerszynski, 2002a).
2   Indeed, 'profane' originally meant the space in front of the temple (*pro-fanum*).
3   Habermas similarly sees societal modernization as involving the clearer separation of different kinds of speech: representing facts ('the' world of external

nature); establishing legitimate interpersonal relations ('our' world of society); and expressing one's own subjectivity ('my' world of internal nature) (Habermas, 1979, 1984).

4   I am adapting Bellah's terminology in order to delineate and name the stages of this history.

5   As Peter Scott (2004) insightfully points out, orthodox understandings of monotheism do not strictly speaking imply a dualistic ontology. He points out that God's transcendence as understood in the doctrine of *creatio ex nihilo* is not one that marks an ontological boundary. The world is internally related to God in such a way that, if God's creatorly distinction from the world makes an appearance in the world, it does so not as a distinction within the world (which would imply an archaic understanding of the sacred), but as a demand to practical engagement.

6   Wars, for example, are no longer the defence of 'the juridical existence of sovereignty; at stake is the biological existence of a population'. And the death penalty is less to do with the enormity of the crime, of attacking the sovereign's will, than the incorrigibility of the criminal – their biological endangerment of others (Foucault, 1979: 137–8).

7   If pressed, I would advocate neither a materialist nor an idealist model of social change, but a hybrid of the two. It seems clear that sometimes ideas lag behind material and technological change, and sometimes vice versa. Similarly, whether contradictions at the level of ideas or of material practice are *perceived* to be contradictions, and hence provoke their own resolution, seems itself to depend on contextual factors both ideational and material. Besides, it is in principle highly problematic to separate the two: the material is always mediated in its effects by culture, and ideas and meanings take on and achieve agency through material form.

Chapter 3   Nature, science and the death of Pan

1   For example, Cox (1965: 22–4); Cox (1967); White (1968); McHarg (1969); Toynbee (1974).

2   See for example Attfield (1983a, 1983b), and the edited collections by Barbour (1972), Spring and Spring (1974) and Hargrove (1986).

3   Though emanationist images of the relationship between God and the world have often been employed as a corrective to the deistic tendencies of images of 'making' (Montefiore et al., 1975: 42).

4   To see nature as divine – as itself God or a god – is not the same as seeing it as containing gods or in some sense under a supernatural being's direct care.

5   Commentators frequently point to animistic or pantheistic cultures, such as the First Nations peoples of America (Reed, 1986) and ancient Greece (Hughes, 1986), or to Asian religions (Callicott and Ames, 1989) as possessing worldviews which by contrast limit environmental depredation.

6   Indeed, in England it was only in the eighteenth century that agriculture turned from a religious activity into a purely economic one, and the marketplace

governed not by ideas of moral obligation but by ideas of the market as 'natural law' (Tribe, 1978).

7 Arendt argues that the idea of the good life as consisting in material abundance is the mark of a society dominated by labouring, rather than by fabrication or action (Arendt, 1958: 126–34).

8 See Robinson (1946): 'The supreme miracle of the Old Testament is the historical development of the religion of Israel, and that is inseparable from the religious interpretation of Nature.'

9 On the Christian symbolic interpretation of trees in terms of the death and resurrection of Christ, see for example Schama (1995: 214–26).

10 Though see Osler (2001) for an argument that Boyle's mechanical philosophy also had space for teleology in nature.

11 It should be pointed out that Bruno does not stand in the same voluntarist tradition as Newton and Boyle; his thought is strongly neo-Platonic, seeing God as immanent in the universe, a first principle guiding its necessary but multiplex unfolding, and matter as active and itself divine. Dupré (1993: 64) argues that once modern scientific thought abandoned the idea of a transcendent, sovereign creator, and nature became seen as self-sufficient, Bruno's neo-Platonic ideas were revived to account for nature's self-organizing powers.

Chapter 4   Modern technology and the sacred

1 There is some evidence, however, that the religious sanctioning of the transformation of nature came after the event, rather than driving it (Coleman, 1976).

2 Though see criticisms of the Merton thesis by Harrison (1998: 5–6) and Morgan (1999).

3 It is possible that Foucault was influenced by Hannah Arendt's earlier analysis of modern society as 'the public organization of the life process' (Arendt, 1958: 46; see also Agamben, 1998).

4 In the rest of the book I will follow the normal practice of using 'biopolitics' to cover both of these sets of practices.

5 Ellul can be read as arguing for a kind of technological determinism – as if technological development follows a predestined path, and thence ineluctably shapes society (e.g. Winner, 1977). It is important for my own argument to reject this idea – to insist that modern technology is a contingent, genuinely historical phenomenon. Yet Ellul himself insists that modern technology is the result of a stake or bet – *The Technological Society* was originally published as *La Technique: L'enjeu du Siècle* ('Technique: the stake of the century'). Technology for Ellul is a gamble made by modern humanity – the gamble that it would be better or even possible to replace the 'natural attitude' towards objects with a technological attitude – and as such could be otherwise (Mitcham, 1994: 60).

6 See previous note.

Chapter 5   The body, healing and the sacred

1   In her study of *Ritual Healing in Suburban America*, Meredith McGuire argues that in contrast to alternative forms of healing, orthodox medicine focuses on the disease entity, and 'unknowingly, reduces the patient's ability to mobilize personal resources against the disease/illness' (McGuire, 1988: 16).

2   Comparative studies have shown that the use of complementary and alternative medicine seems to be on the increase. Thomas et al.'s pilot study in 1993 found 8.5 per cent of the adult population had seen a practitioner for one of the six main therapies in the past 12 months, compared to 10.6 per cent in 1998 – a 25 per cent growth in the proportion of the population using alternative medicine over five years (Thomas et al., 2001). Eisenberg et al. (1998) found an even larger rise in the USA; repeating the same survey in 1990 and 1997, they found a 25 per cent growth in the probability of a respondent having used at least one of sixteen alternative therapies in the last year – from 33.8 per cent to 42.1 per cent. In terms of the use of practitioner-administered therapies there was an increase of 59 per cent – from 12.3 per cent to 19.5 per cent. Measured in terms of numbers of visits to alternative medicine practitioners, the increase was 47 per cent, with most increase being observed in the use of herbal medicine, massage, megavitamins, self-help groups, folk remedies, energy healing and homeopathy.

3   Such as the idea that the late twentieth century has seen an Easternization of Western culture, a shift from transcendental dualism to monism (Campbell, 1999).

4   Fulder acknowledges that not all of these might equally apply to every therapy.

5   See Good (1994) for an anthropological approach to the study of illness and healing in terms of narrative.

6   'The Kendal Project: Patterns of the Sacred in Contemporary Society', funded by the Leverhulme Trust. Paul Heelas, Linda Woodhead and I were the principal investigators, and Ben Seel and Karin Tusting the researchers on the ground. I am grateful to all my colleagues on that project for stimulating discussions on healing and on the changing nature of religion and spirituality. For more information on the project, go to www.kendalproject.org.uk.

7   Similar kinds of argument in terms of cultural change are suggested by Douglas (1994: 23), who sees vegetarianism, new religions, environmentalism and complementary medicine as part of a general 'option for gentleness' in post-1960s culture.

Chapter 6   The birth of 'the environment'

1   From this perspective the miracles of Christ can be seen as the closing act of the archaic sacred.

2   Arendt (1958: 47) argues that the very tendency of 'growth' in modern, capitalist society evidences how much of its character is determined by the eruption of

natural processes into the human world, in the form of labouring, consuming, and the administration of life.

3   See Brooke (2004) on how the early Royal Society presented experimental science as an means of consensus and social cohesion in an age of religious conflict.

4   Although not always perhaps in the most responsible way – Evelyn recommended that most British iron production be transplanted to New England, to prevent the exhaustion of British timber supplies (Merchant, 1980: 239).

5   The discourse of rarity, of course, has always been interwoven with less formalistic criteria for the different evaluation of species. Even in humanitarian discourse, large, spectacular and aesthetically pleasing animals have always tended to receive more concern than others. The particular choice of criteria seems to relate to wider social change. For example, with the founding of national parks in southern Africa in the inter-war years, and the subsequent shift from hunting to tourism, sporting characteristics gave way to viewability as the dominant criterion of animal attractiveness, with a pronounced re-evaluation of the lion in particular (MacKenzie, 1988: 267). But rarity has had an enduring place among these criteria – indeed, endangeredness can itself contribute greatly to the perception of an animal as dramatic.

6   'Unlike Nature and the game-preserver, [collectors] concentrated their destructive power on the rare, and as the number fell so the value of each specimen rose and the stimulus for collecting it increased' (Sheail, 1976: 8).

7   Live trophies, on display in London Zoo, also effectively served as an 'emblem of British dominion over its colonial empire' (Ritvo, 1990: 231). On the individual and class level, Xenos (1989: 86) places the general rise of interest in exotic goods in the nineteenth century against the background of the emergence of a bourgeois society where the overt display of wealth was the main route to social standing.

8   'In most British colonies', MacKenzie reports, 'Africans were excluded from hunting', but even Europeans 'were divided into categories for the issue of licences' (1988: 209).

9   I do not mean to imply that mass extinctions are not really happening, just that this is only one way to represent nature as under threat, and one which has particular reasons for its prominence.

10 Of course, the symbolic has had a strong influence on which endangered species have been the objects of most concern – notably 'the large and dramatic animals such as the whale and the rhinoceros' (Hays, 1987: 209–10).

11 See Nicholas Green on nineteenth-century France: according to Green, 'nature,' for the Parisian bourgeoisie of the time, 'described a structured mode of apprehension, both of the world and of oneself'. Such a communing with nature 'though private, even solitary, … was a profoundly *social* relationship, organised and regulated through ideologies of looking which placed the spectator in relation to the social dynamics of metropolitan class and gender' (Green, 1990: 71).

Chapter 7   The politicization of nature

1 This is not a criticism of non-Western environmentalism; however, it does imply a criticism of Western environmentalists who project their own highly moralized and abstract understanding of environmentalism onto indigenous movements.
2 See Stevens (1989) for an account of the role of psychoactive drugs in the cultural change of the 1960s, and Keniston (1971) and Martin (1981) for more general accounts.
3 Although, of course, the growth of the service sector, especially the 'expressive professions' in education and social services makes the distinction less strong.
4 For studies of the 1970s new religious movements from this perspective, see Westley (1978, 1983) and Robertson and Chirico (1985). For an analysis of global environmental concern, see Beyer (1992).
5 This was not the case with the early CPRE, which originated in a Utopian planning movement. But with the post-war institutionalization of the national planning system for which CPRE was largely responsible, CPRE became an organization with more limited, defensive goals.
6 Of course, neo-Platonic theology is not *wholly* immanentist; however, I do not have the space here to systematically defend the expedient simplification of my argument at this point.

Chapter 8   Nature, virtue and everyday life

1 For a theological critique of deep ecology, see Scott (2003, ch. 3).
2 The study was funded by the ESRC (award number L320253188), and was carried out at the Centre for the Study of Environmental Change, Lancaster University, by myself and Robin Grove-White. Each focus group consisted of between six and nine people, and met for two $1\frac{1}{2}$ hour sessions on separate evenings. All of the focus groups – the vegetarians and the animal rights activists, but also the groups convened for the other case studies on cycling and health – were moderated by myself, and followed broadly the same 'topic guide'. This led the discussion through various aspects of movement membership and practice. A key element of this was the work the participants completed in the week between the two sessions. Here they were asked to write on up to five pieces of card different reasons why they stayed involved in the movement – in this case, why they stayed vegetarian or why they remained involved in animal rights activism. At the beginning of the second session, 30–40 minutes were set aside for the group to sort the cards on the floor into a pattern, by grouping reasons which they felt were similar or related, and to discuss the pattern. Both groups were of mixed gender.
3 Of course, the vegan diet, like other alternative lifestyle choices, also involves significant *inclusions*, equally loaded with symbolic value – in this case items

such as tofu, seeds and home-grown vegetables (Dave Horton, personal communication).

4 It is important not to deny the significant vegetarian strands of other religions, especially Hinduism and Buddhism (Walters and Portmess, 2001), but space does not allow an exploration of the different meanings of meat avoidance in different religions. Here I am using vegetarianism in order to explore the meaning that such lifestyle choices have in the West in the context of its own religious history.

5 I am not interested here in identifying what the higher mode of moral existence is. My point is simply to explore the moral phenomenology involved in the ethical avoidance of meat in the contemporary West, and its dependency on particular orderings of the sacred. Beside which, it is debatable whether the idea of a highest substantive (and hence in principle achievable) moral code is consistent with the sort of social distancing I am describing here.

6 The distinction between the idealist saint–hero and the idealist hero is one that broadly corresponds to that frequently made (though often exaggerated) between what have been called the new social movements, with their more prefigurative, anarchistic praxis, and earlier revolutionary social movements, in which the emphasis was less on the living out of normative principles in the present, and more on sheer political effectiveness – see the next chapter for further discussion of this distinction.

7 Keith Tester captures some of the quality of this mundanity in his description of animal rights as appearing as a universal, self-evident truth to its adherents. However, he goes beyond a phenomenological approach when he sociologically reduces this to the status of a projection or 'fetish' (1991: 172–3).

8 On the contemporary understanding of ill health as something, like the trials of early modern peasant life, that must always be explicable, even if this is by reference to something invisible, see Coward (1989).

Chapter 9 Nature and public speech

1 Stoll also points out that the great moral exemplar Albert Schweitzer was also a Lutheran (Stoll, 1997: 185).

2 For more information on Thoreau, including the full text of 'Civil Disobedience', see www.transcendentalists.com/1thorea.html.

3 For more on Gandhi, see http://web.mahatma.org.in/index.jsp.

4 The version of this that is dramatized in pageant form in the environmentalist roadshows that Taylor describes is projected forward into a future in which feral humans rise up to dismantle the machinery of oppression. For critiques of the idea of primal societies as socially peaceful and ecologically benign, see for example Bradford (1987), Lewis (1992), Luke (1988) and Mellor (1989).

5 Boggs specifically cites Petra Kelly of the Greens as arguing that violence corrupts and undermines legitimacy (1986: 201).

6   At the only point where Pepper allows that there are reasons for joining communes other than the desire for social change, these are described tendentiously
as 'self-seeking' (1991: 54–5).
7   On this distinction between prophecy and apocalyptic, see for example Dodd
(1961) and Ladd (1966).
8   See www.earthcharter.org.

Chapter 10   The global sacred

1   22727 and Earthrise can be viewed by searching for 22727 and 2383 respectively at the NASA JSC Digital Image Collection at http://images.jsc.nasa.gov/.
2   On the analysis of natural history television as employing a mimetic rhetoric
through certain conventional representational devices, see Silverstone (1984).
3   See http://nctn.hq.nasa.gov/innovation/Innovation_84/wnewview.html for a
fuller NASA account of the reception of the image.
4   The full essay is available at: http://cecelia.physics.indiana.edu/life/moon/
Apollo8/122568sci-nasa-macleish.html.
5   There are parallels here with the experience in the United States over the management of deer in the Grand Canyon National Game Preserve in the 1920s
(Worster, 1977: 270).
6   The project, 'Global Citizenship and the Environment,' ran from November
1996 to April 1999, and was supported by the ESRC (award number
R000236768). I would like to thank my colleagues on that project, John Urry,
Greg Myers and Mark Toogood, for the many discussions we had during the
project, discussions which have informed the ideas in this chapter.
7   We conducted a survey of 24 hours of broadcast output on four television
channels available in the United Kingdom: BBC2, one of the two public service
channels paid for by licence fees; ITV, the network of regional UK commercial
terrestrial broadcasters; Channel 4, the national terrestrial television channel
focusing on arts and public affairs programmes and minority interests not provided for on ITV; and CNN, the international satellite news network, based in
Atlanta, but broadcasting throughout the world.
8   The *Soul of Britain* survey was conducted by the Opinion Research Business
(ORB) for the BBC, 1000 telephone interviews being carried out in May 2000.
I would like to thank Gordon Heald of ORB for making available data and
cross-tabulations from the survey.
9   On the concept of globality, see Albrow (1996).

Chapter 11   Nature, technology and the sacred: a postscript

1   Just before completing this book, in February 2004, the bay was again pro-
pelled to international significance by the tragic deaths of Chinese migrant
cockle pickers.

2 See also Fuller (1989), who also connects the development of alternative medicine with aspects of the American religious tradition.
3 For example, see Lyng (1990) for an explicitly Hegelian account of the holistic health movement as a countersystem to orthodox medicine, negating all the characteristics of the latter but thus remaining dependent on it.

References

Adorno, Theodor W. and Horkheimer, Max (1997) *Dialectic of Enlightenment*. Trans. Cumming, John, Verso, London.

Agamben, Giorgio (1998) *Homo Sacer: Sovereign Power and Bare Life*. Trans. Heller-Roazen, Daniel, Stanford University Press, Stanford, CA.

Ahlstrand, Kajsa (2001) Spirituality at the Margins. In: Brosseder, Johannes (ed.) *Verborgener Gott – Verborgene Kirche? Die Kenotische Theologie Und Ihre Ekklesiologischen Implikationen*. Verlag W. Kohlhammer, Stuttgart, pp. 213–17.

Albanese, Catherine L. (1990) *Nature Religion in America: From the Algonkian Indians to the New Age*. University of Chicago Press, Chicago.

Albrow, Martin (1996) *The Global Age: State and Society beyond Modernity*. Polity Press, Cambridge.

Alexander, Jeffrey C. and Smith, Philip (1996) Social Science and Salvation: Risk Society as Mythical Discourse. *Zeitschrift für Sociologie* **25** (4), 251–62.

Allen, Gillian and Wallis, Roy (1992) Pentecostalists as a Medical Minority. In: Saks, Mike (ed.) *Alternative Medicine in Britain*. Clarendon Press, Oxford, pp. 154–65.

Anderson, Benedict (1983) *Imagined Communities: Reflections on the Origin and Spread of Nationalism*. Verso, London.

Ansell, Vera, Coates, Chris, Dawling, Pam, How, Jonathan, Morris, William and Wood, Andy (1989) *Diggers and Dreamers: The 1990/91 Guide to Communal Living*. Communes Network, Townhead, Dunford Bridge, Sheffield.

Anyinam, Charles (1990) Alternative Medicine in Western Industrialized Countries: An Agenda for Medical Geography. *The Canadian Geographer* **34** (1), 69–76.

Arendt, Hannah (1958) *The Human Condition*. University of Chicago Press, Chicago.

Ashby, Eric (1978) *Reconciling Man with the Environment*. Oxford University Press, London.

Astin, J. A. (1998) Why Patients Use Alternative Medicine: Results of a National Survey. *Journal of the American Medical Association* **279** (19), 1548–53.

Attfield, Robin (1983a) *The Ethics of Environmental Concern*. Blackwell Publishers, Oxford.

Attfield, Robin (1983b) Western Traditions and Environmental Ethics. In: Elliot, Robert and Gare, Arran (eds.) *Environmental Philosophy: A Collection of Readings*. Open University Press, Milton Keynes, pp. 201–30.

Augustine, Saint (1960–72) *The City of God against the Pagans*. Vols. 1–7, trans. McCracken, G. E. et al., Heinemann, London.

Bacon, Francis (1960) *The Advancement of Learning, and New Atlantis*. Oxford University Press, London.

Bailey, Edward Ian (1998) *Implicit Religion: An Introduction*. Middlesex University Press, London.

Barbour, Ian G. (ed.) (1972) *Earth might be Fair: Reflections on Ethics, Religion and Ecology*. Prentice-Hall, Englewood Cliffs, NJ.

Barfield, Owen (1954) *History in English Words*. New edn., Faber and Faber, London.

Barr, James (1974) Man and Nature: The Ecological Controversy and the Old Testament. In: Spring, David and Spring, Eileen (eds.) *Ecology and Religion in History*. Harper and Row, New York, pp. 48–72.

Barrell, John (1980) *The Dark Side of the Landscape*. Cambridge University Press, Cambridge.

Barthes, Roland (1973) *Mythologies*. Trans. Lavers, Annette, Paladin, London.

Bate, Jonathan (1991) *Romantic Ecology: Wordsworth and the Environmental Tradition*. Routledge, London.

Bateson, Gregory (1991) *A Sacred Unity: Further Steps to an Ecology of Mind*. Harper-Collins, New York.

Bateson, Gregory and Bateson, Mary Catherine (1987) *Angels Fear: Towards an Epistemology of the Sacred*. Macmillan, New York.

Bauman, Zygmunt (1993) *Postmodern Ethics*. Blackwell Publishers, Oxford.

Bauman, Zygmunt (1998) Postmodern Religion? In: Heelas, Paul (ed.) *Religion, Modernity and Postmodernity*. Blackwell Publishers, Oxford, pp. 55–78.

Bauman, Zygmunt (2001) *Community: Seeking Safety in an Uncertain World*. Polity Press, Cambridge.

Beardsworth, Alan and Keil, Teresa (1992) The Vegetarian Option: Varieties, Conversions, Motives and Careers. *Sociological Review* **40** (2), 253–93.

Beardsworth, Alan and Keil, Teresa (1993) Contemporary Vegetarianism in the UK: Challenge and Incorporation. *Appetite* **20**, 229–34.

Beck, Ulrich (1992) *Risk Society: Towards a New Modernity*. Trans. Ritter, Mark, Sage, London.

Beck, Ulrich (1995) *Ecological Politics in an Age of Risk*. Trans. Weisz, Amos, Polity, Cambridge.

Beck, Ulrich (1996) Risk Society and the Provident State. In: Lash, Scott, Szerszynski, Bronislaw and Wynne, Brian (eds.) *Risk, Environment and Modernity: Towards a New Ecology*. Trans. Chalmers, Martin, Sage, London, pp. 27–43.

Beck, Ulrich (1998) *Democracy without Enemies*. Trans. Ritter, Mark, Polity, Cambridge.

Beck, Ulrich (2000) The Cosmopolitan Perspective: On the Sociology of the Second Age of Modernity. *British Journal of Sociology* 51 (1), 79–106.

Beckford, James A. (1989) *Religion and Advanced Industrial Societies*. Unwin Hyman, London.

Bell, Daniel (1977) The Return of the Sacred? The Argument on the Future of Religion. *British Journal of Sociology* 28 (4), 419–49.

Bell, Daniel (1979) *The Cultural Contradictions of Capitalism*. 2nd edn., Heinemann, London.

Bellah, Robert N. (1970) Religious Evolution. In: *Beyond Belief: Essays on Religion in a Post-traditional World*. Harper & Row, New York, pp. 20–50.

Bennett, Jane (1997) The Enchanted World of Modernity: Paracelcus, Kant and Deleuze. *Cultural Values* 1 (1), 1–28.

Berman, Morris (1981) *The Reenchantment of the World*. Cornell University Press, Ithaca, NY.

Berry, Thomas (1990) *The Dream of the Earth*. Sierra Club Books, San Francisco.

Beyer, Peter (1992) The Global Environment as a Religious Issue: A Sociological Analysis. *Religion* 22 (1), 1–19.

Beyer, Peter (1994) *Religion and Globalization*. Sage, London.

Beyer, Peter (1998) Globalisation and the Religion of Nature. In: Pearson, Joanne, Roberts, Richard H. and Samuel, Geoffrey (eds.) *Nature Religion Today: Paganism in the Modern World*. Edinburgh University Press, Edinburgh, pp. 11–21.

Billig, Michael (1995) *Banal Nationalism*. Sage, London.

Blum, Lawrence A. (1988) Moral Exemplars: Reflections on Schindler, the Trocmes, and Others. In: French, Peter A., Uehling, Theodore E. jun. and Wettstein, Howard K. (eds.) *Midwest Studies in Philosophy*. Vol. 13, *Ethical Theory: Character and Virtue*. University of Notre Dame Press, Notre Dame, pp. 196–221.

Boggs, Carl (1986) *Social Movements and Political Power: Emerging Forms of Radicalism in the West*. Temple University Press, Philadelphia.

Borgmann, Albert (1984) *Technology and the Character of Contemporary Life: A Philosophical Inquiry*. University of Chicago Press, Chicago, IL.

Bossy, John (1985) *Christianity in the West 1400–1700*. Oxford University Press, Oxford.

Bourdieu, Pierre (1977) *Outline of a Theory of Practice*. Trans. Nice, Richard, Cambridge University Press, Cambridge.

Bourdieu, Pierre (1984) *Distinction: A Social Critique of the Judgement of Taste*. Trans. Nice, Richard, Routledge and Kegan Paul, London.

Braathen, Espen (1996) Communicating the Individual Body and the Body Politic: The Discourse on Disease Prevention and Health Promotion in Alternative Therapies. In: Cant, Sarah and Sharma, Ursula (eds.) *Complementary and Alternative Medicines: Knowledge in Practice*. Free Association Books, London, pp. 151–62.

Bradford, George (1987) How Deep is Deep Ecology? A Challenge to Radical Environmentalism. *The Fifth Estate* 22 (3), 5–30.

Bramwell, Anna (1989) *Ecology in the Twentieth Century: A History*. Yale University Press, New Haven.

Brooke, John (2004) Science and Religious Dissent: Some Historiographical Issues. In: Wood, Paul (ed.) *Science and Religious Dissent*. Oxford University Press, Oxford.

Brown, Peter (1981) *The Cult of the Saints: Its Rise and Function in Latin Christianity*. SCM Press, London.

Brown, Peter (1987) The Saint as Exemplar in Late Antiquity. In: Hawley, John Stratton (ed.) *Saints and Virtues*. University of California Press, Berkeley, California, pp. 3–14.

Brubaker, Rogers (1984) *The Limits of Rationality: An Essay on the Social and Moral Thought of Max Weber*. George Allen and Unwin, London.

Bruce, Steve (2002) *God is Dead: Secularization in the West*. Blackwell Publishing, Oxford.

Brunkhorst, Hauke (2000) Equality and Elitism in Arendt. In: Villa, Dana (ed.) *The Cambridge Companion to Hannah Arendt*. Cambridge University Press, Cambridge, pp. 178–98.

Burgess, Jacquelin (1990) The Production and Consumption of Environmental Meanings in the Mass Media: A Research Agenda for the 1990s. *Transactions, Institute of British Geographers* **15** (2), 139–61.

Burgess, Jacquelin (1993) Representing Nature: Conservation and the Mass Media. In: Warren, F. B. and Goldsmith, A. (ed.) *Conservation in Progress*. John Wiley, Chichester, pp. 51–64.

Burgess, Jacquelin, Goldsmith, Barrie and Harrison, Carolyn (1990) Pale Shadows for Policy: Reflections on the Greenwich Open Space Project. In: Burgess, Robert G. (ed.) *Studies in Qualitative Methodology*. Vol. 2, JAI Press, Greenwich, Connecticut, pp. 141–67.

Burke, Edmund (1968) *Reflections on the Revolution in France, and on the Proceedings in Certain Societies in London Relative to that Event*. Ed. O'Brien, Conor Cruise, Penguin, Harmondsworth.

Burke, Edmund (1987) *A Philosophical Enquiry into the Origin of our Ideas of the Sublime and Beautiful*. Rev. edn., ed. Boulton, James T., Blackwell Publishers, Oxford.

Burrell, David B. (1983) The Spirit and the Christian Life. In: Hodgson, Peter and King, Robert (eds.) *Christian Theology: An Introduction to its Traditions and Tasks*. SPCK, London.

Burton-Christie, Douglas (1993) *The Word in the Desert: Scripture and the Quest for Holiness in Early Christian Monasticism*. Oxford University Press, New York.

Button, John (1989) *How to be Green*. Friends of the Earth/Century Hutchinson, London.

Callicott, J. Baird (1994) *Earth's Insights: A Survey of Ecological Ethics from the Mediterranean Basin to the Australian Outback*. University of California Press, Berkeley.

Callicott, J. Baird and Ames, Roger T. (eds.) (1989) *Nature in Asian Traditions of Thought: Essays in Environmental Philosophy*. State University of New York Press, Albany.

Campbell, Colin (1972) The Cult, the Cultic Milieu and Secularization. *A Sociological Yearbook of Religion in Britain* **5**, 119–36.

Campbell, Colin (1987) *The Romantic Ethic and the Spirit of Modern Consumerism*. Blackwell Publishers, Oxford.

Campbell, Colin (1999) The Easternization of the West. In: Wilson, Bryan and Cresswell, Jamie (eds.) *New Religious Movements: Challenge and Response*. Routledge, London, pp. 35–48.

Camporesi, Piero (1988) *The Incorruptible Flesh: Bodily Mutation and Mortification in Religion and Folklore*. Trans. Elsom, Tania and Croft-Murray, Helen, Cambridge University Press, Cambridge.

Cant, Sarah (1996) From Charismatic Teaching to Professional Training: The Legitimation of Knowledge and the Creation of Trust in Homeopathy and Chiropractic. In: Cant, Sarah and Sharma, Ursula (eds.) *Complementary and Alternative Medicines: Knowledge in Practice*. Free Association Books, London, pp. 44–65.

Capra, Fritjof (1975) *The Tao of Physics: An Exploration of the Parallels between Modern Physics and Eastern Mysticism*. Wildwood House, London.

Capra, Fritjof (1983) *The Turning Point: Science, Society and the Rising Culture*. Flamingo, London.

Carson, Rachel (1965) *Silent Spring*. Penguin, Harmondsworth.

Castells, Manuel (1997) *The Power of Identity – the Information Age: Economy, Society and Culture*. Vol 2, Blackwell Publishers, Malden, MD.

Cheney, Jim (1989) The Neo-Stoicism of Radical Environmentalism. *Environmental Ethics* 11 (4), 293–325.

Clark, Nigel (2003) Feral Ecologies: Performing Life on the Colonial Periphery. In: Szerszynski, Bronislaw, Heim, Wallace and Waterton, Claire (eds.) *Nature Performed: Environment, Culture and Performance*. Blackwell/Sociological Review, Oxford, pp. 163–82.

Clark, Stephen R. L. (1984) *The Moral Status of Animals*. Oxford University Press, Oxford.

Coleman, William (1976) Providence, Capitalism and Environmental Degradation: English Apologetics in an Era of Economic Revolution. *Journal of the History of Ideas* 37(1), 27–44.

Collingwood, R. G. (1945) *The Idea of Nature*. Clarendon Press, Oxford.

Commoner, Barry (1963) *Science and Survival*. Viking Press, New York.

Cosgrove, Denis (1994) Contested Global Visions: *One-World, Whole-Earth*, and the Apollo Space Photographs. *Annals of the Association of American Geographers* 84 (2), 270–94.

Coward, Rosalind (1989) *The Whole Truth: The Myth of Alternative Medicine*. Faber and Faber, London.

Cox, Harvey (1965) *The Secular City: Secularization and Urbanization in Theological Perspective*. SCM Press, London.

Cox, Harvey (1967) *On not Leaving it to the Snake*. Macmillan, New York.

Crawford, Robert (1980) Healthism and the Medicalization of Everyday Life. *International Journal of Health Services* 10 (3), 365–87.

Cronon, William (1983) *Changes in the Land: Indians, Colonists, and the Ecology of New England*. Hill and Wang, New York.

Crook, Stephen (1991) *Modernist Radicalism and its Aftermath: Foundationalism and Anti-foundationalism in Radical Social Theory.* Routledge, London.

Dale, Stephen (1996) *McLuhan's Children: The Greenpeace Message and the Media.* Between the Lines, Toronto.

Daly, Robert W. (1970) The Specters of Technicism. *Psychiatry* **33** (4), 417–32.

Darier, Éric (1999) Foucault and the Environment: An Introduction. In: Darier, Éric (ed.) *Discourses of the Environment.* Blackwell Publishers, Oxford, pp. 1–33.

Darley, Gillian (1978) *Villages of Vision.* Paladin, Frogmore, St Albans.

Davis, Natalie Zemon (1981) The Sacred and the Body Social in Sixteenth Century Lyons. *Past and Present* **90**, 40–70.

Dayan, Daniel and Katz, Elihu (1992) *Media Events: The Live Broadcasting of History.* Harvard University Press, Cambridge, MA.

Deason, Gary B. (1986) Reformation Theology and the Mechanistic Conception of Nature. In: Lindberg, David C. and Numbers, Ronald L. (eds.) *God and Nature: Historical Essays on the Encounter between Christianity and Science.* University of California Press, Berkeley, pp. 167–91.

Dennis, John (1693) *Miscellanies in Verse and Prose.* James Knapton, London.

Descartes, René (1968) *Discourse on Method and the Meditations.* Trans. Sutcliffe, F. E., Penguin, Harmondsworth.

Descola, Philippe (1992) Societies of Nature and the Nature of Societies. In: Kuper, A. (ed.) *Conceptualizing Society.* Routledge, London, pp. 107–26.

Descola, Philippe (1994) *In the Society of Nature: A Native Ecology in Amazonia.* Cambridge University Press, Cambridge.

Descola, Philippe and Pálsson, Gísli (1996) *Nature and Society: Anthropological Perspectives.* Routledge, London.

Detienne, Marcel and Vernant, Jean Pierre (1989) *The Cuisine of Sacrifice among the Greeks.* University of Chicago Press, Chicago.

Dietz, Thomas, Frisch, Ann Stirling, Kalof, Linda, Stern, Paul C. and Guagnano, Gregory A. (1995) Values and Vegetarianism: An Explanatory Analysis. *Rural Sociology* **60** (3), 522–42.

Dodd, Charles Harold (1961) *The Parables of the Kingdom.* Rev. edn., Nisbet, Welwyn, Hertfordshire.

Doherty, Brian (1996) Paving the Way: The Rise of Direct Action against Road-Building and the Changing Character of British Environmentalism. Paper presented to the conference Alternative Futures and Popular Protest II, Manchester Metropolitan University, 26–8 March.

Doherty, Brian (1997) Tactical Innovation and the Protest Repertoire in the Radical Ecology Movement in Britain. Paper presented to the European Sociological Association Conference, Essex University, 27–30 August.

Doherty, Brian (2000) Manufactured Vulnerability: Protest Camp Tactics. In: Seel, Benjamin, Paterson, Matthew and Doherty, Brian (eds.) *Direct Action in British Environmentalism.* Routledge, London, pp. 62–78.

Douglas, Mary (1975) Environments at Risk. In: *Implicit Meanings: Essays in Anthropology.* Routledge and Kegan Paul, London, pp. 230–48.

Douglas, Mary (1994) The Construction of the Physician: A Cultural Approach to Medical Fashions. In: Budd, Susan and Sharma, Ursula (eds.) *The Healing Bond: The Patient–Practitioner Relationship and Therapeutic Responsibility.* Routledge, London, pp. 23–41.

Duff, Kat (1994) *The Alchemy of Illness.* Virago, London.

Duffy, Eamon (1992) *The Stripping of the Altars: Traditional Religion in England, c.1400–c.1580.* Yale University Press, New Haven.

Dupré, Louis (1993) *Passage to Modernity: An Essay in the Hermeneutics of Nature and Culture.* Yale University Press, New Haven.

Durkheim, Emile (1915) *The Elementary Forms of the Religious Life: A Study in Religious Sociology.* Allen & Unwin, London.

Durkheim, Emile (1969) Individualism and the Intellectuals. *Political Studies* **17** (1), 14–30.

Eder, Klaus (1996) *The Social Construction of Nature: A Sociology of Ecological Enlightenment.* Sage, London.

Ehrlichman (1989) Fakes Warning to Green Buyers. *Guardian*, 28 September, 3.

Eisenberg, D. M., Davis, R. B., Ettner, S. L. et al. (1998) Trends in Alternative Medicine Use in the United States, 1990–1997. Results of a Follow-up National Survey. *Journal of the American Medical Association* **280** (18), 1569–75.

Eisenberg, David (2001) Complementary and Alternative Medicine Use in the United States: Epidemiology and Trends 1990–2000. In: Ernst, Edzard, Pittler, Max H., Stevinson, Clare and White, Adrian (eds.) *The Desktop Guide to Complementary and Alternative Medicine: An Evidence-Based Approach.* Mosby, Edinburgh, pp. 374–87.

Ekirch, Arthur A. (1963) *Man and Nature in America.* Columbia University Press, New York.

Eliade, Mircea (1954) *The Myth of the Eternal Return or, Cosmos and History.* Trans. Trask, Willard R., Princeton University Press, Princeton, NJ.

Elias, Norbert (1978) *The Civilizing Process.* Vol. 1, *The History of Manners.* Blackwell Publishers, Oxford.

Elkington, John and Burke, Tom (1987) *The Green Capitalists: How to Make Money – and Protect the Environment.* Victor Gollancz, London.

Elkington, John and Hailes, Julia (1988) *The Green Consumer Guide.* Victor Gollancz, London.

Elkington, John, Burke, Tom and Hailes, Julia (1988) *Green Pages: The Business of Saving the World.* Routledge, London.

Ellul, Jacques (1964) *The Technological Society.* Trans. Wilkinson, John, Vintage, New York.

Ernst, Edzard and White, Andrew (2000) The BBC Survey of Complementary Medicine Use in the UK. *Complementary Therapies in Medicine* **8** (1), 32–6.

Eyerman, Ron and Jamison, Andrew (1991) *Social Movements: A Cognitive Approach.* Polity Press, Cambridge.

Faure, Bernard (1991) *The Rhetoric of Immediacy: A Cultural Critique of Chan/Zen Buddhism.* Princeton University Press, Princeton.

Feenberg, Andrew (1999) *Questioning Technology.* Routledge, London.

Fenn, Richard (1982) *Liturgies and Trials.* Blackwell Publishers, Oxford.

Fenn, Richard K. (1978) *Toward a Theory of Secularization.* Society for the Scientific Study of Religion, Storrs, CT.

Ferré, Frederick (1986) Introduction. In: Hargrove, Eugene C. (ed.) *Religion and Environmental Crisis.* University of Georgia Press, Athens, GA, pp. 1–6.

Fischer, Louis (1951) *The Life of Mahatma Gandhi.* Jonathan Cape, London.

Foster, M. B. (1973) The Christian Doctrine of Creation and the Rise of Modern Science. In: Russell, Colin A. (ed.) *Science and Religious Belief: A Selection of Recent Historical Studies.* University of London Press, London, pp. 294–315.

Foucault, Michel (1970) *The Order of Things: An Archaeology of the Human Sciences.* Tavistock, London.

Foucault, Michel (1976) *The Birth of the Clinic: An Archaeology of Medical Perception.* Trans. Sheridan, Alan, Tavistock, London.

Foucault, Michel (1977) *Discipline and Punish: The Birth of the Prison.* Trans. Sheridan, Alan, Allen Lane, London.

Foucault, Michel (1979) *The History of Sexuality.* Vol. 1, *An Introduction.* Trans. Hurley, Robert, Allen Lane, London.

Foucault, Michel (1986) *The History of Sexuality.* Vol. 3, *The Care of the Self.* Trans. Hurley, Robert, Penguin, Harmondsworth.

Foucault, Michel (1988) Technologies of the Self. In: Martin, Luther H., Gutman, Huck, and Hutton, Patrick H. (eds.) *Technologies of the Self: A Seminar with Michel Foucault.* University of Massachusetts Press, Amherst, Mass, pp. 16–49.

Franklin, Adrian (2001) *Nature and Social Theory.* Sage, London.

Franklin, Sarah, Stacey, Jackie and Lury, Celia (2000) *Global Nature, Global Culture: Gender, Race, and Life Itself.* Sage, London.

Freeman, Rich (1994) *Forests and the Folk: Perceptions of Nature in the Swidden Regimes of Highland Malabar.* Pondy Papers in Social Sciences, 15. French Institute of Pondicherry, Pondicherry, India.

French, Peter A., Uehling, Theodore E. jun. and Wettstein, Howard K. (1988) *Midwest Studies in Philosophy.* Vol. 13, *Ethical Theory: Character and Virtue.* University of Notre Dame Press, Notre Dame.

Freund, Peter E. S. and McGuire, Meredith B. (1995) *Health, Illness and the Body: A Critical Sociology.* Prentice Hall, Englewood Cliffs, NJ.

Freund, Peter S. and Fisher, Miriam (1982) *The Civilized Body: Social Domination, Control, and Health.* Temple University Press, Philadelphia.

Fulder, Stephen (1995) Natural Health and Healthy Nature: The Neo-Hippocratic Revolution in Alternative Medicine. In: Johannessen, Helle, Olesen, Søren Gosvig and Andersen, Jørgen Østergåd (eds.) *Studies in Alternative Therapy 2: Body and Nature.* Odense University Press, Odense, pp. 50–64.

Fulder, Stephen (1996) *The Handbook of Alternative and Complementary Medicine.* 3rd edn., Oxford University Press, Oxford.

Fuller, Robert C. (1989) *Alternative Medicine and American Religious Life.* Oxford University Press, New York.

Funkenstein, Amos (1986) *Theology and the Scientific Imagination from the Middle Ages to the Seventeenth Century.* Princeton University Press, Princeton, NJ.

Fürer-Haimendorf, Christoph von (1967) *Morals and Merit: A Study of Values and Social Controls in South Asian Societies.* Weidenfeld & Nicolson, London.

Gadamer, Hans-Georg (1975) *Truth and Method*. Seabury Press, New York.

Gauchet, Marcel (1997) *The Disenchantment of the World: A Political History of Religion*. Trans. Burge, Oscar, Princeton University Press, Princeton, NJ.

Giddens, Anthony (1990) *The Consequences of Modernity*. Polity Press, Cambridge.

Giddens, Anthony (1991) *Modernity and Self-identity: Self and Society in the Late Modern Age*. Polity Press, Cambridge.

Glacken, Clarence J. (1967) *Traces on the Rhodian Shore: Nature and Culture in Western Thought from Ancient Times to the End of the Eighteenth Century*. University of California Press, Berkeley, California.

Gold, Mick (1984) A History of Nature. In: Allen, Doreen and Massey, John (eds.) *Geography Matters!* Cambridge University Press, Cambridge, pp. 12–33.

Goldberg, Vicky (1991) *The Power of Photography: How Photographs Changed our Lives*. Abbeville Press, New York.

Goldsmith, Edward, Allen, Robert, Allaby, Michael, Davoll, John and Lawrence, Sam (1972) Blueprint for Survival. *The Ecologist* **2** (1), 1–43.

Good, Byron J. (1994) *Medicine, Rationality, and Experience: An Anthropological Perspective*. Cambridge University Press, Cambridge.

Goody, Jack (1977) *The Domestication of the Savage Mind*. Cambridge University Press, Cambridge.

Gottlieb, Roger S. (1996) *This Sacred Earth: Religion, Nature, Environment*. Routledge, London.

Gouldner, Alvin W. (1979) *The Future of Intellectuals and the Rise of the New Class*. Macmillan, London.

Graham, Elaine L. (2002) *Representations of the Post/Human: Monsters, Aliens and Others in Popular Culture*. Manchester University Press, Manchester.

Grant, Edward (1986) Science and Theology in the Middle Ages. In: Lindberg, David C. and Numbers, Ronald L. (eds.) *God and Nature: Historical Essays on the Encounter between Christianity and Science*. University of California Press, Berkeley, pp. 49–75.

Green, Martin Burgess (1986) *The Origins of Nonviolence: Tolstoy and Gandhi in their Historical Settings*. Pennsylvania State University Press, University Park.

Green, Nicholas (1990) *The Spectacle of Nature: Landscape and Bourgeois Culture in Nineteenth-Century France*. Manchester University Press, Manchester.

Grove, Richard (1990) Threatened Islands, Threatened Earth: Early Professional Science and the Historical Origins of Global Environmental Concerns. In: Angell, David J. R., Wilkinson, Matthew L. N. and Cromer, Justyn D. (eds.) *Sustaining Earth: Response to the Environmental Threat*. Macmillan, New York.

Grove-White, Robin (1991) *The UK's Environmental Movement and UK Political Culture*. Centre for the Study of Environmental Change, Lancaster University, Lancaster.

Guha, Ramachandra and Martinez-Alier, Juan (1997) *Varieties of Environmentalism: Essays North and South*. Earthscan, London.

Habermas, Jürgen (1971a) *Knowledge and Human Interests*. Trans. Shapiro, Jeremy J., Beacon Press, Boston.

Habermas, Jürgen (1971b) *Toward a Rational Society.* Trans. Shapiro, Jeremy J., Heinemann, London.

Habermas, Jürgen (1979) *Communication and the Evolution of Society.* Trans. McCarthy, T., Beacon Press, Boston.

Habermas, Jürgen (1984) *The Theory of Communicative Action.* Vol. 1, *Reason and the Rationalization of Society.* Trans. McCarthy, Thomas, Heinemann, London.

Habermas, Jürgen (1987a) *The Philosophical Discourse of Modernity.* MIT Press, Cambridge, Mass.

Habermas, Jürgen (1987b) *The Theory of Communicative Action.* Vol. 2, *Critique of Functionalist Reason.* Trans. McCarthy, Thomas, Polity, Cambridge.

Hajer, Maarten (1996) Ecological Modernisation as Cultural Politics. In: Lash, Scott, Szerszynski, Bronislaw and Wynne, Brian (eds.) *Risk, Environment and Modernity: Towards a New Ecology.* Sage, London, pp. 246–68.

Halkier, Bente (2001) Routinisation or Reflexivity? Consumers and Normative Claims for Environmental Consideration. In: Gronow, K. and Warde, A. (eds.) *Ordinary Consumption.* Routledge, London.

Hamilton, Malcolm (2000) Eating Ethically: 'Spiritual' and 'Quasi-religious' Aspects of Vegetarianism. *Journal of Contemporary Religion* 15 (1), 65–83.

Hamilton, Malcolm, Waddington, Peter, Gregory, Susan and Walker, Ann (1995) Eat, Drink and be Saved: The Spiritual Significance of Alternative Diets. *Social Compass* 42 (4), 497–511.

Hand, Carl M. and Van Liere, Kent D. (1984) Religion, Mastery over Nature, and Environmental Concern. *Social Forces* 63 (2), 555–70.

Hardy, Dennis (1979) *Alternative Communities in Nineteenth Century England.* Longman, London.

Hargrove, Eugene C. (ed.) (1986) *Religion and Environmental Crisis.* University of Georgia Press, Athens, GA.

Harrison, Carolyn, Burgess, Jacquelin and Filius, Petra (1994) From Environmental Awareness to Environmental Action? unpublished report, Department of Geography, University College London.

Harrison, Peter (1998) *The Bible, Protestantism, and the Rise of Natural Science.* Cambridge University Press, Cambridge.

Harvey, David (1989) *The Condition of Postmodernity: An Enquiry into the Origins of Cultural Change.* Blackwell Publishers, Oxford.

Hawley, John Stratton (1987) Introduction: Saints and Virtues. In: Hawley, John Stratton (ed.) *Saints and Virtues.* University of California Press, Berkeley, California, pp. xi–xxiv.

Hays, Samuel P. (1969) *Conservation and the Gospel of Efficiency: The Progressive Conservation Movement 1890–1920.* Rev. edn., Atheneum, New York.

Hays, Samuel P. (1987) *Beauty, Health and Permanence: Environmental Politics in the United States.* Cambridge University Press, Cambridge.

Heelas, Paul (1992) The Sacralisation of the Self and New Age Capitalism. In: Abercrombie, Nicholas and Warde, Alan (eds.) *Social Change in Contemporary Britain.* Polity Press, Cambridge, pp. 139–66.

Heelas, Paul (1996) *The New Age Movement: The Celebration of the Self and the Sacralization of Modernity.* Blackwell Publishers, Oxford.

Heelas, Paul, Woodhead, Linda, Seel, Benjamin, Szerszynski, Bronislaw and Tusting, Karin (2004) *The Spiritual Revolution: Why Religion is Giving Way to Spirituality.* Blackwell Publishing, Oxford.

Hegel, Georg Wilhelm Friedrich (1977) *Phenomenology of Spirit.* Trans. Miller, A. V., Oxford University Press, Oxford.

Heidegger, Martin (1962) *Being and Time.* Harper and Row, New York.

Heidegger, Martin (2003) The Question Concerning Technology. In: Scharff, Robert C. and Dusek, Val (eds.) *Philosophy of Technology: The Technological Condition: An Anthology.* Blackwell Publishing, Oxford, pp. 252–64.

Hetherington, Kevin (1997) *The Badlands of Modernity: Heterotopia and Social Ordering.* Routledge, London.

Hilton, Boyd (1988) *The Age of Atonement: The Influence of Evangelicalism on Social and Economic Thought, 1795–1865.* Clarendon Press, Oxford.

Hollyman, Jonathan (1971) *Consumers' Guide to the Planet.* Friends of the Earth/Ballantine, London.

Horkheimer, Max and Adorno, Theodor (1972) *Dialectic of Enlightenment.* Seabury Press, New York.

Horton, Dave (2003) Green Distinctions: The Performance of Identity among Environmental Activists. In: Szerszynski, Bronislaw, Heim, Wallace and Waterton, Claire (eds.) *Nature Performed: Environment, Culture and Performance.* Blackwell/Sociological Review, Oxford, pp. 63–77.

Hughes, J. Donald (1986) Pan: Environmental Ethics in Classical Polytheism. In: Hargrove, Eugene C. (ed.) *Religion and Environmental Crisis.* University of Georgia Press, Athens, GA, pp. 7–24.

Huizinga, J. (1924) *The Waning of the Middle Ages: A Study of the Forms of Life, Thought and Art in France and the Netherlands in the XIVth and XVth Centuries.* Edward Arnold, London.

Ihde, Don (2003) Heidegger's Philosophy of Technology. In: Scharff, Robert C. and Dusek, Val (eds.) *Philosophy of Technology: The Technological Condition: An Anthology.* Blackwell Publishing, Oxford, pp. 277–92.

Inglehart, Ronald (1971) The Silent Revolution in Europe: Intergenerational Change in Post-industrial Societies. *American Political Science Review* **65** (4), 991–1017.

Ingold, Tim (1993) Globes and Spheres: The Topology of Environment. In: Milton, Kay (ed.) *Environmentalism: The View from Anthropology.* Routledge, London, pp. 31–42.

Ingold, Tim (2000) *The Perception of the Environment: Essays in Livelihood, Dwelling and Skill.* Routledge, London.

Ivakhiv, Adrian J. (2001) *Claiming Sacred Ground: Pilgrims and Politics at Glastonbury and Sedona.* Indiana University Press, Bloomington.

Jamison, Andrew (2001) *The Making of Green Knowledge: Environmental Politics and Cultural Transformation.* Cambridge University Press, Cambridge.

Jamison, Andrew, Eyerman, Ron, Cramer, Jacqueline and Læssøe, Jeppe (1990) *The Making of the New Environmental Consciousness: A Comparative Study of the Environmental Movements in Sweden, Denmark and the Netherlands.* Edinburgh University Press, Edinburgh.

Jasper, James M. (1997) *The Art of Moral Protest: Culture, Biography, and Creativity in Social Movements*. University of Chicago Press, Chicago.

Jasper, James M. and Poulsen, Jane D. (1995) Recruiting Strangers and Friends: Moral Shocks and Social Networks in Animal Rights and Anti-nuclear Protests. *Social Problems* **42** (4), 493–512.

Jaspers, Karl (1953) *The Origin and Goal of History*. Routledge and Kegan Paul, London.

Johannessen, Helle (1996) Individualised Knowledge: Reflexologists, Biopaths and Kinesiologists in Denmark. In: Cant, Sarah and Sharma, Ursula (eds.) *Complementary and Alternative Medicines: Knowledge in Practice*. Free Association Books, London, pp. 116–32.

Kamen, Henry (1984) *European Society 1500–1700*. Hutchinson, London.

Kant, Immanuel (1978) *The Critique of Judgement*. Trans. Meredith, James Creed, Clarendon, Oxford.

Katz, Cindi and Kirby, Andrew (1991) In the Nature of Things: The Environment and Everyday Life. *Transactions of the Institute of British Geographers* **16** (3), 259–71.

Keat, Russell, Whiteley, Nigel and Abercrombie, Nicholas (eds.) (1994) *The Authority of the Consumer*. Routledge, London.

Kelsen, Hans (1946) *Society and Nature: A Sociological Inquiry*. Kegan Paul, London.

Keniston, Kenneth (1971) *Youth and Dissent: The Rise of a New Opposition*. Harcourt Brace Jovanovich, New York.

Kepel, Gilles (1994) *The Revenge of God: The Resurgence of Islam, Christianity and Judaism in the Modern World*. Polity, Cambridge.

Kershaw, Baz (1997) Fighting in the Streets: Dramaturgies of Popular Protest, 1968–1989. *New Theatre Quarterly* **13** (51), 255–76.

Kohlberg, Lawrence (1981) *The Philosophy of Moral Development: Moral Stages and the Idea of Justice*. Harper & Row, San Francisco.

Krohn, Wolfgang and Weyer, Johannes (1994) Society as a Laboratory: The Social Risks of Experimental Research. *Science and Public Policy* **21** (3), 173–83.

Kruschwitz, Robert B. and Roberts, Robert C. (eds.) (1987) *The Virtues: Contemporary Essays on Moral Character*. Wadsworth, Belmont, California.

Ladd, George Eldon (1966) *Jesus and the Kingdom: The Eschatology of Biblical Realism*. SPCK, London.

Larner, Christina (1992) Healing in Pre-industrial Britain. In: Saks, Mike (ed.) *Alternative Medicine in Britain*. Clarendon Press, Oxford, pp. 25–34.

Lash, Scott (2000) Risk Culture. In: Adam, Barbara, Beck, Ulrich and van Loon, Joost (eds.) *The Risk Society and Beyond: Critical Issues for Social Theory*. Sage, London, pp. 47–62.

Lash, Scott and Urry, John (1987) *The End of Organized Capitalism*. Polity Press, Cambridge.

Latour, Bruno (1993) *We have Never been Modern*. Trans. Porter, Catherine, Harvester Wheatsheaf, Hemel Hempstead.

Latour, Bruno (1998) From the World of Science to the World of Research? *Science* **280** (5361), 208–9.

Latour, Bruno (2004) *Politics of Nature: How to Bring the Sciences into Democracy.* Trans. Porter, Catherine, Harvard University Press, Cambridge, MA.

Lawrence, C. H. (1984) *Medieval Monasticism: Forms of Religious Life in Western Europe in the Middle Ages.* Longman, London.

Lebeer, Jo (1993) Revealing the Self: Biographical Research as a Method of Enquiry into Health. In: Lafaille, Robert and Fulder, Stephen (eds.) *Towards a New Science of Health.* Routledge, London, pp. 205–23.

Lee, Raymond and Ackerman, Susan Ellen (2002) *The Challenge of Religion after Modernity: Beyond Disenchantment.* Ashgate, Aldershot.

Leon, Derrick (1944) *Tolstoy: His Life and Work.* Routledge, London.

Leopold, Aldo (1966) *A Sand County Almanac, with other Essays on Conservation from Round River.* Oxford University Press, New York.

Lewis, Martin W. (1992) *Green Delusions: An Environmentalist Critique of Radical Environmentalism.* Duke University Press, Durham, North Carolina.

Light, Andrew and Katz, Eric (eds.) (1996) *Environmental Pragmatism.* Routledge, London.

Longinus, Dionysius Cassius (1964) *On the Sublime.* Clarendon, Oxford.

Lovejoy, Arthur O. (1936) *The Great Chain of Being: A Study of the History of an Idea.* Harvard University Press, Cambridge, Massachusetts.

Lovelock, James E. (1987) *Gaia: A New Look at Life on Earth.* Oxford University Press, Oxford.

Lowe, Philip and Goyder, Jane (1983) *Environmental Groups in Politics.* George Allen and Unwin, London.

Lowe, Philip and Morrison, David (1984) Bad News or Good News: Environmental Politics and the Mass Media. *Sociological Review* **32**(1), 75–90.

Lowe, Philip D. (1983) Values and Institutions in the History of British Nature Conservation. In: Goldsmith, A. and Warren, F. B. (eds.) *Conservation in Perspective.* John Wiley, Chichester, pp. 329–52.

Lowenberg, June S. and Davis, Fred (1994) Beyond Medicalisation–Demedicalisation: The Case of Holistic Health. *Sociology of Health and Illness* **16** (5), 579–99.

Lowerson, John (1980) Battles for the Countryside. In: Gloversmith, Frank (ed.) *Class, Culture and Social Change: A New View of the 1930s.* Harvester Press, Brighton, pp. 258–80.

Lowith, Karl (1949) *Meaning in History: The Theological Implications of the Philosophy of History.* University of Chicago Press, Chicago.

Luke, Tim (1988) The Dreams of Deep Ecology. *Telos* **76**, 65–92.

Lyng, Stephen (1990) *Holistic Health and Biomedical Medicine: A Countersystem Analysis.* State University of New York Press, Albany.

Lyotard, Jean-François (1986) *The Postmodern Condition: A Report on Knowledge.* Trans. Massumi, Geoff and Bennington, Brian, Manchester University Press, Manchester.

McGrath, Alister E. (2002) *The Reenchantment of Nature: Science, Religion, and the Human Sense of Wonder.* Doubleday, New York.

McGuire, Meredith B. (1988) *Ritual Healing in Suburban America* (with Debra Kantor). Rutgers University Press, New Brunswick.

McHarg, Ian (1969) *Design with Nature*. Doubleday/Natural History Press, Garden City, NY.

McKay, George (1996) *Senseless Acts of Beauty: Cultures of Resistance since the Sixties*. Verso, London.

MacKenzie, John M. (1988) *The Empire of Nature: Hunting, Conservation and British Imperialism*. Manchester University Press, Manchester.

MacLeish, Archibald (1968) Riders on Earth Together, Brothers in Eternal Cold. *New York Times*, 25 December.

McLuhan, Marshall (1962) *The Gutenberg Galaxy: The Making of Typographic Man*. Routledge and Kegan Paul, London.

Macnaghten, Phil and Urry, John (1998) *Contested Natures*. Sage, London.

Mandelbaum, David G. (1966) Transcendental and Pragmatic Aspects of Religion. *American Anthropologist* **68** (5), 1174–91.

Martin, Bernice (1981) *A Sociology of Contemporary Cultural Change*. Blackwell Publishers, Oxford.

Martin, Calvin (1978) *Keepers of the Game: Indian–Animal Relationships and the Fur Trade*. University of California Press, Berkeley, California.

Martin, David (1993) *Tongues of Fire: The Explosion of Protestantism in Latin America*. Blackwell Publishers, Oxford.

Marx, Karl and Engels, Freidrich (1962) Manifesto of the Communist Party, 1848. In: *The Communist Blueprint for the Future*. E. P. Dutton & Co, New York, pp. 3–44.

Massingham, H. J. (1945) Introduction. In: Massingham, H. J. (ed.) *The Natural Order: Essays in the Return to Husbandry*. J. M. Dent, London, pp. 1–19.

Matzko, David Matthew (1993) Postmodernism, Saints and Scoundrels. *Modern Theology* **9**(1), 19–36.

Meadows, Donella H., Meadows, Dennis L., Randers, Jorgen and Behrens III, William W. (1972) *The Limits to Growth: A Report for the Club of Rome's Project on the Predicament of Mankind*. Earth Island, London.

Mellor, Mary (1989) Turning Green: Whose Ecology? *Science as Culture* **6**, 17–41.

Mellor, Philip A. and Shilling, Chris (1997) *Re-forming the Body: Religion, Community and Modernity*. Sage/TCS, London.

Melucci, Alberto (1989) *Nomads of the Present: Social Movements and Individual Needs in Contemporary Society*. Hutchinson Radius, London.

Melucci, Alberto (1996) *Challenging Codes: Collective Action in the Information Age*. Cambridge University Press, Cambridge.

Merchant, Carolyn (1980) *The Death of Nature: Women, Ecology, and the Scientific Revolution*. Harper and Row, San Francisco.

Merton, Robert K. (1970) *Science, Technology and Society in Seventeenth Century England*. Harper, London.

Micheletti, Michele (2003) *Political Virtue and Shopping: Individuals, Consumerism, and Collective Action*. Palgrave Macmillan, New York.

Milbank, John (1990) *Theology and Social Theory: Beyond Secular Reason*. Blackwell Publishers, Oxford.

Milbank, John (1998) Sublimity: The Modern Transcendent. In: Heelas, Paul (ed.) *Religion, Modernity and Postmodernity*. Blackwell Publishers, Oxford, pp. 258–84.

Milbank, John (2004) The Gift of Ruling: Secularization and Political Authority. *New Blackfriars* **85** (996), 212–38.

Milton, Kay (1999) Nature is Already Sacred. *Environmental Values* **8** (4), 437–49.

Milton, Kay (2002) *Loving Nature: Towards an Ecology of Emotion.* Routledge, London.

Mitcham, Carl (1990) Three Ways of Being-with Technology. In: *From Artifact to Habitat: Studies in the Critical Engagement of Technology.* LeHigh University Press, Bethlehem, PA, pp. 31–59.

Mitcham, Carl (1994) *Thinking through Technology: The Path between Engineering and Philosophy.* University of Chicago Press, Chicago.

Mol, Arthur P. J. (2001) *Globalization and Environmental Reform: The Ecological Modernization of the Global Economy.* MIT Press, Cambridge, MA.

Monk, Samuel H. (1935) *The Sublime: A Study of Critical Theories in Eighteenth-Century England.* University of Michigan Press, Michigan.

Montefiore, Hugh (ed.) (1975) *Man and Nature.* Collins, London.

Montefiore, Hugh, Allchin, A. M., Cupitt, Don, Hesse, Mary, Macquarrie, John and Peacocke, A. R. (1975) Man and Nature: The Report. In: Montefiore, Hugh (ed.) *Man and Nature.* Collins, London, pp. 1–83.

Morgan, John (1999) The Puritan Thesis Revisited. In: Livingstone, David N., Hart, D. G. and Noll, Mark A. (eds.) *Evangelicals and Science in Historical Perspective.* Oxford University Press, Oxford.

Muchembled, Robert (1985) *Popular Culture and Elite Culture in France, 1400–1750.* Trans. Cochrane, Lydia, Louisiana State University, Baton Rouge.

Murdoch, Iris (1970) *The Sovereignty of Good.* Routledge and Kegan Paul, London.

Naess, Arne (1973) The Shallow and the Deep, Long-range Ecology Movement: A Summary. *Inquiry* **16** (1), 95–100.

Nash, Roderick (1973) *Wilderness and the American Mind.* Rev. edn., Yale University Press, New Haven.

Nash, Roderick (1976) *The American Environment: Readings in the History of Conservation.* 2nd edn., Alfred A. Knopf, New York.

Nash, Roderick (1989) *The Rights of Nature: A History of Environmental Ethics.* University of Wisconsin Press, Madison, Wisconsin.

Nelson, Robert H. (1993) Environmental Calvinism: The Judeo-Christian Roots of Eco-theology. In: Meiners, Roger E. and Yandle, Bruce (eds.) *Taking the Environment Seriously.* Rowman & Littlefield, Lanham, MD, pp. 233–55.

Nesti, Arnaldo (1985) *Il Religioso Implicito.* Ianua, Rome.

Nicholson, Max (1972) *The Environmental Revolution: A Guide for the New Masters of the World.* Pelican, Harmondsworth.

Nicholson, Max (1987) *The New Environmental Age.* Cambridge University Press, Cambridge.

Nicolson, Marjorie Hope (1959) *Mountain Gloom and Mountain Glory: The Development of the Aesthetics of the Infinite.* Norton, Ithaca, New York.

Noble, David F. (1999) *The Religion of Technology: The Divinity of Man and the Spirit of Invention.* Penguin, Harmondsworth.

Northcott, Michael N. (1996) *The Environment and Christian Ethics.* Cambridge University Press, Cambridge.

Nye, David E. (1994) *American Technological Sublime*. MIT Press, Cambridge, MA.

Oakley, Francis (1969) Christian Theology and the Newtonian Science. In: O'Connor, Daniel and Oakley, Francis (eds.) *Creation: The Impact of an Idea*. Scribners and Sons, New York, pp. 54–83.

Obelkevich, James (1979) Introduction. In: Obelkevich, James (ed.) *Religion and the People, 800–1700*. University of North Carolina Press, Chapel Hill, pp. 3–7.

Oelschlaeger, Max (1994) *Caring for Creation: An Ecumenical Approach to the Environmental Crisis*. Yale University Press, New Haven.

Ong, Walter J. (1982) *Orality and Literacy: The Technologizing of the World*. Methuen, London.

Opinion Research Business (2000) *Soul of Britain: Analysis by Demographics, Denomination and Values*. Vol. 1, Opinion Research Business, London.

Osler, Margaret J. (2001) Whose Ends? Teleology in Early Modern Natural Philosophy. *Osiris* 16, 151–68.

Otto, Rudolf (1950) *The Idea of the Holy: An Inquiry into the Non-rational Factor in the Idea of the Divine and its Relation to the Rational*. Trans. Harvey, John W., Oxford University Press, Oxford.

Overing Kaplan, Joanna (1975) *The Piaroa: A People of the Orinoco Basin: A Study in Kinship and Marriage*. Oxford University Press, Oxford.

Ovitt, G. (1987) *The Restoration of Perfection*. Rutgers University Press, Brunswick, NJ.

Oyler, Philip (1945) Feeding Ourselves. In: Massingham, H. J. (ed.) *The Natural Order: Essays in the Return to Husbandry*. J. M. Dent, London, pp. 66–77.

Parsons, Talcott (1952) *The Social System*. Routledge, New York.

Passmore, John (1980) *Man's Responsibility for Nature: Ecological Problems and Western Traditions*. 2nd edn., Duckworth, London.

Pearce, Fred (1991) *Green Warriors: The People and the Politics Behind the Environmental Revolution*. The Bodley Head, London.

Pearson, Joanne, Roberts, Richard H. and Samuel, Geoffrey (eds.) (1998) *Nature Religion Today: Paganism in the Modern World*. Edinburgh University Press, Edinburgh.

Pepper, David (1984) *The Roots of Modern Environmentalism*. Croom Helm, Beckenham.

Pepper, David (1991) *Communes and the Green Vision: Counterculture, Lifestyle and the New Age*. Greenprint, London.

Pérez-Ramos, Antonio (1988) *Francis Bacon's Idea of Science and the Maker's Knowledge Tradition*. Clarendon, Oxford.

Pilkington, A. E. (1986) 'Nature' as Ethical Norm in the Enlightenment. In: Jordanova, Ludmilla (ed.) *Languages of Nature: Critical Essays on Science and Literature*. Free Association Press, London, pp. 51–85.

Plutarch (1936) On the Obsolescence of Oracles. In: *Moralia*. Vol. 5, trans. Babbitt, Frank Cole, Heinemann, London, pp. 347–501.

Polanyi, Karl (1977) *The Livelihood of Man*. Academic Press, New York.

Porritt, Jonathon and Winner, David (1988) *The Coming of the Greens*. Fontana, London.

Posey, Darrell Addison (1998) The 'Balance Sheet' and the 'Sacred Balance': Valuing the Knowledge of Indigenous and Traditional Peoples. *Worldviews: Environment, Culture, Religion* 2 (2), 91–106.

Power, Richenda (1991) Ideologies of Holism in Health Care. *Complementary Medical Research* 5 (3), 151–9.

Proctor, James D. and Berry, Evan (forthcoming) Religion and Environmental Concern: The Challenge for Social Science. In: Taylor, Bron and Kaplan, Jeffrey (eds.) *Encyclopedia of Religion and Nature*. Continuum, London.

Proudfoot, Wayne (1985) *Religious Experience*. University of California Press, Berkeley.

Rappaport, Roy A. (1967) *Pigs for the Ancestors*. Yale University Press, New Haven.

Rappaport, Roy A. (1979) *Ecology, Meaning and Religion*. North Atlantic Books, Richmond, California.

Rappaport, Roy A. (1993) Veracity, Verity and *Verum* in Liturgy. *Studia Liturgica* 23 (1), 35–50.

Reed, Gerard (1986) A Native American Environmental Ethic: A Homily on Black Elk. In: Hargrove, Eugene C. (ed.) *Religion and Environmental Crisis*. University of Georgia Press, Athens, Georgia, pp. 25–37.

Reiss, David (1981) *The Family's Construction of Reality*. Harvard University Press, Cambridge, MA.

Reiss, Timothy J. (1982) *The Discourse of Modernism*. Cornell University Press, Ithaca, New York.

Ritvo, Harriet (1990) *The Animal Estate: The English and other Creatures in the Victorian Age*. Penguin, London.

Robbins, Thomas (1988) *Cults, Converts and Charisma: The Sociology of New Religious Movements*. Sage, London.

Roberts, Richard H. (1998) The Chthonic Imperative: Gender, Religion and the Battle for the Earth. In: Pearson, Joanne, Roberts, Richard H. and Samuel, Geoffrey (eds.) *Nature Religion Today: Paganism in the Modern World*. Edinburgh University Press, Edinburgh, pp. 57–73.

Roberts, Richard H. (2004) 'Nature', Post/Modernity and the Migration of the Sublime. *Ecotheology* 9 (3).

Robertson, Roland and Chirico, JoAnn (1985) Humanity, Globalisation and Worldwide Religious Resurgence: A Theoretical Explanation. *Sociological Analysis* 46 (3), 219–42.

Robinson, H. Wheeler (1946) *Inspiration and Revelation in the Old Testament*. Clarendon, Oxford.

Roof, Wade Clark (1999) *Spiritual Marketplace: Babyboomers and the Remaking of American Religion*. Princeton University Press, Princeton.

Rose, Nikolas (2001) The Politics of Life Itself. *Theory, Culture and Society* 18 (6), 1–30.

Rubin, Charles T. (1989) Environmental Policy and Environmental Thought: Ruckelshaus and Commoner. *Environmental Ethics* 11 (1), 27–51.

Ruskin, John (1908) The Storm Cloud of the Nineteenth Century. In: Cook, E. T. and Wedderburn, Alexander (eds.) *The Works of John Ruskin*. Vol. 34, Allen, London, pp. 9–41.

Rutherford, Paul (1993) Foucault's Concept of Biopower: Implications for Environmental Politics. In: Thomas, I. (ed.) *Ecopolitics VI: Interactions and Actions*. Royal Melbourne Institute of Technology, Melbourne.

Rutherford, Paul (1999) The Entry of Life into History. In: Darier, Éric (ed.) *Discourses of the Environment*. Blackwell Publishers, Oxford, pp. 37–62.

Ryder, Richard D. (1989) *Animal Revolution: Changing Attitude towards Speciesism*. Blackwell Publishers, Oxford.

Said, Edward W. (1978) *Orientalism*. Routledge and Kegan Paul, London.

Saks, Mike (1996) From Quackery to Complementary Medicine: The Shifting Boundaries between Orthodox and Unorthodox Medical Knowledge. In: Cant, Sarah and Sharma, Ursula (eds.) *Complementary and Alternative Medicines: Knowledge in Practice*. Free Association Books, London, pp. 27–43.

Scaltsas, Patricia Ward (1992) Do Feminist Ethics Counter Feminist Aims? In: Browning Cole, Eve and Coultrap-McQuin, Susan (eds.) *Explorations in Feminist Ethics: Theory and Practice*. Indiana University Press, Bloomington, pp. 15–26.

Scannell, Paddy (2000) For-Anyone-as-Someone Structures. *Media, Culture and Society* **22** (1), 5–24.

Schama, Simon (1995) *Landscape and Memory*. HarperCollins, London.

Scott, Peter (ed.) (1965) *The Launching of a New Ark: First Report of the President and Trustees of the World Wildlife Fund – an International Foundation for Saving the World's Wildlife and Wild Places – 1961–1964*. Collins, London.

Scott, Peter (2003) *A Political Theology of Nature*. Cambridge University Press, Cambridge.

Scott, Peter (2004) We have Never been Gods: Transcendence, Contingency and the Affirmation of Hybridity. *Ecotheology* **9** (2), 199–220.

Scribner, Robert W. (1987) *Popular Culture and Popular Movements in Reformation Germany*. Hambledon Press, London.

Seed, John, Macy, Joanna, Fleming, Pat and Naess, Arne (1988) *Thinking Like a Mountain: Towards a Council of All Beings*. Neretic Books, London.

Seel, Ben (1996) Frontline Eco-Wars! The Pollok Free State Road Protest Community: Counter Hegemonic Intentions, Pluralistic Effects. Paper presented to the conference Alternative Futures and Popular Protest II, Manchester Metropolitan University, 26–8 March.

Seel, Benjamin, Paterson, Matthew and Doherty, Brian (eds.) (2000) *Direct Action in British Environmentalism*. Routledge, London.

Shaiko, Ronald G. (1987) Religion, Politics, and Environmental Concern: A Powerful Mix of Passions. *Social Science Quarterly* **68** (2), 243–62.

Sharma, Ursula (1995) The Homeopathic Body: 'Reification' and the Homeopathic 'Gaze'. In: Johannessen, Helle, Olesen, Søren Gosvig and Andersen, Jørgen Østergård (eds.) *Studies in Alternative Therapy 2: Body and Nature*. Odense University Press, Odense, pp. 33–49.

Sheail, John (1976) *Nature in Trust: The History of Nature Conservation in Britain*. Blackie and Son, Glasgow.

Sherman, Nancy (1988) Common Sense and Uncommon Virtue. In: French, Peter A., Uehling, Theodore E. jun. and Wettstein, Howard K. (eds.) *Midwest Studies in Philosophy.* Vol. 13, *Ethical Theory: Character and Virtue.* University of Notre Dame Press, Notre Dame, pp. 97–114.

Silverstone, Roger (1984) Narrative Strategies in Television Science: A Case Study. *Media, Culture and Society* 6 (4), 377–410.

Song, Robert (2003) The Human Genome Project as Soteriological Project. In: Deane-Drummond, Celia (ed.) *Brave New World? Theology, Ethics and the Human Genome Project.* T&T Clark, Edinburgh, pp. 164–84.

Sonnenfeld, David A. and Mol, Arthur P. J. (eds.) (2000) *Ecological Modernisation around the World: Perspectives and Critical Debates.* Frank Cass Publishers, London.

Spickard, James V. (1995) Body, Nature and Culture in Spiritual Healing. In: Johannessen, Helle, Olesen, Søren Gosvig and Andersen, Jørgen Østergård (eds.) *Studies in Alternative Therapy 2: Body and Nature.* Odense University Press, Odense, pp. 65–81.

Spring, David and Spring, Eileen (eds.) (1974) *Ecology and Religion in History.* Harper and Row, New York.

Starhawk (1982) *Dreaming the Dark: Magic, Sex & Politics.* Beacon Press, Boston.

Steichen, Edward (ed.) (1983) *The Family of Man.* Museum of Modern Art, New York.

Stevens, Jay (1989) *Storming Heaven: LSD and the American Dream.* Paladin, London.

Stoll, Mark (1997) *Protestantism, Capitalism, and Nature in America.* University of New Mexico Press, Albuquerque.

Strong, Douglas H. (1971) *The Conservationists.* Addison-Wesley, Menlo Park, California.

Swimme, Brian and Berry, Thomas (1992) *The Universe Story: From the Primordial Flaring Forth to the Ecozoic Era – a Celebration of the Unfolding of the Cosmos.* Arkana, London.

Szerszynski, Bronislaw (1991) *Environmentalism, the Mass Media, and Public Opinion.* Report RT91.3, Centre for the Study of Environmental Change, Lancaster University, Lancaster.

Szerszynski, Bronislaw (1993) Uncommon Ground: Moral Discourse, Foundationalism and the Environmental Movement. PhD thesis, Lancaster University.

Szerszynski, Bronislaw (1996) On Knowing what to do: Environmentalism and the Modern Problematic. In: Lash, Scott, Szerszynski, Bronislaw and Wynne, Brian (eds.) *Risk, Environment and Modernity: Towards a New Ecology.* Sage, London, pp. 104–37.

Szerszynski, Bronislaw (1997) The Varieties of Ecological Piety. *Worldviews: Environment, Culture, Religion* 1 (1), 37–55.

Szerszynski, Bronislaw (1999) Performing Politics: The Dramatics of Environmental Protest. In: Ray, Larry and Sayer, Andrew (eds.) *Culture and Economy after the Cultural Turn.* Sage, London, pp. 211–28.

Szerszynski, Bronislaw (2002a) Ecological Rites: Ritual Action in Environmental Protest Events. *Theory, Culture and Society* 19 (3), 305–23.

Szerszynski, Bronislaw (2002b) Wild Times and Domesticated Times: The Temporalities of Environmental Lifestyles and Politics. *Landscape and Urban Planning* 61 (2–4), 181–91.

Szerszynski, Bronislaw (2003a) At Reason's End: The Inoperative Liturgy of Risk Society. In: Deane-Drummond, Celia and Szerszynski, Bronislaw (eds.) *Re-ordering Nature: Theology, Society and the New Genetics.* T&T Clark, Edinburgh, pp. 202–20.

Szerszynski, Bronislaw (2003b) Technology, Performance and Life Itself: Hannah Arendt and the Fate of Nature. In: Szerszynski, Bronislaw, Heim, Wallace and Waterton, Claire (eds.) *Nature Performed: Environment, Culture and Performance.* Blackwell/Sociological Review, Oxford, pp. 203–18.

Szerszynski, Bronislaw (2003c) That Deep Surface: The Human Genome Project and the Death of the Human. In: Deane-Drummond, Celia (ed.) *Brave New World? Theology, Ethics and the Human Genome Project.* T&T Clark, Edinburgh, pp. 145–63.

Szerszynski, Bronislaw and Deane-Drummond, Celia (2003) Re-ordering Nature: A Post-script. In: Deane-Drummond, Celia and Szerszynski, Bronislaw (eds.) *Re-ordering Nature: Theology, Society and the New Genetics.* T&T Clark, Edinburgh, pp. 312–24.

Szerszynski, Bronislaw and Toogood, Mark (2000) Global Citizenship, the Environment and the Media. In: Allan, Stuart, Adam, Barbara and Carter, Cynthia (eds.) *Environmental Risks and the Media.* Routledge, London, pp. 218–28.

Szerszynski, Bronislaw, Urry, John and Myers, Greg (2000) Mediating Global Citizenship. In: Smith, Joe (ed.) *The Daily Globe: Environmental Change, the Public and the Media.* Earthscan, London, pp. 97–114.

Taylor, Bron (2001a) Earth and Nature-Based Spirituality (Part 1): From Deep Ecology to Radical Environmentalism. *Religion* 31 (2), 175–93.

Taylor, Bron (2001b) Earth and Nature-Based Spirituality (Part 2): From Earth First! and Bioregionalism to Scientific Paganism and the New Age. *Religion* 31 (3), 225–45.

Taylor, Bron and Kaplan, Jeffrey (eds.) (forthcoming) *Encyclopedia of Religion and Nature.* Continuum, London.

Tec, Nechama (1986) *When Light Pierced the Darkness: Christian Rescue of Jews in Nazi-occupied Poland.* Oxford University Press, New York.

Tester, Keith (1991) *Animals and Society: The Humanity of Animal Rights.* Routledge, London.

Thomas, K. J., Nicholl, J. P. and Coleman, P. (2001) Use and Expenditure on Complementary Medicine in England: A Population Based Survey. *Complementary Therapies in Medicine* 9, 2–11.

Thomas, Keith (1973) *Religion and the Decline of Magic.* Penguin, Harmondsworth.

Thomas, Keith (1984) *Man and the Natural World: Changing Attitudes in England 1500–1800.* Penguin, Harmondsworth.

Tillich, Paul (1957) *Dynamics of Faith.* Harper & Row, London.

Tipton, Steven M. (1982) *Getting Saved from the Sixties: Moral Meaning in Conversion and Cultural Change.* University of California Press, Berkeley, California.

Tomalin, Emma Louise (2000) Transformation and Tradition: A Comparative Study of Religious Environmentalism in Britain and India. PhD thesis, Lancaster University.

Tomlinson, John (1999) *Globalization and Culture*. Polity, Cambridge.

Toynbee, Arnold (1974) The Religious Background of the Present Environmental Crisis. In: Spring, David and Spring, Eileen (eds.) *Ecology and Religion in History*. Harper and Row, New York, pp. 137–49.

Tribe, Keith (1978) *Land, Labour and Economic Discourse*. Routledge and Kegan Paul, London.

Troeltsch, Ernst (1931) *The Social Teaching of the Christian Churches*. Trans. Wyon, Olive, George Allen and Unwin, London.

Turnbull, Colin (1974) *The Forest People*. Cape, London.

Turnbull, Colin (1978) *Man in Africa*. Penguin, Harmondsworth.

Turner, Bryan S. (1987) A Note on Nostalgia. *Theory, Culture and Society* 4, 147–56.

Twigg, Julia (1983) Vegetarianism and the Meanings of Meat. In: Murcott, Anne (ed.) *The Sociology of Food and Eating: Essays on the Sociological Significance of Food*. Gower, Aldershot, pp. 18–30.

Urry, John (1992a) The Tourist Gaze and the 'Environment'. *Theory, Culture and Society* 9 (1), 1–26.

Urry, John (1992b) The Tourist Gaze 'Revisited'. *American Behavioral Scientist* 36 (2), 172–86.

Urry, John (2000) *Sociology Beyond Societies: Mobilities for the Twenty-first Century*. Routledge, London.

van Gennep, Arnold (1960) *The Rites of Passage*. Trans. Caffee, Monika and Vizedom, Gebrielle, University of Chicago Press, Chicago.

van Lente, Harro (2000) Forceful Futures: From Promise to Requirement. In: Brown, Nik, Rappert, Brian and Webster, Andrew (eds.) *Contested Futures: A Sociology of Prospective Techno-science*. Ashgate, Aldershot, pp. 43–63.

Vogel, David (2002) The Protestant Ethic and the Spirit of Environmentalism: Exploring the Cultural Roots of Contemporary Green Politics. *Zeitschrift für Umweltpolitik und Umweltrecht* 3, 297–322.

Vriezen, Theodorus Christiaan (1960) *An Outline of Old Testament Theology*. Blackwell Publishers, Oxford.

Walters, Kerry S. and Portmess, Lisa (eds.) (2001) *Religious Vegetarianism: From Hesiod to the Dalai Lama*. State University of New York Press, Albany, NY.

Walzer, Michael (1968) *The Revolution of the Saints: A Study in the Origins of Radical Politics*. Atheneum, New York.

Webb, Clement Charles Julian (1915) *Studies in the History of Natural Theology*. Clarendon Press, Oxford.

Weber, Max (1930) *The Protestant Ethic and the Spirit of Capitalism*. Trans. Parsons, Talcott, George Allen & Unwin, London.

Weber, Max (1965) *The Sociology of Religion*. Trans. Fischoff, Ephraim, Methuen, London.

Weber, Max (1985) *The Protestant Ethic and the Spirit of Capitalism*. Trans. Parsons, Talcott, Unwin Paperbacks, London.

Weber, Max (1989) Science as a Vocation. In: Lassman, Peter and Velody, Irving (eds.) *Max Weber's Science as a Vocation*. Trans. John, Michael, Unwin Hyman, London, pp. 1–31.

Weinberger, Jerry (1985) *Science, Faith and Politics: Francis Bacon and the Utopian Roots of the Modern Age – a Commentary on Bacon's Advancement of Learning*. Cornell University Press, Ithaca, New York.

Weinstein, Donald and Bell, Rudolph M. (1982) *Saints and Society: The Two Worlds of Christendom, 1000–1700*. University of Chicago Press, Chicago.

Westermann, Claus (1974) *Creation*. Trans. John J. Scullion, SJ, SPCK, London.

Westley, Frances (1978) The Cult of Man: Durkheim's Predictions and New Religious Movements. *Sociological Analysis* **34** (2), 135–45.

Westley, Frances (1983) *The Complex Forms of the New Religious Life: A Durkheimian View of New Religious Movements*. Scholars Press, Chico, California.

White, Lynn, jun. (1967) The Historical Roots of our Ecologic Crisis. *Science* **155**, 1203–7.

White, Lynn, jun. (1968) The Historical Roots of our Ecologic Crisis. In: *Machina Ex Deo: Essays in the Dynamism of Western Culture*. MIT Press, Cambridge, Mass, pp. 75–94.

Wiener, Martin J. (1985) *English Culture and the Decline of the Industrial Spirit 1850–1980*. Pelican, London.

Williams, Raymond (1976) *Keywords: A Vocabulary of Culture and Society*. Flamingo, London.

Williams, Raymond (1980) Ideas of Nature. In: *Problems in Materialism and Culture*. New Left Bookclub, London, pp. 67–85.

Willis, Roy (1974) *Man and Beast*. Hart-Davis, MacGibbon, London.

Wilson, Bryan (1970) *Religious Sects: A Sociological Study*. Weidenfeld and Nicolson, London.

Wilson, Bryan (1985) Secularization: The Inherited Model. In: Hammond, Phillip E. (ed.) *The Sacred in a Secular Age: Toward Revision in the Scientific Study of Religion*. University of California Press, Berkeley, pp. 9–20.

Wilson, Bryan R. (1982) *Religion in Sociological Perspective*. Oxford University Press, Oxford.

Winner, Langdon (1977) *Autonomous Technology: Technics-out-of-Control as a Theme in Political Thought*. MIT Press, Cambridge, MA.

Wolf, Susan (1982) Moral Saints. *Journal of Philosophy* **79** (8), 419–39.

Woodhead, Linda (2001) The Softening of Christianity. Paper presented to the UK Federation Conference, Cambridge.

Woodhead, Linda and Heelas, Paul (eds.) (2000) *Religion in Modern Times: An Interpretive Anthology*. Blackwell Publishers, Oxford.

Wordsworth, William (1965) *Lyrical Ballads: The Text of the 1798 Edition with the Additional 1800 Poems and the Prefaces*. Methuen, London.

World Commission on Environment and Development (1987) *Our Common Future*. Oxford University Press, Oxford.

Worster, Donald (1977) *Nature's Economy: A History of Ecological Ideas*. Cambridge University Press, Cambridge.

Wynne, Anna (1989) Is it any Good? The Evaluation of Therapy by Participants in a Clinical Trial. *Social Science and Medicine* **29** (11), 1289–97.

Xenos, Nicholas (1989) *Scarcity and Modernity*. Routledge, London.

Index